Lecture Notes in Computer Science

Lecture Notes in Computer Science

Vol. 117: Fundamentals of Computation Theory. Proceedings, 1981. Edited by F. Gécseg. XI, 471 pages. 1981.

Vol. 118: Mathematical Foundations of Computer Science 1981. Proceedings, 1981. Edited by J. Gruska and M. Chytil. XI, 589 pages. 1981.

Vol. 119: G. Hirst, Anaphora in Natural Language Understanding: A Survey. XIII, 128 pages. 1981.

Vol. 120: L. B. Rall, Automatic Differentiation: Techniques and Applications. VIII, 165 pages. 1981.

Vol. 121: Z. Zlatev, J. Wasniewski, and K. Schaumburg, Y12M Solution of Large and Sparse Systems of Linear Algebraic Equations. IX, 128 pages. 1981.

Vol. 122: Algorithms in Modern Mathematics and Computer Science. Proceedings, 1979. Edited by A. P. Ershov and D. E. Knuth. XI, 487 pages. 1981.

Vol. 123: Trends in Information Processing Systems. Proceedings, 1981. Edited by A. J. W. Duijvestijn and P. C. Lockemann. XI, 349 pages. 1981.

Vol. 124: W. Polak, Compiler Specification and Verification. XIII, 269 pages. 1981.

Vol. 125: Logic of Programs. Proceedings, 1979. Edited by E. Engeler. V, 245 pages. 1981.

Vol. 126: Microcomputer System Design. Proceedings, 1981. Edited by M. J. Flynn, N. R. Harris, and D. P. McCarthy. VII, 397 pages. 1982.

Voll. 127: Y. Wallach, Alternating Sequential/Parallel Processing. X, 329 pages. 1982.

Vol. 128: P. Branquart, G. Louis, P. Wodon, An Analytical Description of CHILL, the CCITT High Level Language. VI, 277 pages. 1982.

Vol. 129: B. T. Hailpern, Verifying Concurrent Processes Using Temporal Logic. VIII, 208 pages. 1982.

Vol. 130: R. Goldblatt, Axiomatising the Logic of Computer Programming. XI, 304 pages. 1982.

Vol. 131: Logics of Programs. Proceedings, 1981. Edited by D. Kozen. VI, 429 pages. 1982.

Vol. 132: Data Base Design Techniques I: Requirements and Logical Structures. Proceedings, 1978. Edited by S.B. Yao, S.B. Navathe, J.L. Weldon, and T.L. Kunii. V, 227 pages. 1982.

Vol. 133: Data Base Design Techniques II: Proceedings, 1979. Edited by S.B. Yao and T.L. Kunii. V, 229–399 pages. 1982.

Vol. 134: Program Specification. Proceedings, 1981. Edited by J. Staunstrup. IV, 426 pages. 1982.

Vol. 135: R.L. Constable, S.D. Johnson, and C.D. Eichenlaub, An Introduction to the PL/CV2 Programming Logic. X, 292 pages. 1982.

Vol. 136: Ch. M. Hoffmann, Group-Theoretic Algorithms and Graph Isomorphism. VIII, 311 pages. 1982.

Vol. 137: International Symposium on Programming. Proceedings, 1982. Edited by M. Dezani-Ciancaglini and M. Montanari. VI, 406 pages. 1982.

Vol. 138: 6th Conference on Automated Deduction. Proceedings, 1982. Edited by D.W. Loveland. VII, 389 pages. 1982.

Vol. 139: J. Uhl, S. Drossopoulou, G. Persch, G. Goos, M. Dausmann, G. Winterstein, W. Kirchgässner, An Attribute Grammar for the Semantic Analysis of Ada. IX, 511 pages. 1982.

Vol. 140: Automata, Languages and programming. Edited by M. Nielsen and E.M. Schmidt. VII, 614 pages. 1982.

Vol. 141: U. Kastens, B. Hutt, E. Zimmermann, GAG: A Practical Compiler Generator. IV, 156 pages. 1982.

Vol. 142: Problems and Methodologies in Mathematical Software Production. Proceedings, 1980. Edited by P.C. Messina and A. Murli. VII, 271 pages. 1982.

Vol. 143: Operating Systems Engineering. Proceedings, 1980. Edited by M. Maekawa and L.A. Belady. VII, 465 pages. 1982.

Vol. 144: Computer Algebra. Proceedings, 1982. Edited by J. Calmet. XIV, 301 pages. 1982.

Vol. 145: Theoretical Computer Science. Proceedings, 1983. Edited by A.B. Cremers and H.P. Kriegel. X, 367 pages. 1982.

Vol. 146: Research and Development in Information Retrieval. Proceedings, 1982. Edited by G. Salton and H.-J. Schneider. IX, 311 pages. 1983.

Vol. 147: RIMS Symposia on Software Science and Engineering. Proceedings, 1982. Edited by E. Goto, I. Nakata, K. Furukawa, R. Nakajima, and A. Yonezawa. V. 232 pages. 1983.

Vol. 148: Logics of Programs and Their Applications. Proceedings, 1980. Edited by A. Salwicki. VI, 324 pages. 1983.

Vol. 149: Cryptography. Proceedings, 1982. Edited by T. Beth. VIII, 402 pages. 1983.

Vol. 150: Enduser Systems and Their Human Factors. Proceedings, 1983. Edited by A. Blaser and M. Zoeppritz. III, 138 pages. 1983.

Vol. 151: R. Piloty, M. Barbacci, D. Borrione, D. Dietmeyer, F. Hill, and P. Skelly, CONLAN Report. XII, 174 pages. 1983.

Vol. 152: Specification and Design of Software Systems. Proceedings, 1982. Edited by E. Knuth and E. J. Neuhold. V, 152 pages. 1983.

Vol. 153: Graph-Grammars and Their Application to Computer Science. Proceedings, 1982. Edited by H. Ehrig, M. Nagl, and G. Rozenberg. VII, 452 pages. 1983.

Vol. 154: Automata, Languages and Programming. Proceedings, 1983. Edited by J. Diaz. VIII, 734 pages. 1983.

Vol. 155: The Programming Language Ada. Reference Manual. Approved 17 February 1983. American National Standards Institute, Inc. ANSI/MIL-STD-1815A-1983. IX, 331 pages. 1983.

Vol. 156: M.H. Overmars, The Design of Dynamic Data Structures. VII, 181 pages. 1983.

Vol. 157: O. Østerby, Z. Zlatev, Direct Methods for Sparse Matrices. VIII, 127 pages. 1983.

Vol. 158: Foundations of Computation Theory. Proceedings, 1983. Edited by M. Karpinski, XI, 517 pages. 1983.

Vol. 159: CAAP'83. Proceedings, 1983. Edited by G. Ausiello and M. Protasi. VI, 416 pages. 1983.

Vol. 160: The IOTA Programming System. Edited by R. Nakajima and T. Yuasa. VII, 217 pages. 1983.

Vol. 161: DIANA, An Intermediate Language for Ada. Edited by G. Goos, W.A. Wulf, A. Evans, Jr. and K.J. Butler. VII, 201 pages. 1983.

Vol. 162: Computer Algebra. Proceedings, 1983. Edited by J.A. van Hulzen. XIII, 305 pages. 1983.

Vol. 163: VLSI Engineering. Proceedings. Edited by T.L. Kunii. VIII, 308 pages. 1984.

Vol. 164: Logics of Programs. Proceedings, 1983. Edited by E. Clarke and D. Kozen. VI, 528 pages. 1984.

Vol. 165: T.F. Coleman, Large Sparse Numerical Optimization. V, 105 pages. 1984.

Vol. 166: STACS 84. Symposium of Theoretical Aspects of Computer Science. Proceedings, 1984. Edited by M. Fontet and K. Mehlhorn. VI, 338 pages. 1984.

Lecture Notes in Computer Science

Edited by G. Goos and J. Hartmanis

215

Mathematical Methods of Specification and Synthesis of Software Systems '85

Proceedings of the International Spring School
Wendisch-Rietz, GDR, April 22–26, 1985

Edited by W. Bibel and K.P. Jantke

Springer-Verlag
Berlin Heidelberg New York Tokyo

Editors

Wolfgang Bibel
Institut für Informatik der Technischen Universität München
Postfach 20 24 20, D-8000 München 2

Klaus P. Jantke
Humboldt-Universität zu Berlin, Sektion Mathematik
Unter den Linden 6, DDR-1086 Berlin

CR Subject Classifications (1985): F.1, F.3, I.2.2, I.2.6

ISBN 3-540-16444-8 Springer-Verlag Berlin Heidelberg New York Tokyo
ISBN 0-387-16444-8 Springer-Verlag New York Heidelberg Berlin Tokyo

Printed in the German Democratic Republic

Printing: VEB Kongreß- und Werbedruck, DDR-9273 Oberlungwitz
Binding: Beltz Offsetdruck, Hemsbach/Bergstr.
2145/3140-543210

FOREWORD

Software development is a bottleneck of current information processing practice. Consequently, its fundamental problems constitute a main field of theoretical computer science. The workshop on Mathematical Methods of Specification and Synthesis of Software Systems, organized by the Department of Mathematics and the Computing Center of the Humboldt University Berlin, GDR, was devoted to **several** mathematical approaches to cope with the bottleneck of software design and synthesis. According to the intention of the organizers the topics presented centered around abstract data type theory and inductive inference, and emphasized the use of basic knowledge from mathematical logic and universal algebra.

The workshop featured invited lectures and short research contributions. The papers of the first category are collected in the first part of the present volume. Unfortunately, the paper by H. Rasiowa and A. Skowron could not be presented at the conference. The second part of the volume contains written versions of the short talks.

Some important mathematically based lines of approaches to software development, like program transformation, could not be covered by this first workshop. The organizers at the Computing Center of the Humboldt University Berlin intend to organize a more comprehensive successor workshop in 1987.

The conference program also included a panel discussion under the titel "How to bridge the gap between mathematics and software development", which was opened by introductions given by Jan Bergstra (Amsterdam), Robert P. Daley (Pittsburgh) and Yuri L. Ershov (Novosibirsk). It was not possible to reflect this charged and controversal discussion in the present volume.

The conference was held at Wendisch-Rietz, a nice little village at the lake Scharmützelsee. We would like to express our special thanks to Dr. Thomas Zeugmann, the organizing secretary, for the excellent preparations of this successful conference.

München and Berlin,

Wolfgang Bibel

Klaus P. Jantke

LIST OF PARTICIPANTS

Peter Bachmann, GDR

Hans-Rainer Beick, GDR

Jan Bergstra, Netherlands

Wolfgang Bibel, FRG

Ognian Botusharov, Bulgaria

Jürgen Brunner, GDR

Jolanta Cybulka, Poland

Bernd-Ingo Dahn, GDR

Robert P. Daley, USA

Werner Dilger, FRG

Marek Ejsmont, Poland

Yuri L. Ershov, USSR

Arne Fellien, GDR

Tamas Gergely, Hungary

Jan Grabowski, GDR

Kay Gürtzig, GDR

Zdislaw Habasinski, Poland

Hans-Jürgen Hoehnke, GDR

Christian Horn, GDR

Klaus P. Jantke, GDR

Harald Killenberg, GDR

Steffen Lange, GDR

Wolfgang Lassner, GDR

Jacques Loeckx, FRG

Burkhard Molzan, GDR

Dieter Pötschke, GDR

Joachim Reiss, GDR

Gisela Schäfer-Richter, FRG

Gerhard Schopf, GDR

Takeshi Shinohara, Japan

Dmitri I. Sviridenko, USSR

Zsolt Szabo, Hungary

Bernhard Thalheim, GDR

Helmut Thiele, GDR

Enn Tyugu, USSR

Wolfgang Wechler, GDR

Rolf Wiehagen, GDR

Renate Wenzlaff, GDR

Fritz Wysotzki, GDR

Thomas Zeugmann, GDR

CONTENTS

LECTURES

CONTRIBUTED PAPERS

VERIFICATION OF AN ALTERNATING BIT PROTOCOL BY MEANS OF PROCESS ALGEBRA

J.A. BERGSTRA, J.W. KLOP
Centre for Mathematics and Computer Science
P.O.Box 4079, 1009 AB Amsterdam, The Netherlands

We verify a simple version of the alternating bit protocol in the system ACP_τ (Algebra of Communicating Processes with silent actions) augmented with Koomen's fair abstraction rule.

INTRODUCTION

Let D be a finite set of data. These data are to be transmitted through an unreliable medium from location 1 to location 2, by means of a transmission protocol T.

With r1(d) we denote the act of reading datum d at location 1, whereas w2(d) denotes the act of writing value d at location 2. The external (higher level) specification of the behaviour of T is this:

$$T = \sum_{d \in D} r1(d).w2(d).T$$

From its initial state T is enabled to read any $d \in D$, thereafter T will write d at 2 and subsequently return to its initial state.

A very interesting mechanism to implement T is the alternating bit protocol (from [2]). This protocol turns out to be sufficiently complicated to serve as a test case for protocol verification methods (see HAILPERN & OWICKI [7] and LAMPORT [8] for instance).

We will present a description and verification of ABP (the alternating bit protocol), in terms of process algebra. Our presentation makes extensive use of ACP_τ, Algebra of Communicating Processes with silent actions, as well as of ideas by C.J. Koomen from Philips Research.

The advantage of process algebra in contrast to techniques based on temporal logic and Hoare-style verification is mainly that the entire verification is done in terms of calculations on the protocol itself. Both safety and liveness are simultaneously dealt with in the equational calculus of process algebra.

The structure of this note is as follows:

1. Explanation of the architecture of ABP.
2. Axioms and rules of process algebra.
3. Verification of ABP.

This work was sponsored in part by ESPRIT contract 432 METEOR.

Remark. It must be said that ABP as explained here is only one of the many variations on the same theme, and among these a rather simple one. Process algebra is well suited to specify individual protocols; at present the specification of classes of protocols is not supported by process algebra. For other issues of a philosophical nature we refer to [10] and [11].

1. ARCHITECTURE OF ABP

1.1. The protocol can be visualised as follows:

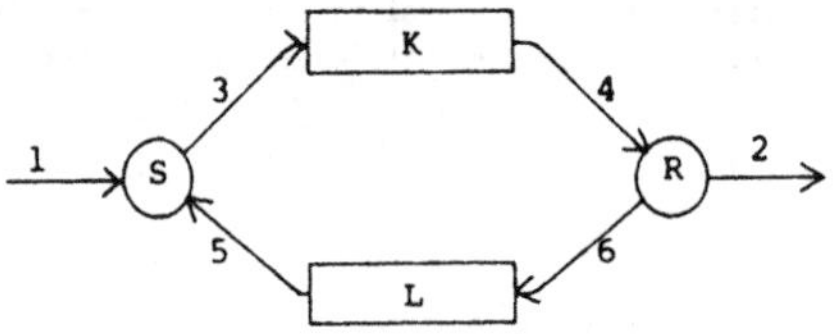

There are four components:

S: sender. S reads data d at 1 ($d \in D$), and communicates the data to channel K until an acknowledgement has been received via channel L.

K: data transmission channel. K communicates data in $D0 \cup D1$ ($Di = \{di \mid d \in D\}$), and may communicate these correctly or communicate an error value e. K is supposed to be fair in the sense that it will not produce an infinite consecutive sequence of error outputs.

R: receiver. R receives data from K, outputs them at 2 and sends back acknowledgements via L.

L: acknowledgement transmission channel. The task of L is to communicate boolean values from R to S. The channel L may yield error outputs but is also supposed to be fair.

The components S,K,R and L are processes. The protocol T is described by

$$\partial_H(S\|K\|R\|L).$$

Here $\|$ denotes parallel composition and ∂_H encapsulates $S\|K\|R\|L$ by requiring that no external processes may interfere in the communications at ports 3,4,5 and 6.

In order to obtain an abstract view of the protocol the operator τ_I is applied, which replaces internal actions (in I) by the silent action τ. Thus:

$$\boxed{T = \tau_I \partial_H(S\|K\|R\|L)}$$

Verification amounts to a proof that this T satisfies the equation

$$T = \sum_{d \in D} r1(d).w2(d).T$$

1.2. Structure of the components of ABP.

1.2.1. Data and actions.

D is the finite set of data that is to be transmitted by ABP. For $d \in D$, d0 and d1 are new data, obtained by appending 0 resp. 1 to d. We write:

$$D0 = \{d0 \mid d \in D\}$$
$$D1 = \{d1 \mid d \in D\}$$
$$\mathbb{D} = D \cup D0 \cup D1 \cup \{0,1,e\}.$$

$\mathbb{D}$ is the set of data that occur as parameter of atomic actions.

For $t \in \{1,\ldots,6\}$ there are read and write actions:

rt(a), read $a \in \mathbb{D}$ at t

wt(a), write $a \in \mathbb{D}$ at t.

Here $t \in \{1,\ldots,6\}$ is called a port (or location, but we prefer port). Communication takes place at ports only:

$$rt(a) \mid wt(a) = j,$$

where j is an internal action. Another kind of internal action is i. It corresponds to internal choices made by K and L. The entire alphabet A of proper actions is then as follows:

$$A = \{rt(a) \mid 1 \leq t \leq 6,\ a \in \mathbb{D}\} \cup \{wt(a) \mid 1 \leq t \leq 6,\ a \in \mathbb{D}\} \cup \{i,j,\delta\}.$$

The communication function $.|. : A \times A \rightarrow A$ yields δ (deadlock or failure) except in the case mentioned before: $rt(a) \mid wt(a) = j$.

Of course the abstraction operator will introduce Milner's silent action τ and the universe of discourse consists of the processes over $A_\tau = A \cup \{\tau\}$. Furthermore H, the set of subatomic (or communication) actions is:

$$\bigcup_{t \in \{3,4,5,6\}} \ \bigcup_{a \in \mathbb{D}} \{rt(a), wt(a)\},$$

and I, the set of internal actions is just $\{i,j\}$.

1.2.2. The individual components.

We will first give the well-known state transition diagrams (or 'process graphs') for S,K,L and R. Here a node is a state and an arrow denotes an action (i.e. state transition of the process). Both state and actions can be parametrised by data.

Channels:

K:

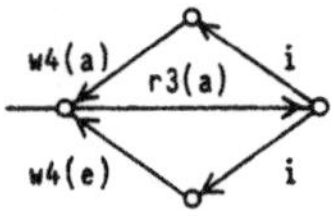

(a∈ D0 ∪ D1)

$$K = \sum_{a \in D0 \cup D1} r3(a).(i.w3(a) + i.w3(e)).K$$

L:

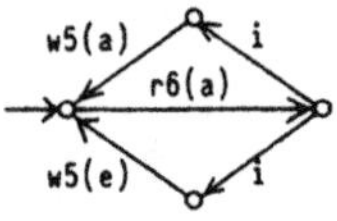

$$L = \sum_{a \in \{0,1\}} r6(a).(i.w5(a) + i.w5(e)).L$$

Note that K and L, after receiving input, have a nondeterministic choice, by doing one of both i actions.

At the level of this equational specification of K and L fairness is not yet mentioned. Fairness will come in when abstraction is applied to remove the i's.

Sender:

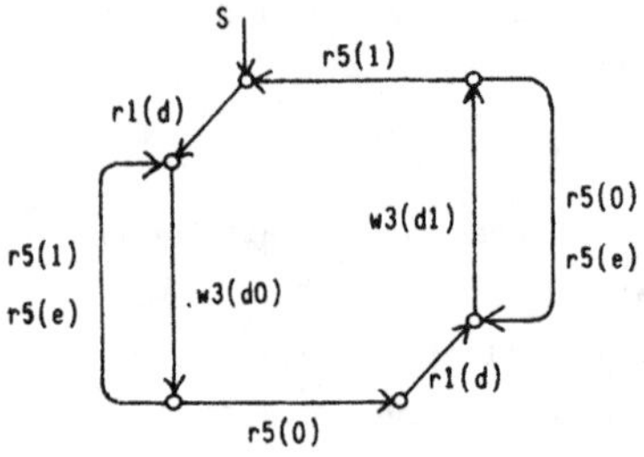

$$S = S^0.S^1.S$$

$$S^n = \sum_{d \in D} r1(d).S^n_d \qquad (n = 0,1)$$

$$S^n_d = w3(dn).U^n_d$$

$$U^n_d = (r5(1-n) + r5(e)).S^n_d + r5(n)$$

Receiver:

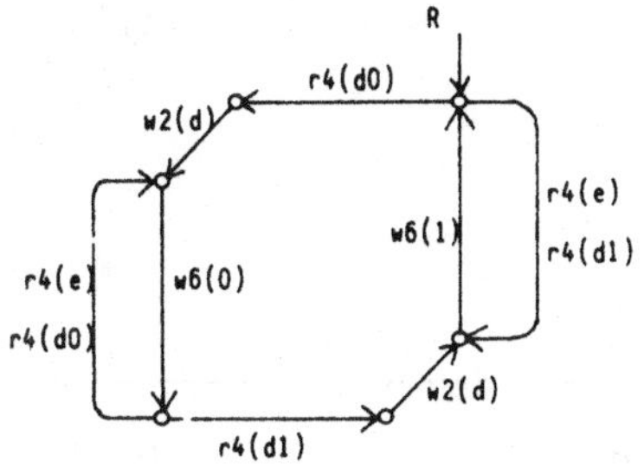

$$R = R^1 . R^0 . R$$

$$R^n = \left(\sum_{d \in D} r4(dn) + r4(e)\right) . w6(n) . R^n +$$

$$+ \sum_{d \in D} r4(d(1-n)) . w2(d) . w6(1-n)$$

$(n = 0,1)$

2. PROCESS ALGEBRA

2.1. ACP_τ.

Let A be a set of atomic actions and $.|. : A \times A \longrightarrow A$ a communication function, which is commutative and associative and for which δ acts as a zero. A_τ denotes $A \cup \{\tau\}$; τ is the silent action, that results from application of the abstraction operator.

The signature of operations of processes that we will use is this:

$+$	*alternative composition (sum)*
$\cdot$	*sequential composition (product)*
$\parallel$	*parallel composition (merge)*
$\lfloor\!\lfloor$	*left-merge*
$\mid$	*communication merge*
∂_H	*encapsulation*
τ_I	*abstraction*
δ	*deadlock/failure*
τ	*silent action*

Table 1.

An ACP_τ algebra is an algebra of the above signature (where | extends the communication function on atoms) and which satisfies the axioms in Table 2. Here $H \subseteq A$, $I \subseteq A$, $\delta \notin I$ and a,b,c range over A.

ACP_τ

$x + y = y + x$	A1	$x\tau = x$	T1
$x + (y + z) = (x + y) + z$	A2	$\tau x + x = \tau x$	T2
$x + x = x$	A3	$a(\tau x + y) = a(\tau x + y) + ax$	T3
$(x + y)z = xz + yz$	A4		
$(xy)z = x(yz)$	A5		
$x + \delta = x$	A6		
$\delta x = \delta$	A7		
$a \mid b = b \mid a$	C1		
$(a \mid b) \mid c = a \mid (b \mid c)$	C2		
$\delta \mid a = \delta$	C3		
$x \parallel y = x \,⌊\!⌊\, y + y \,⌊\!⌊\, x + x \mid y$	CM1		
$a \,⌊\!⌊\, x = ax$	CM2	$\tau \,⌊\!⌊\, x = \tau x$	TM1
$(ax) \,⌊\!⌊\, y = a(x \parallel y)$	CM3	$(\tau x) \,⌊\!⌊\, y = \tau(x \parallel y)$	TM2
$(x + y) \,⌊\!⌊\, z = x \,⌊\!⌊\, z + y \,⌊\!⌊\, z$	CM4	$\tau \mid x = \delta$	TC1
$(ax) \mid b = (a \mid b)x$	CM5	$x \mid \tau = \delta$	TC2
$a \mid (bx) = (a \mid b)x$	CM6	$(\tau x) \mid y = x \mid y$	TC3
$(ax) \mid (by) = (a \mid b)(x \parallel y)$	CM7	$x \mid (\tau y) = x \mid y$	TC4
$(x + y) \mid z = x \mid z + y \mid z$	CM8		
$x \mid (y + z) = x \mid y + x \mid z$	CM9		
		$\partial_H(\tau) = \tau$	DT
		$\tau_I(\tau) = \tau$	TI1
$\partial_H(a) = a$ if $a \notin H$	D1	$\tau_I(a) = a$ if $a \notin I$	TI2
$\partial_H(a) = \delta$ if $a \in H$	D2	$\tau_I(a) = \tau$ if $a \in I$	TI3
$\partial_H(x + y) = \partial_H(x) + \partial_H(y)$	D3	$\tau_I(x + y) = \tau_I(x) + \tau_I(y)$	TI4
$\partial_H(xy) = \partial_H(x).\partial_H(y)$	D4	$\tau_I(xy) = \tau_I(x).\tau_I(y)$	TI5

Table 2.

ACP_τ algebras satisfy the combinatorial identities shared by finite processes. In order to deal with infinite processes we will further assume that the following second order principles and rules are satisfied in the process algebra in which we model ABP, the alternating bit protocol.

I. Recursive specification principle (RSP)
II. Koomen's fair abstraction rule (KFAR)
III. Handshaking axiom (HA)
IV. Expansion Theorem (ET)

We will explain I-IV below. First, however, we allow ourselves some methodological remarks.

Remark 1. At present it is not possible to provide a remotely complete axiomatisation of processes that is of use "in general". But the equational (sub)-systems ACP and ACP_τ are a fixed kernel. Here ACP consists of the axioms A1-7,C1-3,CM1-9,D1-4, i.e. the left column of Table 2.

Remark 2. The system ACP was introduced in [3], and ACP_τ was introduced in [4]. We view ACP_τ as a reformulation of the basic issues of Milner's CCS [9] Comments on the relation between ACP_τ and CCS are in [4].

Remark 3. Koomen's fair abstraction rule has been derived from an idea that C.J. Koomen and R. Schutten used in experimental work on protocol verification . At Philips Research Eindhoven they have developed a formula manipulation package based on CCS.

2.2. Explanation of the principles I,II,III,IV.

2.2.1. The recursive specification principle.

Let X, Y, X_i, Y_i $(i\in\omega)$ be variables for processes. We write $\mathbb{X}$ for $\{X_i \mid i\in\omega\}$ and $\mathbb{Y}$ for $\{Y_i \mid i\in\omega\}$. If Z is a collection of variables then t(Z) denotes an ACP_τ term over Z.

Let $E \subseteq A$. We call the term t(Z) E-guarded if each variable in t(Z) is preceded by an atom in E and t(Z) does not contain an operator τ_I. Here 'preceded' is defined thus: if t is a subterm (occurrence) in x and s in y, then t precedes s in x.y; likewise in $x \lfloor\!\lfloor y$ (but not in $x\|y$).
Example: $a.(X\|Y) + b.X$ and $a.X.(X\|Y) + \tau.(b \lfloor\!\lfloor X)$ are $\{a,b\}$-guarded, but $\tau.X + b.Y$, $\tau X|aY$ and $(aX\|Y) \lfloor\!\lfloor bZ$ are not E-guarded for any E.

We call an equation X = t(Z) E-guarded if t(Z) is E-guarded.

Remark. The reason for excluding operators τ_I in an E-guarded term is that it is problematic to find a suitable definition of guardedness in the presence of such operators. Here 'suitable' refers to our wish to obtain unique processes (by RSP; see below) as solutions of systems of guarded equations. E.g. the following system has infinitely many solutions:

$$X = a.\tau_{\{b\}}(Y)$$

$$Y = b.\tau_{\{a\}}(X).$$

Namely, every X = a.p with a,b not in the alphabet of p is a solution.

DEFINITION. A recursive specification $S_E(X;\mathcal{X})$ is a collection of E-guarded equations (over ACP):

$$X_i = t_i(\mathcal{X})$$

together with an equation

$$X = t(\mathcal{X}).$$

Remark. If P,P_i $(i\in\omega)$ satisfy the system of equations $S_E(P;P_i|i\in\omega)$ then we want to view $S_E(X;X_i|i\in\omega)$ as a specification of P involving auxiliary processes P_i $(i\in\omega)$.

Of course this definition includes the case of a finite specification.

The recursive specification principle (RSP) states that a recursive definition singles out a unique process (if any). In more formal notation:

$$\text{(RSP)}\qquad \frac{S_E(X;\mathcal{X})\qquad S_E(Y,\mathcal{Y})}{X=Y}$$

2.2.2. Koomen's fair abstraction rule (KFAR).

This rule allows to compute $\tau_I(X)$ for certain X, thereby expressing the fact that certain steps in I will be fairly scheduled in such a way that eventually a step outside I is performed. This is the formal description of KFAR:

$$\text{(KFAR)}\qquad \frac{\forall n\in\mathbb{Z}_k\quad X_n = i_n.X_{n+1} + Y_n \qquad (i_n\in I)}{\tau_I(X_n) = \tau.\tau_I(Y_0+\ldots+Y_{k-1})}$$

Here $\mathbb{Z}_k = \{0,\ldots,k-1\}$ and addition in subscripts works modulo k.

We illustrate the effect of KFAR in two simple examples:

(i) Suppose $X = i.X + a$ where $a \notin I$. Then an application of KFAR yields: $\tau_I(X) = \tau.a$. This expresses the fact that, due to some fairness mechanism, i resists being performed infinitely many times consecutively.

(ii) Let $Y = i.Y$, then $\tau_I(Y) = \tau.\delta$. To see this note that $Y = i.Y + \delta$ and apply KFAR.

For a different approach to fairness in processes we refer to DE BAKKER & ZUCKER [1].

2.2.3. Axioms of standard concurrency.

We will adopt the following axioms of 'standard concurrency'; all axioms (1)-(6) hold for finite processes from ACP_τ. In [5] these axioms are proved simultaneously with induction on term formation; we will only need here axioms (3)-(6).

(1)	$(x \lfloor\!\lfloor y) \lfloor\!\lfloor z = x \lfloor\!\lfloor (y \| z)$
(2)	$(x \mid ay) \lfloor\!\lfloor z = x \mid (ay \lfloor\!\lfloor z)$
(3)	$x \mid y = y \mid x$
(4)	$x \| y = y \| x$
(5)	$x \mid (y \mid z) = (x \mid y) \mid z$
(6)	$x \| (y \| z) = (x \| y) \| z$

2.2.4. Handshaking axiom (HA).

The handshaking axiom expresses the fact that all communications are binary, i.e. work by means of handshaking.

(HA)	$x \mid y \mid z = \delta$

2.2.5. Expansion Theorem (ET).

This theorem, in the context of CCS due to MILNER [9] and for ACP_τ formulated in [4], can be shown for finite processes from ACP_τ. (See [5].) The Expansion Theorem presupposes HA and the axioms of standard concurrency (except (1),(2)). The following notation is used: Let $x_1,\ldots,x_k$ be processes. With X^i we denote merge of all x_n such that $n \in \{1,\ldots,k\} - \{i\}$. With $X^{i,j}$ we denote the merge of all x_n such that $n \in \{1,\ldots,k\} - \{i,j\}$.

ET is then formulated as follows (for $k \geq 3$):

$$(ET) \quad x_1 \| \ldots \| x_k = \sum_{1 \leq i \leq k} x_i \lfloor\!\lfloor X^i + \sum_{1 \leq i < j \leq k} (x_i | x_j) \lfloor\!\lfloor X^{i,j}$$

ET is an indispensable tool for the calculation of terms of the form $x_1 \| \ldots \| x_k$. Essentially it is a generalisation of the axiom CM1 of ACP_τ.

3. A VERIFICATION OF ABP

Let $T^* = \sum_{d \in D} r1(d).w2(d).T^*$ and $T = \tau_I \partial_H(S \| K \| L \| R)$ in the notation of Section 1. Section 1 fixes a set of atomic actions A and a communication function on it.

Using ACP_τ + RSP + KFAR + HA + ET we will show: $T = T^*$. Stated differently:

$$\tau_I \partial_H(S \| K \| L \| R) = \sum_{d \in D} r1(d).w2(d).\tau_I \partial_H(S \| K \| L \| R)$$

For the proof we use the following notation:

$$(x_1 \| x_2 \| x_3 \| x_4) = \left(\begin{array}{c|c} x_1 & x_2 \\ \hline x_3 & x_4 \end{array}\right).$$

Using this notation we have:

$$T = \tau_I \partial_H \left(\begin{array}{c|c} S & K \\ \hline L & R \end{array}\right) = \tau_I \partial_H \left(\begin{array}{c|c} S^0.S^1.S & K \\ \hline L & R^1.R^0.R \end{array}\right).$$

For $b \in \{0,1\}$ we write

$$T^b(X,Y) = \tau_I \partial_H \left(\begin{array}{c|c} S^b.S^{1-b}.X & K \\ \hline L & R^{1-b}.R^b.Y \end{array}\right).$$

In particular, $T = T^0(S,R)$.

<u>CLAIM</u>: $$T^b(X,Y) = \sum_{d \in D} r1(d).w2(d).\tau_I \partial_H \left(\begin{array}{c|c} S^{1-b}.X & K \\ \hline L & R^b.Y \end{array}\right).$$

The claim proves $T = T^*$ as follows:

$$T = T^0(S,R) = \sum_{d \in D} r1(d).w2(d).\tau_I \partial_H \left(\begin{array}{c|c} S^1.S & K \\ \hline L & R^0.R \end{array}\right) =$$

$$\sum_{d\in D} r1(d).w2(d).\tau_I\partial_H\left(\begin{array}{c|c} S^1.S^0.S^1.S & K \\ \hline L & R^0.R^1.R^0.R \end{array}\right) =$$

$$\sum_{d\in D} r1(d).w2(d).T^1(S^1.S,\ R^0.R) =$$

$$\sum_{d\in D} r1(d).w2(d).\ \sum_{a\in D} r1(a).w2(a).\tau_I\partial_H\left(\begin{array}{c|c} S^0.S^1.S & K \\ \hline L & R^1.R^0.R \end{array}\right) =$$

$$\sum_{d\in D} r1(d).w2(d).\ \sum_{a\in D} r1(a).w2(a).T\ .$$

Thus T satisfies an (A-guarded) recursion equation which is also satisfied by T*. It follows by RSP that T = T*.

<u>PROOF OF THE CLAIM</u>. We write

$$G^b(X,Y) = \partial_H\left(\begin{array}{c|c} S^b.S^{1-b}.X & K \\ \hline L & R^{1-b}.R^b.Y \end{array}\right)$$

and

$$G^b_d(X,Y) = \partial_H\left(\begin{array}{c|c} S^b_d.S^{1-b}.X & K \\ \hline L & R^{1-b}.R^b.Y \end{array}\right)$$

Terms like $G^b(X,Y)$ and $G^b_d(X,Y)$ can be rewritten using the Expansion Theorem. ET will yield 4 + 6 = 10 terms and in all cases in this proof at most 2 of these terms are not equal to δ. In the sequel we will use applications of ET as a single calculation step. (Note that it is entirely feasible to verify all these applications of ET automatically.)

Now:

$$T^b(X,Y) = \sum_{d\in D} r1(d).\tau_I\partial_H\left(\begin{array}{c|c} S^b_d.S^{1-b}.X & K \\ \hline L & R^{1-b}.R^b.Y \end{array}\right) =$$

$$\sum_{d\in D} r1(d).\tau_I G^b_d(X,Y).$$

We will derive a recursive specification for $G^b_d(X,Y)$:

$$G^b_d(X,Y) = j.\partial_H\left(\begin{array}{c|c} U^b_d.S^{1-b}.X & (i.w4(e) + i.w4(db)).K \\ \hline L & R^{1-b}.R^b.Y \end{array}\right) =$$

$$= j.\left[i.\partial_H\left(\begin{array}{c|c} U^b_d.S^{1-b}.X & w4(e).K \\ \hline L & R^{1-b}.R^b.Y \end{array}\right) + i.\partial_H\left(\begin{array}{c|c} U^b_d.S^{1-b}.X & w4(db).K \\ \hline L & R^{1-b}.R^b.Y \end{array}\right)\right] =$$

$$= j.\left[i.j.\partial_H \left(\begin{array}{c|c} U_d^b.S^{1-b}.X & K \\ \hline L & w6(1-b).R^{1-b}.R^b.Y \end{array} \right) + \right.$$

$$\left. + \ i.j.\partial_H \left(\begin{array}{c|c} U_d^b.S^{1-b}.X & K \\ \hline L & w2(d).w6(b).R^b.Y \end{array} \right) \right] =$$

$$= j.\left[i.j.j.\partial_H \left(\begin{array}{c|c} U_d^b.S^{1-b}.X & K \\ \hline (i.w5(e) + i.w5(1-b)).L & R^{1-b}.R^b.Y \end{array} \right) + i.j.Z \right]$$

$$\text{(with } Z = \partial_H \left(\begin{array}{c|c} U_d^b.S^{1-b}.X & K \\ \hline L & w2(d).w6(b).R^b.Y \end{array} \right) \text{)} =$$

$$= j.\left[i.j.j.\left\{ i.\partial_H \left(\begin{array}{c|c} U_d^b.S^{1-b}.X & K \\ \hline w5(e).L & R^{1-b}.R^b.Y \end{array} \right) + \right.\right.$$

$$\left.\left. + \ i.\partial_H \left(\begin{array}{c|c} U_d^b.S^{1-b}.X & K \\ \hline w5(1-b).L & R^{1-b}.R^b.Y \end{array} \right) \right\} + i.j.Z \right] =$$

$$= j.\left[i.j.j.\left\{ i.j.\partial_H \left(\begin{array}{c|c} S_d^b.S^{1-b}.X & K \\ \hline L & R^{1-b}.R^b.Y \end{array} \right) + \right.\right.$$

$$\left.\left. + \ i.j.\partial_H \left(\begin{array}{c|c} S_d^b.S^{1-b}.X & K \\ \hline L & R^{1-b}.R^b.Y \end{array} \right) \right\} + i.j.Z \right] =$$

$$= j.\left[i.j.j.i.j.G_d^b(X,Y) + i.j.Z \right].$$

We can now apply KFAR for $k = 6$ and $Y_0 = \delta$, $Y_1 = i.j.Z$, $Y_2 = \ldots = Y_5 = \delta$. This gives:

$$\tau_I(G_d^b(X,Y)) = \tau.\tau_I(i.j.Z) \ .$$

Hence:

$$T^b(X,Y) = \sum_{d\in D} r1(d).\tau_I(G_d^b(X,Y)) = \sum_{d\in D} r1(d).\tau.\tau_I(i.j.Z) =$$

$$= \sum_{d\in D} r1(d).\tau.\tau.\tau.\tau_I(Z) = \sum_{d\in D} r1(d).\tau_I(Z) =$$

$$= \sum_{d\in D} r1(d).\tau_I\partial_H\left(\begin{array}{c|c} U_d^b.S^{1-b}.X & K \\ \hline L & w2(d).w6(b).R^b.Y \end{array}\right) =$$

$$= \sum_{d\in D} r1(d).\tau_I\left[w2(d).\partial_H\left(\begin{array}{c|c} U_d^b.S^{1-b}.X & K \\ \hline L & w6(b).R^b.Y \end{array}\right)\right] =$$

$$= \sum_{d\in D} r1(d).w2(d).\tau_I(K_d^b(X,Y))$$

$$\text{(with } K_d^b(X,Y) = \partial_H\left(\begin{array}{c|c} U_d^b.S^{1-b}.X & K \\ \hline L & w6(b).R^b.Y \end{array}\right)\text{)}.$$

The next part of the proof of the claim consists in deriving a recursion equation for $K_d^b(X,Y)$:

$$K_d^b(X,Y) = j.\partial_H\left(\begin{array}{c|c} U_d^b.S^{1-b}.X & K \\ \hline (i.w5(b) + i.w5(e)).L & R^b.Y \end{array}\right) =$$

$$= j.\left[i.\partial_H\left(\begin{array}{c|c} U_d^b.S^{1-b}.X & K \\ \hline w5(b).L & R^b.Y \end{array}\right) + i.\partial_H\left(\begin{array}{c|c} U_d^b.S^{1-b}.X & K \\ \hline w5(e).L & R^b.Y \end{array}\right)\right] =$$

$$= j.\left[i.j.\partial_H\left(\begin{array}{c|c} S^{1-b}.X & K \\ \hline L & R^b.Y \end{array}\right) + i.j.\partial_H\left(\begin{array}{c|c} S_d^b.S^{1-b}.X & K \\ \hline L & R^b.Y \end{array}\right)\right] =$$

$$= j.\left[i.j.V + i.j.j.\partial_H\left(\begin{array}{c|c} U_d^b.S^{1-b}.X & (i.w4(e) + i.w4(db)).K \\ \hline L & R^b.Y \end{array}\right)\right]$$

$$\text{(with } V = \partial_H\left(\begin{array}{c|c} S^{1-b}.X & K \\ \hline L & R^b.Y \end{array}\right)\text{)} =$$

$$= j.\left[i.j.V + i.j.j.\left\{i.\partial_H\left(\begin{array}{c|c} U_d^b.S^{1-b}.X & w4(e).K \\ \hline L & R^b.Y \end{array}\right) + \right.\right.$$

$$\left.\left. + \; i.\partial_H\left(\begin{array}{c|c} U_d^b.S^{1-b}.X & w4(db).K \\ \hline L & R^b.Y \end{array}\right)\right\}\right] =$$

$$= j.\left[i.j.V + i.j.j.\left\{i.j.\partial_H\left(\begin{array}{c|c} U_d^b.S^{1-b}.X & K \\ \hline L & w6(b).R^b.Y \end{array}\right) + \right.\right.$$

$$\left.\left. + \; i.j.\partial_H\left(\begin{array}{c|c} U_d^b.S^{1-b}.X & K \\ \hline L & w6(b).R^b.Y \end{array}\right)\right\}\right] =$$

$$= j.\left[i.j.V + i.j.j.i.j.K_d^b(X,Y)\right].$$

Applying KFAR we get:

$$\tau_I(K_d^b(X,Y)) = \tau.\tau_I(i.j.V) = \tau.\tau.\tau.\tau_I(V) = \tau.\tau_I(V) =$$

$$\tau.\tau_I\partial_H\left(\begin{array}{c|c} S^{1-b}.X & K \\ \hline L & R^b.Y \end{array}\right).$$

We conclude:

$$T^b(X,Y) = \sum_{d\in D} r1(d).w2(d).\tau_I(K_d^b(X,Y)) =$$

$$= \sum_{d\in D} r1(d).w2(d).\tau.\tau_I\partial_H\left(\begin{array}{c|c} S^{1-b}.X & K \\ \hline L & R^b.Y \end{array}\right) =$$

$$= \sum_{d \in D} r1(d).w2(d).\tau_I \partial_H \left(\begin{array}{c|c} S^{1-b}.X & K \\ \hline L & R^b.Y \end{array} \right).$$

This finishes the proof of the claim and the verification of ABP.

REFERENCES

[1] DE BAKKER, J.W. & J.I. ZUCKER, *Compactness in semantics for merge and fair merge*, Report IW 238/83, Mathematisch Centrum Amsterdam 1983.

[2] BARTLETT, K.A., R.A. SCANTLEBURY & P.T. WILKINSON, *A note on reliable full-duplex transmission over half duplex lines*, CACM 12,No.5(1969).

[3] BERGSTRA, J.A. & J.W. KLOP, *Process Algebra for Synchronous Communication*, Information and Control, Vol.60, Nos.1-3, 1984, 109-137.

[4] BERGSTRA, J.A. & J.W. KLOP, *Algebra of Communicating Processes*, to appear in Proc. of the CWI Symposium Mathematics and Computer Science (eds. J.W. de Bakker, M. Hazewinkel and J.K. Lenstra), North-Holland, Amsterdam 1985.

[5] BERGSTRA, J.A. & J.W. KLOP, *Algebra of Communicating Processes with abstraction*, to appear in Theoretical Computer Science, 1985.

[6] HAILPERN, B.T., *Verifying concurrent processes using temporal logic.* Springer LNCS 129, 1982.

[7] HAILPERN, B.T. & S. OWICKI, *Verifying network protocole using temporal logic*, in: Trends and applications symposium, National Bureau of Standards 1980.

[8] LAMPORT, L., *Specifying concurrent program modules*, ACM Toplas, Vol.5, No.2, p.190-222.

[9] MILNER, R., *A Calculus of Communicating Systems*, Springer LNCS 92, 1980.

[10] SCHWARTZ, R.L. & P. MELIAR SMITH, *From state machine to temperal logic, specification methods for protocol standards*, IEEE Transactions on communication, Vol.30, No.12 (1982) p.2486-2496.

[11] YEMINI, Y. & J.F. KUROSE, *Can current protocol verification techniques guarantee correctness?* Computer networks, Vol.6, No.6 (1982), p. 377-381.

PREDICATIVE PROGRAMMING REVISITED

W. Bibel
TU München, Germany,
and
Duke University, Durham NC USA

Abstract.

This paper analyzes the problem of program synthesis at various levels of detail. At the highest level we distinguish a number of problem areas which are addressed in the subject as a whole. The goals, achievements and perspectives of each of these areas are briefly reviewed. At the next lower level we outline techniques which have been applied partially in the context of the LOPS project, or which, to our opinion, are worth further elaboration. Occasionally, we work out at the technical level specific features which seem to need clarification. The connection method will be the deductive tool on this level of detail, where especially two new results of interest are achieved. One concerns the functionalization of PROLOG programs, the other the extension of PROLOG's relative efficiency to formulas beyond those in Horn-form.

Keywords: predicative programming, program synthesis, program construction, LOPS, connection method

Introduction

Software production is one of the most rapidly expanding sectors in economy ranging in the tens of billions of dollars per year. Yet the way of production still appears to be rather archaic. The consequences are well-known and may be experienced by anyone who makes any kind of use of any sort of software:

- production is slow and costly
- reliability is questionable for larger systems
- changes require an inadequate amount of efforts
- different packages never fit together
- numerous further problems

It has been argued in Bibel (1974) that these problems are inherent in the way software is developed. At that time we proposed a higher level approach for which we coined the name *predicative programming.*

The fundamental thesis of predicative programming is that programming problems and solutions must be allowed to be stated in a descriptive way, in the sense that the objects involved are described by way of their relationships. This philosophy is meant to be applied for the entire process spanning the informal and the machine level. Formally, such relationships would be captured by predicates from where the name originates, then (Hehner 1984 used the term in a related but yet significantly different context).

Since logic is the canonical formalism dealing with predicates, clearly our approach has always been deeply committed with modeling the entire program construction process in terms of logic as a uniform formalism. We share this commitment with the logic programming community, although predicative programming from the very beginning was designed to include a number of important features which so far are not considered in the context of, say, PROLOG.

This research program has continuously been pursued (unfortunately with poor resources of all sorts) during the last decade leading to an experimental system called LOPS - for LO*gical* P*rogram* S*ynthesis* - as well as to a number of publications. Some of them are listed in the references and discussed elsewhere in the paper.

Although fifth generation computer systems have drawn the attention of computer scientists and software engineers to logic oriented programming, the commitment still is poor in view of the task that had to be accomplished for making this way feasible. This is to a large degree true also for theoretical issues which are emerging under such an approach.

It is the purpose of the present paper to review briefly the whole approach of predicative programming. In particular, we identify (in section 1) a number of levels of specification along with the issues raised by the transformations between them. (This keyword clearly reminds of the transformational approach to programming; in a sense any approach to programming will be transformational in some way; the "transformational camp" in the more specific sense of this term would, however, not agree with a number of basic features of our approach.) This level structure is meant to support a clarifying comparison of various constructive methods known under the headings of *program synthesis* or *program construction.*

All these levels are then discussed bottom up, one section for each. Especially, the paper focuses on the problem of *functionalizing* recursive logic programs. This is discussed in section 3 where we revisit and refine the program synthesis method by Manna and Waldinger (1971). A further technical result of interest is introduced in Section 4, which shows a promising way of extending PROLOG's relative efficiency in a natural way to the whole class of formulas in first-order logic, by imposing a restriction on proofs rather than on formulas.

As the deductive technique supporting this approach we use the *connection method* (Bibel 1982, 1983). In lack of space the reader is sort of assumed to be familiar with its flavor.

1. An analysis of the problem

On the highest level of abstraction and informality the problem of program synthesis or program construction amounts to the following. We are given an informal description of some problem that usefully involves some computations for solving it. Our goal is to construct a piece of software that would perform these computations, hopefully in a correct and efficient way. Typically the stated problem in fact consists of a class of problems that are considered similar in their nature so that the software eventually may support any instance in this class.

It might be worthwhile to alert the reader to the fact that by the nature of our subject we have to talk here about problems on different levels of language. This is for the simple reason that our topic is concerned with the problem of solving problems. It is our hope that this warning already helps to avoid any confusions from this fact. In addition we will make an attempt to stick to the notion of "task" in the context of the problems that are supposed to be solved by the resulting programs. Hence our topic rather is the problem of solving tasks.

In a problem of this complexity it is mandatory to make every attempt to break it down into as many independent pieces as possible. Unfortunately such a pre-structuring process to some extent predetermines the class of possible solutions since most of the pieces involved are in fact not really independent. Moreover there is a wide variety of possible structures. The selection we have made is based on the following considerations.

It seems reasonable to identify subproblems that differ in their feasibility with current technology. This goes along with a "feeling" of hardness of these subproblems with respect to the state of the art. In this sense the problem of transforming an informal description in natural language, say, into a formal one is felt to be harder than compiling a FORTRAN program into machine code. Further we would like to take full advantage of existing capabilities both theoretical and practical. At the same time we are aiming at the greatest possible uniformity in the formal treatment of our problem.

With considerations of that sort in mind the global structure of the problem as shown in figure 1 has emerged over the last decade. This structure distinguishes between various levels of task specification. When we have spoken of an informal task description above, it is meant that this description might be provided at any of these levels. On the one extreme the description might be provided by the ***s***ystem ***e***ngineer (***se***) in a way which can directly be executed by the machine. On the other topmost extreme we think of the ***c***asual ***u***ser (***cu***) who is neither trained in formal descriptions in some field of expertise nor in programming in general. These extremes span the range of all these levels.

In this model we allow an "informal task description" be provided at any level although the choice of wording is meant to suggest that our emphasis is more on the problems related with descriptions provided on the higher rather than the lower levels. Nevertheless it should be noted that a classical program, say, is not excluded from our considerations. The description might even be provided in a mixed way at more than one level.

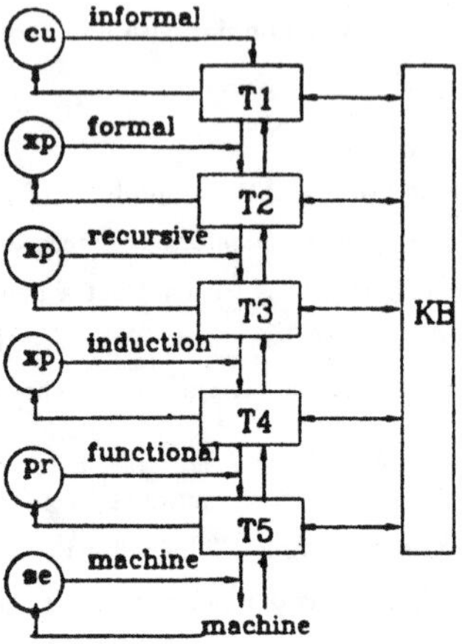

Figure 1. The structure of the program construction problem

Let us now informally discuss the various levels starting from top. Clearly the most convenient way of programming for a casual user would be by describing his problem in his own natural way which usually is in natural language supported by some graphics. In our structure a component (T1) would have to transform such informal input into a specification in a formal language that we propose to be an enriched version of predicate logic (see below).

Lack of formality is only one deficiency in a task description as provided by a casual user. His description will in most cases feature a certain degree of incompleteness. For this reason the model forsees an ongoing interaction of the user (at any level) with the system in the process of program development. This interaction is meant to be carried out at the same level of language as his original description. As a result of this interaction missing details may be identified and integrated into the description at a later stage if necessary in a joint effort of man and machine. Let us ignore this additional problem for a while and assume that the result of the transformation carried out by T1 is a complete logical specification, say S.

By nature the description will also be naive in view of the capabilities of the machine in the following sense. Any machine may carry out a number of basic functions, say $f\,1,...,fn$, along with a number of basic operators, say $p\,1,...,pm$. Our basic problem may now be stated in the following way. We want to synthesize a term t (representing an executable functional or algorithmic program) over these function and operator symbols such that $z=tx$ holds for any pair x,z that satisfies the (input-output) specification S. In addition t should to some degree be optimal in terms of efficiency.

In order to be able to solve this problem one must know both all these basic functions and operators, and their behaviour in terms of computational resources needed for their execution. Even at the level of a classical programmer this cannot be seriously expected to be provided by the user. Thus the problem of program synthesis clearly includes the problem of an appropriate selection of f 's and p 's. To some extent it is realistic to assume that this selection is deferred until the last transformation T5.

The second level from top is meant to be the one of an *expert* (*xp*) capable of stating his task in a formal way. It will not necessarily use logic, although we can consider logic as a canonical form of representation. At this level we assume that the description merely defines the input-output behavior without providing any extra knowledge specifically aimed at an algorithmic solution.

It is meant to be the task of component T2 to transform such a purely descriptive specification into one that explicitly includes a recursive solution. As an example think of any PROLOG program. However, in contrast to PROLOG we are not thinking of the restriction to Horn clause logic in this context.

For the first time we consider in this paper a level between that of, say, PROLOG and the one of typical programming. At this intermediate level, the specification is meant to include in addition to the recursive description mentioned just before also an appropriate formal statement of the induction principle underlying the recursion under consideration along with the well-founded ordering relation on the domain.

On the level of ordinary *pr*ogramming (*pr*) we may think of a purely functional programming language which allows us to regard any program as a term in predicate logic. In view of mathematical semantics of conventional programming languages this is not a serious restriction of any relevance. It provides, however, the advantage of a uniform representational language, namely predicate logic, on all levels except the top-most (informal) and the bottom-most (machine) ones.

This concludes a first overview of these levels of specification. They structure the problem of program construction into the subproblems $T1$ through $T5$ in the most difficult case of an informal task description. Each of these subproblems requires appropriate support by a knowledge base (KB) in a system that would to some degree automatically attempt their solution. Each of these tasks will be discussed in more detail in the following sections along with the level they are taking their input from.

2. Functional programs

The level of language of functional programs is meant to cover all of standard programming (i.e., we do not restrict ourselves here to what today is called "functional programming"). There is certainly no need in our context of automatic programming to go into any details of how such programs are handled in computers. Most of the literature in Computer Science is concerned with this issue in one or another way. Nevertheless our way of abstracting from the many individual features of different standard programming languages might not be so familiar for which reason we are going to briefly illustrate this view.

In logic a term is built from variables and n-ary function symbols, $n \geq 0$. Both the variables and the function symbols are taken from any alphabet. Semantically terms are the syntactic equivalent of functions in a model. If we take this definition in its full generality, any program in a standard programming language may in fact be regarded as a term in an appropriate first-order language.

For algorithmic programming languages the justification of such an abstract view is provided by their mathematical semantics which defines the meaning of programs in terms of functions as well. Since their meaning is the same, programs may well be considered as terms if the alphabets are defined adequately.

For functional programming languages such as LISP this view is more obvious anyway. Still many people seem to be surprised being reminded that first-order terms may well include *λ-expressions*. We only have to require that λ be a symbol in the alphabet of function symbols. Then the *λ-expression*
$\lambda x.t$ is just another syntactic way of writing the term $\lambda(x,t)$ where t now is considered changed this way recursively all the way through. Similarly the λ-expression $(\lambda x.t)a$ would have to be considered as an

abbreviated form of writing *apply*[$\lambda(x,t),a$] where again *apply* is a symbol from the alphabet of functions.

Although I could not keep track of all the many recent publications on combining LISP with PROLOG (such as Derschowitz and Plaisted 1984), it is my impression that few or even none of them take this approach which I would consider the most direct one. In fact pretty standard work in theorem proving including generalized unification, procedural attachment, and so forth cover the main theoretical issues of this combination.

The reason why we are interested in taking this particular view lies in our aiming at a treatment of all the levels including this bottom-most functional one within a single uniform formalism. So once we have achieved a specification of the given task on this level, either directly or through a number of transformational steps starting from one of the higher levels, we may consider the task to be solved since compiling standard programs is certainly no issue anymore.

It might still be worth some consideration, however, which of the many programming languages available would best suit an approach to automatic programming like ours. Although I will not enter this discussion here, it is my belief that eventually some sort of a functional programming language (in contrast to any of the algorithmic languages) would offer an advantage in the present context. This is because they are close enough to the term part of the logic formalism and still offer the expressive power and flexibility needed for human interaction.

Meanwhile the reader may think of a program in any standard programming language when we speak of a term in the following sections.

3. Program synthesis through skolemization

Above the level, that we discussed in the last section, all levels (except the informal one) are considering a task specification in terms of logical formulas rather than just terms. In the present section we are considering a very specific way of defining a particular task in logic. It is restricted in a way so that the logical formula can be compiled into a term (i.e. a standard program according to the last section) by way of an automated theorem prover.

Let us consider the non-trivial and familiar example of appending one list to (the front of) another. The reader might find it useful to compare our treatment with the one in Nilsson (1980) of the same problem. We begin with stating the task description in logical terms.

In mathematical notation lists are constructs of the form $(a,b,\ldots,c)$. A complete specification would have to include a precise definition of this notion of lists (possibly provided by the knowledge base). There are several ways of defining it. Here we adopt the one from LISP which represents lists as nested dotted pairs of the form $a.(b.\ldots(c.nil)\ldots)$. When the same is represented in prefix form, the dot operation usually is denoted by *cons*. Thus the list then reads $cons(a,cons(b,\ldots cons(c,nil)\ldots))$. This is the form which fits into our logical framework since it is simply a term in it (recall what we said in the previous section about the relation of PROLOG and LISP).

In terms of a formal representation the task of appending one list to another is perhaps most naturally stated in the following form (for a different way of representation see Section 5).

P1 $$\forall x\,\forall y\,\exists z\,[x=cons(x1,\ldots cons(xm,nil)\ldots)\wedge y=cons(y1,\ldots cons(yn,nil)\ldots)\rightarrow z=cons(x1,\ldots cons(xn,cons(y1,\ldots cons(yn,nil)\ldots))\ldots)]$$

Given lists x and y as displayed by the term in the antecedent of P1, the append problem consists in finding a result z of the form displayed by the term in the consequence which is the list of elements from the first followed by those from the second input list. It is this form which, for instance, we want to permit as a legitimate input from the user denoted by xp in figure 1 on the formal level.

In the present section we substantially reduce this problem, however, first by explicitly providing a recursive definition of z in terms of x and y within the task specification. Informally, this recursive definition defines appending as *cons*-ing the first element of x with the result of appending the rest of x with y. In its formal form, which follows further below, it involves the following parts in which we use the three predicates A (for APPEND), N (for NULL), and S (for SUBLIST).

F1 $Nx \rightarrow A(x,y,y)$

F2 $\neg Nu \wedge A(cdr(u),v,w) \rightarrow A(u,v,cons(car(u),w))$

With these definitions alone we were only able to run this task specification in the way of a PROLOG program (provided that some more information on N and a goal statement be given) as discussed in the next section. In order to attain the desired functional program, however, an important additional piece of information has to be provided. For instance, an adequate induction scheme will serve this purpose.

Since there are a number of such induction schemes, whereby each may be used with a different well-founded ordering relation in order to provide a concrete induction rule, we substantially reduce our problem once more by explicitly providing an adequate such induction rule. How to have the system support this selection will be the topic of the next section. The scheme we are going to use here includes the notion of a sublist. So we must provide also statements defining this notion in terms of the notions used before. The proof below will require only the following one out of these.

F3 $\neg Nx' \rightarrow S(cdr(x'),x')$

Now we are ready to introduce the induction rule. Informally, it states that, suppose we know how to append sublists of a list and how to carry over such knowledge to appending the list itself, then this shows us how to append any list. It is the usual induction scheme with the well-founded ordering "sublist of". Formally, this reads as follows.

F4 $\forall cd\ \{\forall y'u'[S(y',c) \rightarrow \exists f\, A(y',u',f)] \rightarrow \exists z' A(c,d,z')\} \rightarrow \forall v'w' \exists g\ A(v',w',g)$

Our overall goal in this task is to determine the result of appending two given lists which simply reads as follows.

G1 $\forall ab\ \exists z\ A(a,b,z)$

So the task as a whole may now fully be stated in a way that is familiar from program synthesis: under the assumption of all the facts F1 through F4 we claim that the goal holds. Formally this is expressed by the following formula.

P2 $F1 \wedge F2 \wedge F3 \wedge F4 \rightarrow G1$

Altogether from the task description P1 we arrived at an equivalent specification P2 that is much more specific in view of a potential computation. We will see now that it is even straightforward, at least in principle, to obtain a functional program out of P2. This can be achieved by proving P2 automatically with a theorem prover.

Any theorem prover for first-order logic would in fact serve for this purpose. For instance, we might use a resolution-type prover after transformation of P2 into clause form. Or we might prefer a more natural deduction-like setting. It just happens that the author has developed a proof method called the connection method for which reason the reader hopefully may understand our preference for this particular type of proofs. But let us emphasize again that this choice is not relevant for the final result. We will raise this point once more later on.

As we mentioned in the introduction there is no space in this paper to introduce once more any details of the connection method that are described elsewhere. Nevertheless we will comment the connection proof of P1 shown in figure 2 to an extent so that even the casual reader may get a feeling for how it might be understood.

The first step in arriving at the representation of P2 as shown in figure 2 consists of the usual procedure for getting rid of the quantifiers. This is done by introducing the Skolem functions *a* ,*b* , *c* ,*d* ,*f* , and *append*, and this way being able to delete all quantifiers.

Basically, a proof for the resulting quantifier-free formula in the connection method consists of a set of connections that connect pairs of complementary literals in it so that certain criteria are fulfilled. One of the criteria is best understood if we represent the formula in a two-dimensional way as is done with the present formula in the matrix shown in figure 2.

It consists of 5 columns that we might call (generalized) clauses which are to be combined in a disjunctive way in order to yield the whole formula. The subparts of each clause are to be understood as conjuncts. They are all literals in the present case except for the second one from the right. This one consists of 2 conjuncts where one is a whole matrix again, namely a disjunction of 2 clauses. In other words P1 is transformed into an AND/OR form displayed in a 2-dimensional way (AND vertically, OR horizontally). Note that this transformation is carried out for illustrative reasons only, and is not actually needed. A fortiori there is no need for the connection method to transform further into the usual clause form as is necessary for a resolution proof which is one of the (minor) reasons for our preference for this particular method.

Now we must find a set of connections so that, no matter which way you go when traversing the matrix strictly from left to right, you always meet a pair of connected literals. In this test you may take into account different copies of the clauses as if these different copies would be represented as different columns instead of a single one in the matrix. This is in fact necessary for a number of clauses in the matrix below in the sense that we would not find a set of connections meeting all criteria just with a single copy of each column. The different copies are indicated simply by numbering the endpoints of the connections into the literals of the clauses. In the present case this means that we never need more than just 2 copies of any clause.

Another criterion that must be fulfilled in order to be accepted as a proof is unifiability of the respective terms in the connected literals. Thereby variables in different copies may be considered different. In our illustration this is realized by indexing the variables with the number of the copy in which they occur. For instance *z* in the first copy of the last clause is denoted by *z*. 1, while in the second it is denoted *z*. 2. The reader might now want to check that the substitutions given along with the connections in figure 2 in fact unify all the terms as described before.

Recall that *z* is the variable the value of which we want to determine in this problem. As we see *z* obtains two different values in this proof stored in *z.1* and *z.2*. So the question arises which one applies for a given input. There is a simple way to determine this by inspecting the established proof.

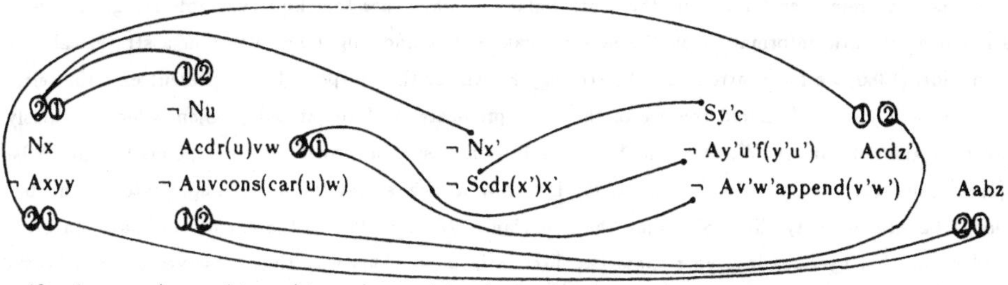

unifications: *x.1\a, y.1\b, z.1\b, u.1\a, v.1\b, v\cdr(a), w\b, w.1\append(cdr(a),b), z'.1\d, x.2\c, y.2\d, u.2\c, v.2\d, z'.2\cons(car(c),f(cdr(c),d)), u\d, y\cdr(c), w.2\f(cdr(c),d), x\c, z.2\cons(car(a),append(cdr(a),b))*

the substitutions of the result variable combined as a conditional substitution:
z \ (if Na then b else cons(car(a),append(cdr(a),b))

Figure 2. A connection proof for P2 together with all unifications

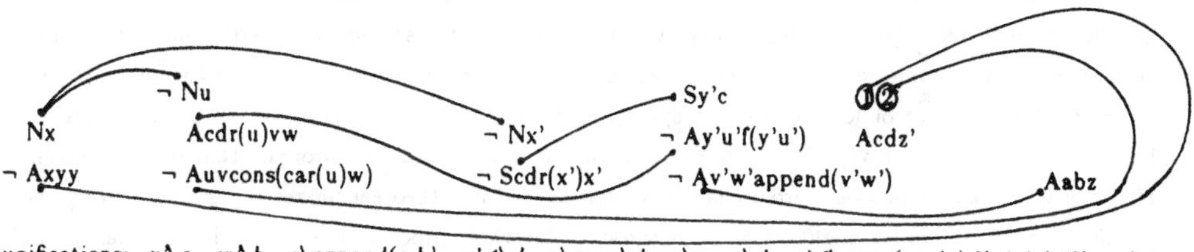

unifications: *v\a, w\b, z\append(a,b), z'.1\d, x\c, y\d, u\c, v\d, z'.2\cons(car(c),f(cdr(c),d)), u\d, y\cdr(c), w\f(cdr(c),d), x\c*

Figure 3. A different connection proof for P2

Consider the following chain of connections (pairs of connected literals with their variables being substituted) from the first into the second copy of the goal clause:
(Aabb, ¬ Aabb), (Na, ¬ Na), ¬ A(a,b,cons(car(a),append(cdr(a),b))), A(a,b,cons(car(a),append(cdr(a),b))),
Note that the second literal of a pair is always in the same (copy of a) clause as the first literal in the next pair. We select *(Na,¬ Na)* out of this chain for reasons discussed below. If its first literal holds the first value of *z* applies otherwise the second one (note the relevance of the order in which the literals are listed).

This fact may be written in form of the conditional substitution shown in figure 2.

We observe that the general way of determining such a chain is purely mechanical and can be performed fast with standard cycle algorithms. In principle any pair of literals in any chain of this kind might be used for the conditional substitution provided that after its deletion no such chain can be found any more (which is the case for our selected connection). In view of the intended computational purpose, however, we have a preference for literals the truth values of which are (quickly) evaluable for given input. This requires semantic information on the systems capabilities and might be settled in a strategical way only. In Bibel (1980) we have introduced the strategy EVAL for this purpose. In the present case the selection is unique if we simply avoid the use of the main predicate A of the stated problem which obviously cannot be evaluated quickly. We mention that the selection of such a connection corresponds to what Nilsson (1980) calls restricted goal resolution (RGR). Logically it means that the proof is split into two unconnected parts. Also we may think of adding the new clause $Na \vee \neg Na$ to the axioms and substitute the selected connection by ones involving these two literals in an obvious way that preserves the connection proof.

It happens that a proof for an example of the kind discussed in this section is not unique; rather there is an even simpler one shown for the present example in figure 3 again with all involved substitutions. It requires a second copy of a single (sub-) clause only; also it may be noticed that most connections in it are actually present in the previous proof as well along with their substitutions. Here the result variable obtains the value *append(a,b)*. So altogether we obtain two different results by two different proofs. If we insist that our problem defines a function then the result cannot vary with the particular proof chosen. In other words the two results must be the same. This gives us the following equation.

$$append(a,b) = (if\ Na\ then\ b\ else\ cons(car(a),append(cdr(a),b)))$$

This clearly is a functional program of the sort considered in the previous section (with some knowledge from recursive function theory it may be easily represented as a term), and thus can be evaluated with the standard methods considered there, assuming *cons*, *car*, and *cdr* are basic operations. In summary, for the class of logical program specifications on the level discussed in the present section we have a purely mechanical way of compiling the specification into a machine program that seems to be feasible for a wide class of practical programs. All that is needed is a theorem prover capable of proving those specifications. (The reader might wish to go through the whole process once more with another example like counting the items in a list which structurally is quite similar as the append problem.)

Let us point out a number of issues that are of relevance in this context. The first is concerned with terminology. As we said in the beginning of the present section the most difficult part of program synthesis has not been considered with the technique described here since we simply jumped from P1 to P2. In our view the work reported in this section should therefore rather be described as *functionalization of recursive logic programs*. As we have seen this can be done in the presence of an induction rule.

We already emphasized the fact that the proof method might have been any standard method for first-order logic. Unfortunately, Manna and Waldinger (1984) have caused some confusion with their statements made there in section A (p.34): "the difficulty of representing the principle of mathematical induction in a resolution framework hampered ...". With their ongoing remarks concerning their own framework they leave the reader with the impression that they have overcome these alleged difficulties.

In order to clarify this confusion it must be clearly stated that there is no single technical feature of any relevance in their system that has not been studied in the context of other systems such as resolution or the connection method. Someone familiar with any of these systems will easily recognize the correspondences. Their recent contribution rather lies in the appealing way of representing the reasoning steps for carrying out the synthesis by hand.

For an implementation their representation has major drawbacks, however. For instance, they need a polarity strategy (p.47) for preventing fruitless resolution applications that become possible in their way of representation only; an analogue application would not even be possible in the representation used by the connection method, thus no such strategy is needed here.

On the other hand let us emphasize that the basic technique reported in this section is in fact due to Manna and Waldinger (1971). In our presentation we might have contributed a minor refinement only; for instance, the existence of a second proof has perhaps not been taken into explicit consideration in previous treatments, a point which seems to further clarify the technique. Also we have introduced a new mechanical way of detecting the condition for the conditional substitution. Altogether it should be clear that the whole method is fully general.

As a concluding remark let us point out that the technique presented in this section is quite capable of dealing with purely sequential (i.e. non-recursive) problems in the absence of any induction rule. This has an important application in the area of plan generation (e.g. for robots) that is discussed in detail in Bibel (1985).

4. Recursive logic programs

Consider again our problem of appending two given lists to obtain a single one as stated in P1. On the level to be discussed in the present section we liberalize our requirements on a suitable specification by abandoning the request for an induction scheme. So instead of jumping to the specification called P2 in the previous section, we only proceed from P1 to the following formula obtained from P2 by deletion of the induction scheme F4 and the property F3 of the corresponding ordering relation S.

P3 $\quad F1 \wedge F2 \rightarrow G1$

Let us consider this formula with a particular input term $cons(c, cons(d, nil))$ instead of the variable a. Figure 4 shows a connection proof for this case given in the matrix representation for the reasons mentioned in the previous section. It realizes the computation for a particular input by deduction in accordance with the logic programming paradigm. In the present example the output variable z gets the resultant value $cons(c,cons(d,b))$.

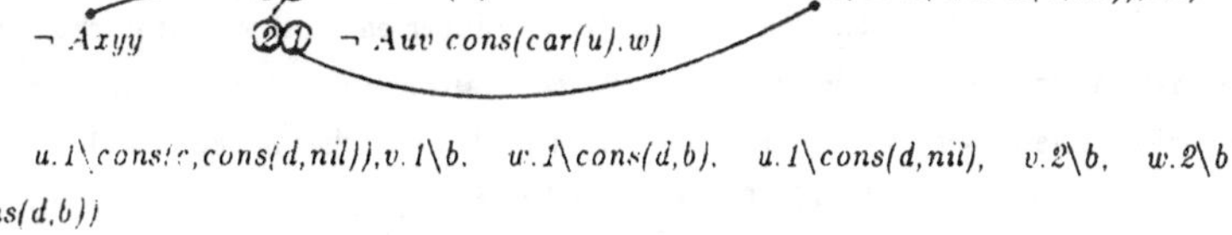

Unifications: $u.1\backslash cons(c,cons(d,nil)), v.1\backslash b, \quad w.1\backslash cons(d,b), \quad u.1\backslash cons(d,nil), \quad v.2\backslash b, \quad w.2\backslash b \quad x\backslash nil, \quad y\backslash b, \quad z\backslash cons(c,cons(d,b))$

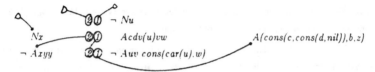

Figure 4. The connection proof for P3

As a remark concerning this particular connection proof we mention that we have in fact made use of a more generalized form of unification that involves evaluations. The same applies to literals - such as *Nnil* - evaluating to ***true***, which is syntactically captured by an open-ended connection (see Bibel 1982, section V.4, for more details). These features are not principally necessary, but are quite useful w.r.t. both performance and representation for better human understanding.

The matrix in figure 4 may be regarded as a PROLOG program since it can immediately be transformed into one by the following logically justified manipulations. Since PROLOG is sensitive for the order of clauses the control would not switch to the second clause unless ¬ Nu holds; thus this literal may be deleted from it so that the matrix now consists of a set of 3 Horn clauses (at most one negative literal in the positive representation). A turn of 90° together with a switch to the negative representation and insertion of implication in fact yields

$$
\begin{array}{lcl}
Axyy & \leftarrow & Nx \\
Auv\ cons(car(u),w) & \leftarrow & A\ cdr(u)vw \\
 & \leftarrow & A(cons(c,cons(d,nil)),b,z)
\end{array}
$$

So our proof in figure 4 is just one way of demonstrating how a PROLOG interpreter might work. Hence the level discussed in this section includes the level of PROLOG, but is actually more general since we do not restrict ourselves to Horn formulas. In fact, the attraction of PROLOG certainly is due to the relative efficiency of the proof mechanism in its restriction to Horn clauses. We are now going to define a restriction on the proof mechanism (rather than on the formulas) that does not affect the process in the case of Horn clause programs but results in the same degree of efficiency (as PROLOG) for *arbitrary* formulas. This restriction was first introduced in Bibel (1975) in a related context.

Definition: A connection proof is called (strictly) *linear* if each instance of a literal is contained at most in one connection required for establishing the proof.

For instance, the connection proof in figure 4 is linear while those in figure 2 and 3 are not (because of *Nx* occuring in two connections). The following result is a simple observation.

Theorem: Any PROLOG interpreter generates linear proofs only.

The proof is obvious since each connection, i.e., each match of a goal with the head of a clause, leads into a new instance of that clause, and each goal is considered only once. So on the set of Horn clauses, this is not a restriction at all.

On the other hand, there are (many) formulas which are non-Horn but have linear connection proofs. Figure 4 shows an example (the second clause is non-Horn). The efficiency, however, remains that experienced in PROLOG if we restrict the interpreter to searching for linear connection proofs only. This way the flavor of PROLOG in terms of efficiency may be extended to arbitrary formulas beyond Horn-clauses, a generalization considered desirable in many recent publications.

On the set of all formulas the restriction most likely is a proper one, although it might not be easy to prove it. Note that, while the proofs in the figures 2 and 3 are non-linear, there might be linear ones involving more copies. The reason for why that claim most likely holds, lies in the fact that on the propositional level the restriction reduces the proof-search problem to a polynomial one. Namely, for a given matrix with *n* literals any linear connection proof has *O(n)* connections and there are at most *O(n)* different sets of connections that might contain a spanning set of connections for a linear proof; but the test for the latter property is (e.g., by linear chaining) linear in n again. So, only if $P = NP$, could the claim be false.

Now, even with this promising concept of linear connection proofs, there remains an important difference between the way of computation discussed in the present section, which is computation by proving, and the way discussed in the previous section. Here the search for the proof has to be carried out for each input anew; there the proof search has to be done once to yield a functional program that requires no search anymore for any given input. Even with machines of the new generation we believe that this difference will continue to be relevant in terms of feasibility in other but experimental or prototyping systems.

It is therefore amazing how little work is being done in this direction of functionalizing recursive logic programs. Bibel (1974) has proposed a method of abstracting a connection scheme from a number of explicitly generated proofs on given test inputs. For instance, such a scheme would be obvious for the present example P3 since any further list element in a would just add another connection like the one between the first and second copy of the second clause. Clearly, any of the "synthesizing LISP functions from examples" methods (e.g. Kodratoff and Jouannaud 1984) would have no difficulty in detecting such a scheme after some adaption of the two kinds of representation. Moreover, the restriction to linear connection proofs, which seems to cover a wide class of practical problems, the inductive inference would be even simpler. Once a scheme has been found this way a functional program can be extracted from it. In addition the correctness might be verified by a theorem prover capable of induction.

An alternative approach to functionalization is suggested by the technique from the previous section. Since the choice of the induction rule F4 only depends on the data structure present in the recursion (since the scheme itself is standard) it seems to be pretty straightforward to put together a knowledge base that provides this information in all practical cases so that in combination with that technique we would obtain a system capable of transforming recursive logic programs into functional programs.

The researchers studying program transformations (e.g. Broy 1983) are certainly contributing in some way to the problem we are describing here. Unfortunately it seems that their approach focuses the attention on particular cases in special contexts rather than striving towards solvable cases in the general setting that we are proposing.

5. The general logic level

A glimpse at the difference between the specification given in P1 and that in P3 may easily convince the reader that even for relatively simple examples there seems to be a long way to go in order to obtain a recursive logic program starting from a relatively natural (which is to say mostly non-resursive) formal specification. This is the challenging task which has been undertaken in the LOPS project (Bibel 1980, Bibel and Hörnig 1984, Fronhöfer 1984). Since this project has been well documented elsewhere we are not going into any details here again except for a few general remarks.

A problem specification as the one in P1 is certainly not complete in the sense that it does not explicitly state the properties defining $=$, *cons, nil,* the meaning of "...", the domain of the variables etc. We assume such information being provided by the KB so that the user needs not undertake this exercise in each particular case.

Now in some cases, if these formal definitions are taken into consideration together with a specification as the one provided by P1, the resulting formula as a whole will in fact turn out to be of recursive nature. This is because the structures involved are recursive by nature, a feature that is imposed on the problem as a whole in such a case. (This is probably even true for the append problem but I did not check the tedious technical details.)

But the cases where this is the case certainly amount only to a small fraction of the interesting programming problems since the majority of them require the discovery (or retrieval) of suitable mathematical lemmas or theorems for their solution (even for the append problem we might have started out with an even "less recursive" specification). This seems to be beyond the capabilities of any system in existence. The LOPS system is an attempt into such a direction and is based on the belief gained from experience that these lemmas can be identified following certain strategic guidelines, a thesis that has proved correct for a variety of problems.

Yet LOPS is still far from being able to tackle automatic programming problems in a realistic application due mainly to the restricted efforts we are able to put into it, not least the still very limited computer facilities available for this project. On the other hand, there seems to be no other system that has gone that far in terms of creative power (versus mere quantity of information stored in the knowledge base, the importance of which not being questioned, of course).

Of course, it is not the idea behind LOPS to discover algorithms even for problems where such algorithms are well-known and thus may be stored in the knowledge base for activation whenever needed. But even in this seemingly simple situation we may face the problem of matching the given task specification with that accompanying the algorithm in the knowledge base, since they may obviously be different. In this case a theorem prover has to figure out whether one specification implies the other.

This problem gets real tough when we even consider the case where the two task specifications refer to analogue rather than identical tasks. Little work is known tackling with this problem.

6. The informal level

A casual user would definitely not feel comfortable with being requested to accomodate with the precision of logic. Quantifiers, for instance, typically frighten even people educated in computer science. Although those in P1 could be easily understood by a system (like LOPS), without explicitly being mentioned by the user it still requires a high level of skill in formal thinking to get together all the rest.

People typically would prefer to explain their problem in terms of a few examples. For instance, we would say that appending two lists such as *(a,b)* and *(c,d,e)* yields *(a,b,c,d,e)*, accompanied by a couple of further explanatory remarks. This has motivated quite a bit of research on synthesizing functions from a number of such input-output pairs.

Although this research has yielded nice theoretical theorems, and in some cases gives impressive results indeed, the technique yet has not found its way into systems of practical importance. One of the reasons for this to my opinion lies in a crucial omission of an important detail in this research. With this I am referring to the phrase "accompanied by a couple of further explanatory remarks" above.

For if we give an example as the one above, we usually also point out the generic features of such an example. For instance, in the previous explanation we would more or less explicitly make clear the distinction between accidental and crucial features in the example; such as the names *a,b,c,...*, the number of elements being accidental, but the change in the parenthesis structure being crucial.

It seems that no one has taken such an approach in the past. This may have something to do with a tendency which sometimes may be observed in theoretical computer science; namely, the advantage of obtaining clear theorems is traded-off against dealing with the reality as it is, a tendency which in the extreme sometimes leads even to blaming the work of those stumbling around in the mud of reality for their alleged lack of scientific quality. We believe that the work of Shapiro (1983) would provide a solid basis for such an approach.

Informality, of course, would also mean that we would allow some sort of "artificial natural language" as an interface between the casual user and the system. This paper is not the right place to pursue this particular topic any further. Finally, informality also means to allow for incompleteness of the specification. To some extent the synthesis is in fact possible for incompletely specified tasks (Guiho and Gresse 1980). Beyond that it is mainly a matter of intelligent interaction of the system with the user.

Acknowledgements. This paper was written during a period of inspiring discussions with A. Biermann on the subject which greatly influenced this paper. I express my gratitude for this ongoing exchange of ideas as well as for his helpful comments on an earlier draft of the paper. Thanks are also due to A. Davis for the typescript.

References

Bibel, W. (1974), Programmieren in der Sprache der Prädikatenlogik, Habilitationsarbeit (rejected), Technische Universität München; shortened version appeared as: Prädikatives Programmieren, LNCS *33*, Springer, Berlin, 274-283 (english version available as a report entitled: Predicative programming).

Bibel, W. (1976), A uniform approach to programming, Technical Report 7633, Technische Universität München.

Bibel, W. (1980), Syntax-directed, semantics-supported program synthesis, Artificial Intelligence *14*, pp.243-261.

Bibel, W. (1981), Logical program synthesis; In: Proceedings Int. Conference on Fifth Generation Computer Systems, (T. Moto-oka, ed.), North-Holland.

Bibel, W. (1982), Automated theorem proving, Vieweg, Braunschweig.

Bibel, W. (1983), Matings in matrices, CACM *26*, 844-852.

Bibel, W. (1984), Software - Eine Studie aus der Perspektive der Künstlichen Intelligenz, Report ATP-27-IV-84, Technische Universität München.

Bibel, W. (1985), A deductive solution for plan generation, Technical Report CS-1985-7, Duke University (submitted to New Generation Journal).

Bibel, W., Hörnig, K.M., (1984), LOPS - A system based on a strategical approach to program synthesis; In: Biermann et al. (1984).

Biermann, A.W., Automatic programming: A tutorial on formal methodologies, Journal on Symbolic Computation, vol. *1*, no.2 (to appear).

Biermann, A.W., Guiho, G., eds. (1983), Computer program synthesis methodologies, Reidel, Dordrecht.

Biermann, A.W., Guiho, G., Kodratoff, Y., eds. (1984), Automated program construction techniques, Macmillan, NewYork.

Broy, M. (1983), Program constructions by transformations; In: Biermann et al. (1983), pp. 1-49.

Dershowitz, N., Plaisted, D. (1984), Logic programming *cum* applicative programming. Symposium on Logic Programming, Boston, July 1985, (to appear).

Fronhöfer, B. (1984), Heuristics for recursion improvement, ECAI-84 (T. O'Shea, ed.), North-Holland, Amsterdam.

Green, C. (1969), Application of theorem proving to problem solving, IJCAI-69, Kaufmann, Los Altos CA, 219-239.

Guiho, G., Gresse, C., Program synthesis from incomplete specifications, 5th Conf. Automated Deduction (W. Bibel et al., eds.), Lecture Notes in CS *87*, Springer, Berlin.

Hehner, E. (1984), Predicative programming, CACM *27*, 134-151.

Kodratoff, Y., Jouannaud, J.-P., Synthesizing LISP programs working on the list level of embedding; In: Biermann et al. (1984), pp. 325-374.

Kowalski, R. (1979), Logic for problem solving, North Holland, New York NY.

Manna, Z., Waldinger, R. (1971), Toward automatic program synthesis, CACM *14*, pp. 151-165.

Manna, Z., Waldinger, R. (1984), A deductive approach to program synthesis; In: Biermann et al. (1984), pp. 33-68.

Nilsson, N.J. (1980), Principles of Artificial Intelligence, Tioga, Palo Alto CA.

Shapiro, E. (1983), An algorithm that infers theories from facts, IJCAI-81, Kaufmann, Los Altos, pp. 446-451.

SOME PROBLEMS ON INDUCTIVE INFERENCE FROM POSITIVE DATA

by

Takeshi SHINOHARA

Computer Center, Kyushu University 91,

Fukuoka, 812 Japan

Abstract: This paper describes some problems on inductive inference of formal languages from positive data: polynomial time inference and its application to practical problem, inference of unions, and inference from negative data.

1. Introduction

The theory of inductive inference should be useful for us not only to understand the mechanism of learning and generalizing processes but also to make computer systems more intelligent by applying it to practical problems. Concerned with deductive inference, many studies on theories and practices cover a wide range from theoretical problems to practical problems: mechanical theorem proving, logic program, etc. Although some theories of inductive inference have been developed, few of them have reached practical applications to computer softwares. This study presents an approach to practical application of inductive inference and give its theoretical basis.

In general, there are two kinds of inductive inferences. One is from positive and negative data and the other is only from positive data. In most practical problems, inference only from positive data is more natural than that from positive and negative data. However inference from positive data has been considered not so interesting to study, since Gold[1] proved a strong theorem which asserts that any class of laguages that contains every finite language and at least one infinite language is not inferable from positive data. For example, by his theorem, we can easily see that the class of all regular sets is not inferable from positive data.

Angluin[2,3] gave new life to the study of inference by characterizing the class of languages inferable from positive data and showing non-trivial and interesting classes. The class of pattern languages is one of the classes introduced by her.

The direct motivation of the present work is to develop a data entry system with learning function, proposed by Arikawa[4]. The system must infer or learn the structure of input data from the user. The information, the system can use, is only the input data. Hence we should consider inference from positive data. The computational complexity problem is another important point in discussing such practical problems as the learning data entry system. Polynomial time inference is carried out by a machine which makes every guess in polynomial time.

The present paper is basically a summary of the author's works[5,6,7,8] which describe several topics on inductive inference from positive data.

First, in Section 3, we briefly describe the data entry system with learning function which directly motivates the present approach.

In Section 4 we discuss the problem of polynomial time inference of pattern languages. A pattern is a string of constant symbols and variable symbols. The language of a pattern p is the set of all strings obtained by substituting any non-empty constant string for each variable symbol in p. We show that a subclasse of pattern languages, named regular pattern languages, is polynomial time inferable. A regular pattern has at most one occurrence of each variable.

The extended languages of a pattern p is the set of all strings obtained by substituting any (possibly empty) constant string for each variable symbol in p. In Section 5 we discuss the problem of polynomial time inference for extended regular pattern languages. We also discussed the relation between the inference of extended regular pattern languages and the longest common subsequence problem.

The third problem, we discuss in Section 6, is the inference for unions of two languages. We show that the class of pattern languages is not closed under union. Without this property, considering inference for unions would make no sense. The class of unions of two pattern languages is shown to be inferable from positive data.

Finally, in Section 7, we discuss the problem of inference from negative data, which is based on strings not in the language. In other words inference of a language from negative data is inference of the complement from positive data. We show that it is not the case that the inferability of a class of laguages always guarantees the inferability from negative data. We also show that some non-trivial classes are inferable both from positive data and from negative data.

2. Preliminaries

We start with a brief review of inductive inference from positive data and pattern languages according to Angluin[2,3].

Let Σ be a finite alphabet of symbols. The set of all finite strings over Σ is denoted by Σ^*. A language is a subset of Σ^*.

A class of languages $L = L_1, L_2, \ldots$ is said to be an indexed family of recursive languages if there exists a computable function f such that

$$f(i,x) = \begin{cases} 1, & \text{if } x \text{ is in } L_i; \\ 0, & \text{otherwise.} \end{cases}$$

From here on, the classes of languages are assumed to be indexed family of recursive languages.

A positive presentation of a non-empty language L is an infinite sequence $\tilde{s} = s_1, s_2, \ldots$ such that the set of all strings in $\tilde{s}$ is equal to L.

Inference machine M is an effective procedure that requests input from time to time and produces output from time to time. M on input sequence $\tilde{s} = s_1, s_2, \ldots$ converges to g iff the sequence of outputs $\tilde{g} = g_1, g_2, \ldots$ produced by M when elements in $\tilde{s}$ are successively given to M is either a finite sequence ending with g or an infinite sequence such that all but finitely many elements in $\tilde{g}$ are equal to g.

A class of languages $\mathbf{L} = L_1, L_2, \ldots$ is said to be inferable from positive data if there exists an inference machine M such that M on input $\tilde{s}$ converges to j with $L_j = L_i$ for any i and any positive presentation $\tilde{s}$ of L_i.

The following theorem essentially characterizes classes inferable from positive data.

Theorem 1. [2] A class L of non-empty languages is inferable from positive data if and only if there exists an effective procedure P which enumerates elements in T_i for any index i such that

1) T_i is finite,
2) $T_i \subseteq L_i$, and
3) $T_i \subseteq L_j \Rightarrow \neg(L_j \subsetneq L_i)$ for all j.

The right part of Theorem 1 is called Condition 1. T_i is called a tell-tale finite subset of L_i. Note that L_i is a minimal language containing T_i.

Corollary 2. [2] If L is a class of languages such that $C(F)=\{L \in \mathbf{L} \mid F \subseteq L\}$ is finite for any non-empty finite language F then L is inferable from positive data.

The assumption part of Corollary 2 is called Condition 2. Although Condition 2 is not necessary for inferability from positive data, it is convenient because it is independent of indexing. In fact, many classes including the class of pattern languages of Angluin are shown to be inferable from positive data by using Corollary 2.

Let $X = \{x_1, x_2, \ldots\}$ be a countable set of symbols disjoint from . Elements in are called constants and elements in X are called variables. A pattern is any string over $\Sigma \cup X$. The set $(\Sigma \cup X)^*$ of all patterns is denoted by P. The length of srting w is denoted by $|w|$.

Let f be a non-erasing homomorphism from P to P. If f(a) = a for any constant a, then f is called s substitution. If f is a substitution, f(x) is in X, and $f(x) = f(y)$ implies $x = y$ for any variables x and y, then f is called a *renaming of variables*. We use a notation $[a_1/v_1, \ldots, a_k/v_k]$ for the substitution which maps each variable symbol v_i to a_i and every other symbol to itself. Two binary relations on P, $='$ and $\leq'$, are defined as follows:

1) $p =' q$ iff $p = f(q)$ for some renaming of variables f,

2) $p \leq' q$ iff $p = f(q)$ for soma substitution f.

The *language of a pattern* p, denoted by L(p), is the set $\{w \in {}^{*}; w \leq' p\}$. The class of pattern languages is $\mathbf{PL} = \{L(p); p \in P\}$. Syntactic relations $='$ and $\leq'$ are characterized by the following lemma.

Lemma 3. [2] For any patterns p and q,

1) $p =' q \Longleftrightarrow L(p) = L(q)$,

2) $p \leq' q \Longrightarrow L(p) \subseteq L(q)$, and

3) if $|p| = |q|$ then $p \leq' q \Longleftrightarrow L(p) \subseteq L(q)$.

3. Data Entry System with Learning Function

The author has developed, with his co-workers, an information system SIGMA at Kyushu University[9]. Data dealt with in SIGMA are texts or strings of symbols, whose structure should be the most simple. Arikawa, the project head, has proposed to add a data entry system with learning function. The present approach is directly motivated by his idea. In this section, we describe the outline of the idea.

At the stage of data entry from a keyboard, a user types, for example, some bibliographic data in the following way:

$

Author: Angluin, D.

Title: Inductive Inference of Formal Languages from Positive Data

Journal: Inform. Contr. 45

Year: 1980

$

Author: Hirschberg, D.S.

Title: Algorithms for the Longest Common Subsequence Problems

Journal: JACM 24

Year: 1977

$

...,

where $ is a special symbol to mark off records. A halfway through this entry process, the system will learn or infer a structure of records of the form

"Author: "<w>"Title: "<x>"Journal: "<y>"Year: "<z>,

where <w>, <x>, <y>, and <z> stand for any string, and the system will successively emits "Author: ", "Title: ", "Journal: ", and "Year: " as prompts for user's input. Then the user may only types the data coresponding to <w>, <x>, <y>, and <z>.

It is clear thet the pattern languages can represent the structure that the data entry system needs. The data entry system is a man-machine system. Hence the learning process should not be computationally hard. The data which is used by learning or inferring of the system is only from user's input. Therefore we must concentrate our attention to the problem of the inference from positive data.

4. Polynomial Time Inference of Pattern Languages

In this section we introduce polynomial time inference from positive data and show the class of regular pattern languages to be polynomial time inferable from positive data.

An inference by a machine M is said to be consistent if a language L_g contains all inputs given so far whenever M produces output g. An inference is said to be conservative if an output g produced by M is never changed unless L_g fails to contain some of the inputs. These two properties should be natural and valuable in inference problems. Angluin, however, showed that inferability does not always mean consistency and conservativeness[3].

A class **L** is said to be polynomial time inferable from positive data if there exists an inference machine M which infers **L** consistently and conservatively from positive data, and requests a new input in polynomial time (with respect to the length of the inputs read so far) after the last input has been received.

MINL calculation for a class $\mathbf{L} = L_1, L_2, \ldots$ is defined as follows:

MINL(S) = "Given non-empty finite set S of strings, find an index i such that $S \subseteq L_i$ and for no index j, $S \subseteq L_j \subsetneq L_i$."

The following theorem indicates the importance of MINL calculation.

Theorem 4. [2] If a class $\mathbf{L} = L_1, L_2, \ldots$ satisfies Condition 2 and MINL for L is computable, then the following procedure infers L consistently and conservatively from positive data.

```
begin
g := "none";  S := ∅;
for each input s_i do
     begin
     S := S ∪ {s_i};
     if s_i ∉ L_g then
          begin
          g := MINL(S);
          output g;
          end
     end
end
```

Corollary 5. If a class **L** satisfies Condition 2 and the membership decision and MINL calculation for **L** are computable in polynomial time, then the class **L** is polynomial time inferable from positive data.

Angluin[2] showed that the membership decision of pattern languages is NP-complete. Therefore the procedure in Theorem 4 can not respond in polynomial time for the class of pattern languages. Angluin presented polynomial time algorithms of the membership decision and MINL calculation for the class of one-variable pattern languages.

Since one-variable patterns contain one variable, they are not suitable to apply to the data entry system with learning function. The data structure needed by the data entry system might be more simple than the general patterns. In other words, patterns which have at most one occurrence of each variable symbol can represent the structure satisfactorily.

A pattern is called <u>regular</u> if it has at most one occurrence of each variable symbol. The rest of this section is devoted to show that the class of regular pattern languages is polynomial time inferable.

Lemma 6. For any regular pattern p and any string w, whether w is in L(p) or not is decided in $O(|p|+|w|)$ time.

Proof. Let $p = w_1 x_1 w_2 x_2 \ldots x_n w_{n+1}$ be a given regular pattern, where each w_i ($i = 1, 2, \ldots, n+1$) is any (possibly empty) string of constant symbols and $x_1, x_2, \ldots, x_n$ are distinct variable symbols. Then we can construct a deterministic finite automaton DFA_1 which recognizes the language $\{w_1\}$ in $O(|w_1|)$ time. For each $i = 1, 2, \ldots, n+1$, we can also construct a deterministic finite automaton DFA_i which recognizes the language represented by regular expression $\Sigma^+ w_i$ in $O(|w_i|)$ time by using the method of pattern matching machine bu Aho-Corasick[10]. By catenating DFA_i and DFA_{i+1} for all $i = 1, 2, \ldots, n$, we can obtain a deterministic finite automaton DFA[p] which recognizes the languages L(p). We can determine whether DFA[p] accepts the given string w or not in $O(|w|)$ time. Therefore the time required to determine whether w is in L(p) or not is $O(|p|+|w|)$.

Lemma 7. MINL(S) for the class of regular pattern languages is computable in $O(m^2 n)$ time, where $m = \max\{|w|; w \in S\}$ and n is the cardinality of S.

Proof. Consider the following procedure, where S is a given non-empty finite set of strings and $w = a_1 \ldots a_k$ ($a_i \in \Sigma$) is one of the shortest strings in S.

```
begin
p1 := x1...xk;
for i:=1 to k do
    begin
    q := pi[ai/xi];
    if S ⊆ L(q) then pi+1 := q;
                else pi+1 := pi;
    end
output pk+1;
end
```

We show first the correctness and then show the time complexity.

1) Correctness. Since pattern languages are recursive, the procedure is effective. Clearly it always halts. We show, by a contradiction, that the output p_{k+1} is a correct answer to MINL(S) for the class of regular pattern languages. Suppose that p is the output of the procedure and there exists a regular pattern r such that $S \subseteq L(r) \subsetneq L(p)$. Since w is in L(r), $|r| \leq |w|$. Suppose $|r| < |w|$. Then, $|p| = |w|$, $r \not\leq' p$, and hence we have $L(r) \not\subseteq L(p)$ by Lemma 3 which contradicts to our assumption for r. Therefore $|r| = |w|$. Again by Lemma 3, we get $r \leq' p$ and $r \not\equiv' p$. Hence there exists an integer i such that the variable x_i occurs in p and $r \leq' p[a_i/x_i]$. Let p_i is the regular pattern determined by the procedure. Then $p = f(p_i)$ for some substitution f which maps each variable x_j in p to itself. Since $r = p[a_i/x_i] = f(p_i)[a_i/x_i] = f(p_i[a_i/x_i])$, we have $r \leq' p_i[a_i/x_i]$. By Lemma 3 S is contained by $L(p_i[a_i/x_i])$, and hence the variable x_i can not appear in p. Therefore p is a correct answer of MINL(S).

2) Time complexity. The procedure decides whether S is contained in L(q) just k times. Each decision is done by at most n membership decisions. The membership of regular pattern languages is computable in O(k+m) time by Lemma 6. Therefore the time complexity of the procedure is $O(kn(k+m)) = O(m^2n)$.

From Corollary 5, Lemma 6, and Lemma 7, we have the following theorem.

Theorem 8. The class of regular pattern languages is polynomial time inferable from positive data.

5. Extended Regular Pattern Languages

In the previous section we see that the class of regular pattern languages is polynomial time inferable from positive data. The inference machine for regular patterns uses MINL calculation. The procedure presented in Lemma 7 calculates a special case of MINL, called l-MINL that finds a regular pattern of maximum possible length which represent a minimal regular pattern language containing given set S of strings. There are some difficulties when the inference machine using l-MINL for regular patterns is applied to practical use such as the data entry system. The main reasons are in

1) restriction on the length of pattern, and

2) prohibition against substituting empty string for any variable.

We present some examples to explain these problems.

Example 1. Let S be the set {ABCdeFGh, ABCiFGjk}. Then any answer of 1-MINL calculation is eight symbols long. In fact the answer of the procedure in Lemma 7 is $ABCx_1x_2x_3x_4$. Let p be any regular pattern of the form p_1FGp_2, where p_1 and p_2 are any regular patterns. Assume S is contained by L(p). Then, clearly, ABCi e in $L(p_1)$ and h e $L(p_2)$, therefore

$$|p| = |p_1| + |FG| + |p_2| \leq 4 + 2 + 1 = 7 < 8.$$

Hence the string "FG" does not appear in any answer of 1-MINL(S).

On the other hand the pattern $ABCx_1FGx_2$ is a possible answer of MINL(S). Thus MINL(S) may have an answer which contains more constant symbols than any answer of 1-MINL(S).

Exapmle 2. Let S = {aBcde, GHcdBiii}. Then both patterns $p_1 = x_1Bx_2x_3x_4$ and $p_2 = x_1x_2cdx_3$ are correct answers of 1-MINL(S). The procedure in Lemma 7 returns p_1 for S. If we change the order of substitutions in the algorithm, we can get p_2 as the answer of the procedure.

Example 3. Let S = {ABC, AC}. Then MINL(S) does not have any answer containing both symbols A and C because we can not substitute empty string for any variable.

To solve these problems, we might extend the definition of pattern languages to allow erasing substitutions. We give new definitions of pattern languages. The definitions of patterns and regular patterns are the same.

A substitution is any (possibly erasing) homomorphism from P to P which maps each constant symbol to itself. A special substitution which maps every variable to empty string is denoted by c. For example, if $\Sigma = \{0, 1, 2\}$ and X = {x, y, ... }, then c(0x1y2) = 012. We define two binary relations $\leq'$ and $='$ as follows:

1) $p \leq' q$ iff $p = f(q)$ for some substitution f,

2) $p =' q$ iff $p \leq' q$ and $q \leq' p$.

The language of a pattern p, denoted by L(p), is the set $\{w \in \Sigma^* \mid w \leq' p\}$. Hereafter in this section we use the term "pattern languages" in the sense defined just above.

Proposition 9.

1) $p \leq' q \Rightarrow L(p) \subseteq L(q)$,

2) $p =' q \Leftrightarrow L(p) = L(q)$.

We say that a pattern $\hat{p}$ is in canonical form if

$\hat{p} =' q \Rightarrow |\hat{p}| \leq |q|$ for any pattern q, and

$\hat{p}$ contains exactly k variables $x_1, x_2, \ldots, x_k$ for some integer k and the leftmost occurrence of x_i is to the left of the leftmost occurrence of x_{i+1} for i = 1, 2, ... , k-1. The following two lemmas are obvious.

Lemma 10. There exists a unique canonical pattern $\hat{p}$ equivalent(=') to p for any regular pattern p.

Lemma 11. If p is a canonical regular pattern, then $|\hat{p}| \leq 2|c(\hat{p})| + 1$.

Theorem 12. The class of (extended) regular pattern languages satisfies Condition 2 and it is inferable from positive data.

Proof. Let S be any non-empty finite set of constant strings and let w be one of the shortest strings in S. Assume S is contained by $L(\hat{p})$, where $\hat{p}$ is any canonical regular pattern. Then $|w| \geq |c(\hat{p})|$ because w is in $L(\hat{p})$. By Lemma 11, $|\hat{p}| \leq 2|c(\hat{p})| + 1 \leq 2|w| + 1$. Therefore the number of such patterns $\hat{p}$ is finite. Since $\{S \subseteq L(p) \mid p \text{ is regular}\} = \{S \subseteq L(\hat{p}) \mid \hat{p} \text{ is canonical and regular}\}$, the class of extended regular pattern languages satisfies Condition 2, and hence by Corollary 2 it is inferable from positive data.

To show the polynomial time inferability of extended regular pattern languages, we discuss MINL calculation which is closely related to the longest common subsequence (LCS for short) problem. First we give some definitions on subsequences:

1) For any string $w = a_1 \ldots a_k$ ($a_i \in \Sigma$) and $s_i \in \Sigma^*$, $s \leq w$ (or $w \geq s$) iff $s = a_{i_1} \ldots a_{i_m}$ ($1 \leq i_1 < \ldots < i_m \leq k$). We say that s is a <u>subsequence</u> of w (or w is a <u>supersequence</u> of s).

2) The set of <u>common subsequences</u> to a set S of strings is $CS(S) = \{ s \in \Sigma^* \mid s \leq w \text{ for any string } w \text{ in } S \}$.

3) The set of <u>maximal common subsequences</u> to S is $MCS(S) = \{ s \in CS(S) \mid s = t \text{ or } s \not\leq t \text{ for any } t \in CS(S) \}$.

4) The set of <u>longest common subsequences</u> to S is $LCS(S) = \{ s \in CS(S) \mid |s| \geq |t| \text{ for any } t \in CS(S) \}$.

Proposition 13. Let w be any string, p and q be any regular patterns, and S be any non-empty set of strings. Then

1) $w \in L(p) \Rightarrow w \geq c(p)$,

2) $L(p) \subseteq L(q) \Rightarrow c(p) \geq c(q)$,

3) $L(p) = L(q) \Rightarrow c(p) = c(q)$, and

4) $S \subseteq L(p) \Rightarrow c(p) \in CS(S)$.

For any string $w = a_1 \ldots a_n$, $w\langle i:j\rangle$ denotes the substring $a_i \ldots a_j$ if $1 \leq i \leq j \leq |w|$ and empty string otherwise.

Lemma 14. Let the number of constant symbols be greater than or equal to three and p and q be any refular patterns. Then $L(p) \subseteq L(q)$ implies $p \leq' q$.

Proof. We may assume, without loss of generality, that p and q are canonical regular patterns. We prove by a contradiction. Assume that the constant alphabet Σ contains three or more symbols, $L(p) \subseteq L(q)$, and $p \not\leq' q$. Let $q = w_0 x_1 w_1 \ldots w_{n-1} x_n w_n$, where w_0 and w_n are any (possibly empty) constant strings and each w_i ($i = 1,\ldots,n-1$) is any non-empty constant string. Since c(p) is a supersequence of c(q) and $p \not\leq' q$, there exist integers i, j, and k such that

$0 \leq i \leq n$, $1 \leq j < k \leq |p|$, and $p = p<1:j>p<j+1:k-1>p<k:|p|>$, where

$c(p<1:j>) \in L(w_0x_1...x_{i-1}w_{i-1})$,

$c(p<1:j'>) \notin L(w_0x_1...x_{i-1}w_{i-1})$ for any integer $j' < j$,

$p<j+1:k-1> \neq rw_ir'$ for any regular patterns r and r',

$c(p<k:|p|>) \in L(w_{i+1}x_{i+2}...x_nw_n)$, and

$c(p<k':|p|>) \notin L(w_{i+1}x_{i+2}...x_nw_n)$ for any integer $k' > k$.

Let $p_1 = p<1:j>$, $p_2 = p<j+1:k-1>$, and $p_3 = p<k:|p|>$. Then $L(p_2) \subseteq L(x_iw_ix_{i+1})$ because $L(p) \subseteq L(q)$ and $c(p_1)p_2c(p_3) \leq' p$. Let a be any constant symbol except $w_i<1>$ and $w_i<|w_i|>$ and let be $v_1,...,v_m$ be all variables in p_2. Then

$p[a^{|w_i|}/v_1,...,a^{|w_i|}/v_m] \in L(p_2) - L(x_iw_ix_{i+1})$.

This contradicts $L(p_2) \subseteq L(x_iw_ix_{i+1})$.

We should note that the condition card(Σ) $\geq$ 3 in Lemma 14 is necessary. In fact, when $\Sigma = \{0, 1\}$, $p = x_101x_20x_3$, and $q = x_10x_210x_3$, $p \not\leq' q$ and $q \not\leq' p$, but $L(p) = L(q)$. Hereafter in this section we assume that contains at least three symbols.

Theorem 15. For any maximal common subsequence $s \in MCS(S)$, there exists an answer p of MINL(S) for the class of extended regular pattern languages such that $c(p) = s$.

Proof. Let $s = a_1...a_k$ be any maximal common subsequence to a non-empty set S of strings. Then the regular pattern q_{k+1} defined as follows is an answer of MINL(S):

$$q_i = \begin{cases} x_1a_1x_2...a_kx_{k+1} & (i = 0) \\ \text{if } S \subseteq L(q_{i-1}[\varepsilon/x_i]) \text{ then } q_{i-1}[\varepsilon/x_i] \text{ else } q_{i-1} & (i = 1,...,k+1). \end{cases}$$

We show that $L(q_{k+1})$ is a minimal regular pattern language containing S by a contradiction. Assume that $L(q_{k+1})$ is not minimal, that is, there exists a regular pattern q' such that $S \subseteq L(q') \subsetneq L(q_{k+1})$. Then $c(q') \geq c(q_{k+1}) = s$. Since s is a maximal common subsequence to S, $c(q') = c(q_{k+1}) = s$. By Lemma 14, $q' \leq' q_{k+1}$ and $q' \neq' q_{k+1}$. There exists a substitution f which maps q_{k+1} to q'. The substitution f erases some variable x_j in q_{k+1} because $q_{k+1} \neq' q'$. Let j be the minimum integer such that $f(x_j) = \varepsilon$. Then $q' \leq' q_{j-1}[\varepsilon/x_j]$. Therefore $S \subseteq L(q_{j-1}[\varepsilon/x_j])$ and $q_j = q_{j-1}[\varepsilon/x_j]$. Hence the variable x_j can not appear in q_{k+1}. This contradicts our selection of j.

Here we should note that we can construct an answer of MINL(S) in $O(m^2n)$ time from any maximal common subsequence to a set S of strings, where m is the maximal length of strings in S and n is the number of strings on S.

We may think of the longest common subsequence better than the maximal common subseqeunces. However the problem to find one of the longest common subseqeunces to a set of strings is known to be NP-complete[11]. Therefore finding an answer of MINL(S) containing constants as many as possible does not seem to be done in polynomial time. To find an answer of MINL(S) for the class of extended regular pattern languages, is it necessary to select one of the maximal common subsequences to S? The following theorem asserts that it is not the case.

Theorem 16. There exists an answer p of MINL(S) for the class of regular pattern languages such that c(p) is not maximal common subsequence to S.

Proof. Let S = {01020, 0212}. Then 02 $\notin$ MCS(S) because 012 e CS(S). However the pattern $p = x_1 02 x_2$ represents a minimal regular pattern language containing S.

In the proof of Theorem 16, the pattern $q = 0x_1 1x_2 2x_3$ is a possible answer of MINL(S) and c(q) = 012 e LCS(S). In some cases q is not always better answer of MINL(S) than p because p contains a longer constant string "02" than q. Finally, from this observation, we get a MINL algorithm by using a method to find common strings in length decreasing order. The correctness is easily shown by using Lemma 14 and the computing time is $O(m^4 n)$, where m is the maximal length of strings in S and n is the number of strings in S.

In our MINL algorithm We use some notations for simplicity. Let W = $w_1,\ldots,w_n$ be a sequence of strings. we denote the regular pattern language $L(x_1 w_1 x_2 \ldots w_n x_{n+1})$ by L(W), the number of strings in W by $|W|$, and the sum of the length of strings in W by $\|W\|$.

```
Procedure MINL(S);
     (* Input S: non-empty finite set of strings *)
     (* Output p: a pattern representing a minimal extended regular
         pattern language containing S *)
     begin
     s := one of the shortest strings in S;
     W := empty; (* sequence of common strings *)
     n := |s|; (* length of candidate common string *)
     while n > 0 do
          begin
          for i := 1 to |s| - n + 1 do
more:          for j := 0 to |W| do
                    if S ⊆ L(W<1:j>,s<i:i+n-1>,W<j+1:|W|>) then
                    begin
                    W := W<1:j>s<i:i+n-1>W<j+1:|W|>;
                    go to more;
                    end
          n := min(|s|-||W||,n-1);
          end
     p := x1W<1>x2W<2>...W<|W|>x|W|+1;
     if S ⊆ L(p[ɛ/x1]) then p := p[ɛ/x1];
     if S ⊆ L(p[ɛ/x|W|+1]) then p := p[ɛ/x|W|+1];
     output p;
     end
```

Theorem 17. The class of extended regular pattern languages is polynomial time inferable from positive data.

6. Inference of Unions

Inference of unions from positive data, we are concerning with in this section, is an inference of languages when given enumeration is not of one language but of two languages, and is found in the following problems.

1) Bilingual learning of children whose parents are internationallv married.

2) Error detection when correct data and wrong data are shuffled.

Let $L = L_1, L_2, \ldots$ be a class and $I = \{1, 2, \ldots\}$ be the set of indexes. We define $I^2 = \{(i,j) \mid i,j \in I\}$, $L_{(i,j)} = L_i \cup L_j$, $\mathbf{L}^2$ is the class of languages whose index set is I^2. Let **PL** denote the class of pattern languages. Then inference of unions of two pattern languages is nothing less than the inference of $\mathbf{PL}^2$. In our case the set of indexes is the set of all pairs (p,q) of patterns. By L(p,q) we denote L(p) ∪ L(q).

In this section we show that for the class of pattern languages, which is defined in Section 1 and not extended, inference of unions is possible, that is, $\mathbf{PL}^2$ is inferable from positive data. When the class is not closed under union, inference of unions should make no sence. First we show that the class of pattern languages is not closed under union. The following lemma is used in the proof. By $L^s(p)$ we denote the set of shortet strings in L(p).

Lemma 18.[2] Let p and q be any patterns and $|p| = |q|$. Then

$$L^s(p) \subseteq L(q) \Rightarrow L(p) \subseteq L(q) \text{ and } p \leq' q.$$

Theorem 19. If the constant alphabet has three or more symbols, then for any pattern p, q, and r,

$$L(p) \cup L(q) = L(r) \Rightarrow p =' r \text{ or } q =' r.$$

Proof. Asuume L(p) L(q) = L(r), $|p| \leq |q|$, $p \neq' r$, and $q \neq' r$. The minimum lengths of strings in L(p) ∪ L(q) and L(r) are equal to $|p|$ and $|r|$ respectively. Therefore

$$|p| = |r|.$$

From our assumtion we have $L(p) \subseteq L(r)$ and hence by Lemma 3

$$p \leq' r.$$

If $L^s(r) - L(p)$ is empty then $L^s(r) \subseteq L(p)$ and hence by Lemma 18 $r \leq' p$. This contradicts our assumption $p \neq' r$. Therefore $L^s(r) - L(p)$ is not empty. Let w be any element in $L^s(r) - L(p)$. Then the string w must belong to L(q) and $|r| = |w| \geq |q|$. Therfore

$$|p| = |q|.$$

Again by Lemma 3

$$q \leq' r.$$

Here we should note that if $|s| = |t|$, $s \leq' t$, and $s \neq' t$, then

s_i is a constant and t_i is a variable for some i, or

s_i, s_j, t_i, and t_j are variables, $s_i = s_j$, and $t_i \neq t_j$ for some i and j, where v_i denotes the i-th symbol in v from the left. Typical exapmles of s and t for $\Sigma = \{0, 1, 2\}$ and $X = \{x, y, \ldots\}$ are

$s = 012$, $t = 0x2$, and

$s = x1x$, $t = x1y$, respectively.

Clearly from our observation, there exists a string w in $L^s(r)$ satifying the following conditions:

1) If p_i is a constant and r_i is a variable for some i, then

$w_i \neq p_i$, or

if p_i, p_j, r_i, and r_j are variables, $p_i = p_j$, and $r_i \neq r_j$ for some i and j, then

$w_i \neq w_j$, and

2) If $q_{i'}$ is a constant and $r_{i'}$ is a variable for some i', then

$w_{i'} \neq q_{i'}$, or

if $q_{i'}$, $q_{j'}$, $r_{i'}$, and $r_{j'}$ are variables, $q_{i'} = q_{j'}$, and $r_{i'} \neq r_{j'}$ for some i' and j', then

$w_{i'} \neq w_{j'}$.

Then we get $w \notin L(p)$ from 1) and $w \notin L(q)$ from 2). Hence, by a contradiction, our proof is completed.

The condition in Theorem 19 that the constant alphabet has three or more constant symbols is necessary because if p_i and q_i are constants, $p_i \neq q_i$, and r_i is a variable, then we need at least three constant symbols to satisfy two conditions

$w_i \neq p_i$ and $w_i \neq q_i$.

In fact, $L(0x) \cup L(1x) = L(xy)$ when $\Sigma = \{0, 1\}$. Even if the constant alphabet has only two symbols, it is clear that the class of pattern languages is not closed under union.

Now we state the main theorem of this section and prove it.

Theorem 20. $\mathbf{PL}^2$ is inferable from positive data.

Proof. We show that $\mathbf{PL}^2$ satisfies Condition 1 of Theorem 1. We present an effective procedure which enumerates elements in a tell-tale finite subset of L(p,q) for any pair of patterns. Consider the following procedure, where (p,q) is the given pair of patterns, $|p| \leq |q|$, and additions to T is regarded as the enumeration.

```
        begin
start:  T := L^s(p);                                                        (1)
        F := {(r,s); |p|=|r|=|s|, r and s are canonical, T⊆L(r,s)};         (2)
        start enumeration of Σ+;                                            (3)
        for each w ∈ Σ+ do                                                  (4)
            if w ∈ L(p) then                                                (5)
                begin
                F1 := {(r,s) ∈ F; w ∉ L(r,s)};                              (6)
                if F1 ≠ ∅ then T := T ∪ {w};                                (7)
                F := F - F1;                                                (8)
                end
            else if w ∈ L(q) then go to restart;                            (9)
restart: T := T ∪ L^s(q) ∪ {w};                                             (10)
        F := {(r,s); |p| = |r| ≤ |s| ≤ |w|,
                           r and s are canonical, T ⊆ L(r,s)};              (11)
        restart enumeration of Σ+;                                          (12)
        for each w ∈ Σ+ do                                                  (13)
            if w ∈ L(p,q) then                                              (14)
                begin
                F2 := {(r,s) ∈ F; w ∉ L(r,s)};                              (15)
                if F2 ≠ ∅ then T := T ∪ {w};                                (16)
                F := F - F2;                                                (17)
                end
        end
```

The numbers of elements in T at (1), F at (2), T at (10), and F at (11) are all finite. It is clear that the procedure enumerates elements in a finite subset of L(p,q). We must show that T^*, the finite subset of L(p,q) enumerated by the procedure, is a tell-tale, that is, no pair (r,s) of patterns satisfies

$$T^* \subseteq L(r,s) \subsetneq L(p,q). \qquad (*)$$

We prove by a contradiction. Assume T^* is not a tell-tale finite subset of L(p,q). Then, there exists a pair (r,s) satifying (*). Without loss of generality we assmume that $|r| \leq |s|$, r and s are canonical. As L(p) is not properly contained in L(q), we consider two cases according to whether L(p) - L(q) is empty or not.

Case 1. Assume $L(q) - L(p) = \emptyset$. Then the condition "$w \in L(q)$" at (9) is never satisfied and hence the **for** loop (4) never terminates and statements (10)-(17) are never executed. Note that L(p,q) = L(p) holds in this case.

Since $\min\{|w|;\ w \in L(p,q)\} = |p| \leq \min\{|w|;\ w \in L(r,s)\} = |r|$ and $L^s(p) \subseteq T^* \subseteq L(r,s)$,

$$|p| = |r|.$$

By Lemma 18, there exists a string $w \in L^s(p) - L(r)$. The string w must be in L(s) and $|w| = |p| = |s|$. Hence

$$|p| = |r| = |s|.$$

Therefore the pair (r,s) appears in F at (2) and never appears in F1 at (6).

However any string $w' \in L(p,q) - L(r,s)$ will appear in the enumeration of Σ^+ in time and then the pair (r,s) will appear in F1 at (6). This is a contradiction.

Case 2. Assume $L(q) - L(p) \neq \emptyset$. Then the **for** loop (4) terminates and statements (10)-(17) are executed. If we can show that the pair (r,s) satisfying (*) appears in F at (11), then a contradiction is easily derived in a similar way to Case 1. It should be noticed that

$$L^s(p) \cup L^s(q) \cup \{w\} \subseteq T$$

holds at (10). Obviously $|p| = |r|$. There are two cases to consider. Let w the w at (10).

1) Assume $L^s(p) \not\subseteq L(r)$. Then clearly $|s| = |p| \leq |w|$.

2) Assume $L^s(p) \subseteq L(r)$. Then $L(p) \subseteq L(r)$ by Lemma 18. If $L(p) = L(r)$, then $w \notin L(r)$ and hence $w \in L(s)$ and $|s| \leq |w|$. Otherwise, if $L(p) \subseteq L(r)$, then there exists a string v such that $v \in L^s(r) - L(p)$. Since the string v must be in $L(q)$, $|p| = |q|$. Clearly by Lemma 18 $L^s(q) \not\subseteq L(r)$ and hence there exists a string $v' \in L^s(q)$ $L(s)$. Therfore

$$|s| = |q| \leq |w|.$$

In either 1) or 2), $|p| = |r| \leq |s| \leq |w|$ is holds and hence the pair (r,s) appears in F at (11).

7. Inference from Negative Data

In this section we discuss the relation between inferability from positive data and that from negative data. Formally inference from positive data is defined as the inference based on negative presentations.

A negative presentation of a language L not equal to Σ^* is an infinite sequence $\bar{s} = s_1, s_2, \ldots$ such that the set of all strings in $\bar{s}$ is equal to the complement $\Sigma^* - L$.

Let $L^c = \Sigma^* - L$ and $\mathbf{L}^c = L_1^c, L_2^c, \ldots$. Then, clearly from definitions, a class $\mathbf{L}$ of languages not equal to * is inferable from negative data if and only if $\mathbf{L}^c$ is inferable from positive data. Thus we can apply Theorem 1 or Corollary 2 to the class of the complements to show that a class is inferable from negative data.

The first question we may ask is whether a class of languages which is inferable from positive data is still inferable from negative data. The following theorem answers in the negative to this question.

Theorem 21. $\mathbf{F} = \{L \subseteq \Sigma^* \mid L \text{ is non-empty and finite}\}$ is inferable from positive data but not inferable from negative data.

Proof. It is clear that **F** is inferable from positive data. Assume that $\mathbf{L}$ is inferable from negative data. Then $\mathbf{L}^c$ is inferable from positive data. By Theorem 1, for any $L_i^c = \Sigma^* - L_i$, there exits T_i such that

1) T_i is finite,

2) $T_i \subseteq L_i^c$, and

3) $T_i \subseteq L_j^c \Rightarrow \neg(L_j^c \subsetneq L_i^c)$ for all j.

Let T_i be any set satisfying both 1) and 2). Then $L_i^c - T_i$ is nonempty. For any element x in $L_i^c - T_i$, $L_i \cup \{x\}$ is finite and there exits j such that

$L_j = L_i \cup \{x\}$, and $T_i \subseteq L_j^c \subsetneq L_i^c$.

Therefore T_i can not satify 3).

The next question should be this. Does there exit a class that is inferable both from positive data and from negative data ? The answer is clearly "yes". Any class which consists of finitely many languages is trivially inferable both from positive data and from negative data. As already mentioned, many classes inferable from positive data satisfy Condition 2. The following theorem shows that such classes are also inferable from negative data.

Theorem 22. A class of languages not equal to Σ^* which satisfies Condition 2 is inferable from negative data.

Proof. Let **L** be any class of languages which satisfies Condition 2. It sufficies to show that $\mathbf{L}^c$ satisfies Condition 1, that is, there exists an effective procedure which enumerates the elements in T_i for **L** any i such that

1) T_i is finite,

2) $T_i \subseteq L_i^c$, and

3) $T_i \subseteq L_j^c \Rightarrow \neg(L_j^c \subsetneq L_i^c)$ for all j.

Consider the following procedure, where we regard additions to the set A as the enumeration by this procedure.

begin

u := any element in L_i;

A := empty;

loop

  begin

  find (j,x) such that

    $u \in L_j$ and

    $A \subseteq L_j^c$ and

    $x \in L_i^c - L_j^c$

  if found **then** A := A $\cup$ {x};

  end

end

Since we can find out all the pairs (j,x) of index j and string x, the procedure is obviously effective.

For input i, let T_i be the set enumerated by this procedure in the limit. It is clear that T_i satisfies 2).

Now we show that 1) holds for T_i. Let u be the element in L_i selected at the first stage in the procedure. Then the number of languages in **L** containing u is finite, because **L** satisfies Condition 2, that is,

$C(\{u\}) = \{ L \in \mathbf{L} \mid u \in L \}$

is finite. The number of indexes j such that $u \in L_j$ may be naturally infinite. However, once a pair (j,x) is found, the string x is added to A. Then as L_j^c does not include A, any pair (j',x) with $L_{j'} = L_j$ can not be found.

Therefore T_i is finite.

Finally we show that 3) is satisfied. Assume that 3) is violated. Then, for some index j,

$$T_i \subseteq L_j^c \text{ and } L_j^c \subsetneq L_i^c \ (\Leftrightarrow L_i \subsetneq L_j).$$

Since u belongs to L_i,

$$u \in L_j.$$

Therefore a pair (j,x) should be found for some string x not in T_i, and then x must be enumerated. This contradicts our assumption that T_i is the set enumerated by the procedure in the limit.

8. Concluding and Remarks

In this paper we have discussed some problems on inductive inference from positive data. Our purpose is to apply inductive inference to practical problems and realize higher intelligence on computer softwares. Recently several works have been developed in a similar approach to the present study by Nix[12] and Janke[13].

Nix developed a learning system named EBE (Editing By Example) which infers or synthesizes text transformation program from examples. The inference by EBE can be seen as a polynomial time inference from positive data. Jantke showed that the class of general pattern languages is polynomial time inferable from positive data. Botusharov[14] applies it to re-structuring of a relational database and intelligent data entry.

Although inference from positive data has strictly less power than that from positive and negative data, it should be more natural in considering practical applications. In fact, almost all of a few successful applications of inductive inference are based on inference from positive data. Thus we should pay more attention to inference from positive data.

We also could not ignore the work on model inference from facts by Shapiro[15]. His model inference system is carried out essentially by negative facts in a sence that it can not infer any theory but a contradiction without negative facts. It should be natural and valuable to consider model inference from positive facts.

We have dealt with inference from positive data other than from positive and negative data. We also may think that inference in practical problems is based almost on positive data and slightly on negative data. For example, inference from positive data with one negative data is defined as inference based on positive presentation with one negative data. A <u>positive presentation with one negative data</u> of a language L which is not empty and not equal to Σ^* is an infinite sequence $\tilde{s} = s_1, s_2, \ldots$ such that $s_1 \notin L$ and the set of all strings in $\tilde{s}$ but s_1 is equal to L. It should be an another interesting problem whether inference from positive data with one negative data is strictly more powerful than that only from positive data or not.

The discussion in Section 7 on inference from negative data is directly motivated by the problem just mentioned.

Assume that there exists a class **L** of languages which satisfies Condition 2 and is not inferable from negative data. Then the class L^c of the complements is not inferable from positive data but it is inferable from positive data with one negative data, because the number of languages in L^c which does not contain a string given by negative data is finite. Unfortunately our result (Theorem 22) says that any class of languages satisfying Condition 2 is always inferable from negative data. Thus our problems on the contribution of negative data to inference remains open.

REFERENCES

[1] Gold,E.M.: Language Identification in the Limit, Inform. Contr. **10**, (1967), 447-474.

[2] Angluin,D.: Finding Patterns Common to a Set of Strings, Proc. 11th Annual Symposium on Theory of Computing, (1979), 130-141.

[3] Angluin,D.: Inductive Inference of Formal Languages from Positive Data, Inform. Contr. **45**, (1980), 117-135.

[4] Arikawa,S.: A personal communication.

[5] Shinohara,T.: Polynomial Time Inference of Pattern Languages ant Its Applications, Proc. 7th IBM Symposium on Mathematical Foundations of Computer Science, (1982), 193-209.

[6] Shinohara,T.: Polynomial Time Inference of Extended Regular Pattern Languages, Proc. RIMS Symposia on Software Science and Engineering, LNCS **147**, (1982), 115-127.

[7] Shinohara,T.: Inferring Unions of Two Pattern Languages, Bull. Informatics and Cybernetics, **20**, (1983), 83-87.

[8] Shinohara,T.: Inductive Inference from Negative Data, ibid., **21**, (1985), 67-68.

[9] Arikawa,S., Shinohara,T., Shiraishi,S. and Tamakoshi,Y.: SIGMA - An Information System for Researchers Use, ibid., **20**, (1982), 97-114.

[10] Aho,A.V. and Corasick,M.J.: Efficient String Matching, Commun. ACM, **18**, (1975), 333-340.

[11] Maier,D.: The Complexity of Some Problems on Subsequences and Supersequences, JACM **25** (1978) 322-336.

[12] Nix,R.P.: Editing by Example, Res. Report 280, Dept. Comp. Sci., Yale Univ., (1983).

[13] Jantke,K.P.: Polynomial Time Inference of General Pattern Languages, Proc. STACS'84, LNCS **166**, 1984, 314-325.

[14] Botusharov,O.: Learning on the Basis of a Polynomial Time Pattern Synthesis Algorithm, Proc. MMSSSS'85, (to appear).

[15] Shapiro,E.: Inductive Inference of Theories from Facts, Res. Report 192, Dept. Comp. Sci., Yale Univ., (1981).

LANGUAGE AND EXAMPLE OF KNOWLEDGE-BASED PROGRAMMING

E. Tyugu [1)]

1. Introduction

The aim of this paper is to give a precise representation of semantics of a specification language and to demonstrate its usage. The formal means needed for that purpose are also simple - a restricted form of the intuitionistic propositional calculus. Nevertheless, the meaning of the semantics can be understood better, if a realisation of intuitionistic formulas is considered.

The language considered in this paper forms the core of the input language of the PRIZ system, a software product which is widely installed in the Soviet Union [1]. During the last five years, PRIZ has been installed on approximately one thousand "Ryad" computers and has been ported also to SM-4 and Besm-6 computers. Most features of the language, which are not considered formally here, can be modelled in quite a simple way using a technique similar to macro preprocessing. We introduce some extentions of the language in p. 5 and use the extended language for specifying data description and data handling concepts in p. 6.

2. The Specification Language

The language is intended for specifying problems in such a form that, given a specification S, it is possible to execute statements of the form

$$(S \mid\!- x \to y)\ (\xi)$$

obtaining the value for y depending on the given value ξ of the variable x. (Obviously, the variables x and y must be specified in S.)

A shorter variant of the problem statement is

$$S \mid\!- y$$

In this case it is assumed that input values are present in the specification S itself.

1) Institute of Cybernetics of Academy of Sciences of The Estonian SSR 200026 Tallinn, Akadeemia tee 21

Actually we shall do more than calculating the value of y. We shall prove the solvability of the problem and derive a program from this proof, which calculates the value. If the solvability can't be proved, then we say that the problem statement is semantically invalid.

A specification written in the language is of the form

$$a : t$$

where a is a new identifier and t is a type specifier. It can be

(1) A primitive type : <u>numeric</u> or <u>text</u>;

(2) A name of an object which has been already specified;

(3) A structure of the following form :

$$(x_1 : t_1 ; \ldots ; x_k : t_k \quad [;<relations>])$$

Where $x_i : t_i$ are specifications, and relations are either equations or pre-programmed functions, separated by semicolons.

The specification a:t specifies a new object a with the properties given by t.

Due to the nested structure of specifications, a hierarchy of objects can be declared. In the case of the specification

$$x:(x_1:t_1;\ldots;x_k:t_k;\ <relations>)$$

$x_1,\ldots,x_k$ are components of x.

Compound names can be used for naming the components of an object. The following rule is valid:

A component a of an object b is called b.a outside of b. If b in its turn is a component of an object c, then outside of c , the name of the inner object will be c.b.a. An equation is of the following form:

$$E_1 (x_1,\ldots,x_k) = E_2 (x_1,\ldots,x_k),$$

Where E_1, E_2 are arithmetic expressions, and $x_1,\ldots,x_k$ are names of objects of the numeric type. (Any of $x_1,\ldots,x_k$ may be absent on either side of the equation.)

A pre-programmed function is represented in the language by its visible part which contains the name of the function and its parameter list. For every parameter it is shown in the parameter list whether the parameter is an input or an output parameter of the functions. The form is as follows:

$$\underbrace{x_1,\ldots,x_k}_{\text{input}} \to \underbrace{y}_{\text{output}} \ \underbrace{(F)}_{\text{name}}$$

The function may have input parameters which are functions. For every functional parameter its non-functional input and output parameters are shown.

For instance, in

$$(g : u \to v),\ x \to y \quad (G)$$

$(g : u \to v)$ denotes a functional parameter g which has u as the input and v as the output. x,y,u,v are names of objects, but g is not.

3. The semantic language

The semantic language includes only propositional formulas of the following two forms:

$$X_1 \ \ldots \ X_k \to Y, \qquad (1)$$

or in a shorter way:

$\underline{X} \to Y$;

$$(\underline{U}^1 \to V^1 \ \ldots \ (\underline{U}^m \to V^m) \to (\underline{X} \to Y), \qquad (2)$$

or in a shorter way

$\underline{(\underline{U} \to V)} \to (\underline{X} \to Y)$.

Logically these formulas are implications. But from a computational point of view they can be considered as functional dependencies. The formulas (2) express functional dependencies of higher order (with functions as arguments). To be precise: Functional dependencies can be introduced as realisations of formulas (1) and (2) or, otherwise, the formulas (1) and (2) can be regarded as abbrevisations for specific formulas of the predicate calculus, as it is shown in Appendix 1.

Bearing in mind the fact that a realisation for an implication $A \to B$ is a function that computes the realisation of B from a given realisation of A, we extend the formulas (1) and (2). We show the realisation of an implication under the arrow as follows:

$$\underline{X} \underset{f}{\to} Y \qquad (3)$$

and

$$\underline{(\underline{U} \underset{\underline{g}}{\to} V)} \to (\underline{X} \underset{F(\underline{g})}{\longrightarrow} Y) \qquad (4)$$

where $\underline{g} = g_1, \ldots, g_m$.

Propositional variables X,Y etc will express the computability (existence) of values of objects presented by a specification. Let us denote objects with small letters: a, b, x, y, a_1, a_2, ... For any object x we define a propositional variable X which denotes the computability of x. (X is true iff x is computable or x already has a value). The computability of y from x is now denoted by X -> Y, or by $X \xrightarrow{f} Y$ if the function f for computations is also given. So we have come to the semantics.

4. The Semantics

Let us define a function sem which computes a set AS of formulas of the form (3), (4) for any specification S. These formulas are axioms which describe the possible computations specified by S, i.e. they determine the statements (S |- x -> y)() which are semantically correct and can be executed. A statement (S |- x -> y)() is semantically correct if the sequent AS |- X -> Y is valid. Then the realisation of the implication X -> Y is the desired program for computing y from x.

Appendix 2 represents inference rules called structural synthesis rules (SSR) for building proofs in theories with formulas of the form (3) and (4). Correctness and completeness of the SSR for intuitionistic propositional logic has been shown in (1). A method for deriving programs from proofs which enables us to build a realisation for X -> Y from a proof of AS |- X -> Y is also presented there (see Appendix 3). It is worth mentioning that in the case where all axioms in AS are of the form (1) there exists a procedure for building a proof for AS - X -> Y, which has linear time complexity.

The function sem is the following:

(1) Let t be a primitive type, then

$$\text{sem } (x:t) = 0 \quad \text{(the empty set)}$$

(2) Let Γ be the set of axioms for the type t and Γ^{x}_{t} is obtained from Γ by substituting x instead of t for every occurence of t, then

$$\text{sem } (x:t) = \Gamma^{x}_{t}$$

(3) $\text{sem } (x:(x_1:t_1;\ldots;x_k:t_k)) = \{X_1 \mathbin{\&} \ldots \mathbin{\&} X_k \to X;$

$X \to X_1;\ \ldots;\ X \to X_k\}$

(4) $\text{sem } (E_1(x_1,\ldots,x_k) = E_2(x_1,\ldots,x_k)) =$

$= \{X_1 \mathbin{\&} \ldots \mathbin{\&} X_{i-1} \mathbin{\&} X_{i+1} \mathbin{\&} \ldots \mathbin{\&} X_k \to X_i$ / the equation

$E_1(X_1,\ldots,x_k) = E_2(x_1,\ldots,x_k)$ is solvable for $x_i\}$

(5) $sem((g:u \to v), x \to y (G)) = \{(U \to V) \to (X \to Y)\}$

(6) $sem(x:(x_1:t_1;\ldots;x_k:t_k;\ R_1;\ldots;R_m) =$

$= sem(x:(x_1:t_1;\ldots;x_k:t_k)) \cup sem(R_1) \cup \ldots \cup sem(R_m)$, where

$R_1,\ldots,R_m$ are relations (equations or pre-programmed functions).

5. Extended language

We introduce the following extentions of the language:

(1) Instead of

$$x_1:t;\ \ldots;\ x_k:t$$

we shall write

$$x_1,\ \ldots,\ x_k:t$$

(2) We shall use equations

$$x = y$$

for any objects x and y of one and the same type. Using such an equation induces automatically an equation x.a = y.a for any component a of x and y.

(3) If t is specified as $t:(a:t_a;\ldots;b:t_b;\ldots)$ then we shall write

$$x:t\ \ a = u,\ldots,b = v$$

instead of x:t; x.a = u;...;x.b = v.

(4) We add to the language the following primitive types:
<u>space</u> for any incapsulated type the properties of which are not specified in the language itself;
<u>undefined</u> for any type which can be redefined (can be made precise) before it is used in a problem statement.

(5) We introduce virtual components of objects. For this purpose we extend the definition of specification of structured objects as follows:

$x:(x_1:t_1;\ldots;x_k:t_k$

$[;$<u>vir</u> $y_1:s_1;\ldots;y_m:s_m][;$<relations>$])$

where $x_i:t_i$ and $y_j:s_j$ are specifications. The objects denoted by y_j

are called virtual components of x. Their values are not included into the value of x, so that

$$sem(x:(x_1:t_1;\dots;x_k:t_k;\underline{vir,}\ y_1:s_1;\dots;y_m:s_m))=$$

$$=sem(x:(x_1:t_1;\dots;x_k:t_k)).$$

But virtual components can be used in any relation as other components.

(6) copy x is used for inserting all specifications of components and relations of x into the specification where copy x is used.

6. Example of conceptual programming

The language described here is suitable for using in a completely new style which we call conceptual programming or knowledge based programming. Conceptual programming is a programming methodology which enables the programmer to build its own intelligent software capable of understanding the language of the user. As an example of conceptual programming, we shall consider here systematic construction of concepts for data description and data handling.

As an example of application of the language we shall consider here systematic constuction of concepts for data description and data handling: sets, subsets, operations over sets and some other concepts of data models.

Set

Let us specify a concept of a set with the following properties:

(1) A set is an object the value of which is represented by its single nonvirtual components "val".

(2) A set can contain elements of any type, its component "elem" has type undefined. All elements of one and the same set must have one and the same type.

(3) Knowing a property of elements of a set, which determines any element uniquely, it is possible to retrieve the element from the set. This property is represented by a component "key" of the set. We don't put any restrictions here on the representations of keys in the elements.

(4) It is always possible to select an arbitrary element from a set. If the set is empty, then the result of the selection will be the value empty.

(5) All sets are finite, and we can arrange the selection of elements in such a way that repeating the selection we can get all elements of a set once at a time and after that get the value empty.

In order to express the last two properties we must introduce a component "selector" which controls the selection of elements. If it has the value true then one particular element of a set is selected. If the value of the selector is false then an element which is different from previously selected elements is selected.

The following specification can be used for describing a concept with the properties listed above:

```
set1:(val:space;
     vir;
        elem:any;
        key :any;
        selector:bool;
        r1:val,selector->elem(A);
        r2:val,key->elem(B))
```

This concept doesn't possess any facilities for changing a value of a set. These facilities are added in the following version of a set concept:

```
set:(copy set1;
    create: ->val(C);
    addelem:elem,val->val(D);
    deletelem:elem,val->val(E))
```

We don't discuss implementation of the functions A,B,C,D,E which represent the relations r1,r2, create, addelem and deletelem. But the properties of the set described above must be taken into consideration when the functions are being programmed. A special care must be taken for satisfying the restrictions (4) and (5).

Subset

We shall specify a concept of a subset also in the most general way -- as a relation between two sets which is determined by a predicate p:

$$B=\{x \mid x \quad A \ \& \ p(x)\}.$$

The value of a subset will be the single nonvirtual component of this concept.

```
subset:(copy:set;
        vir of:set;
          cond:bool;
      R:(of.selector->cond),of->val(F))
```

In this specification we have used the names "val", "of" and "cond" for the sets B, A and for the predicate p respectively. The following are some examples of application of these concepts:

```
people:set elem=person;
children:subset of=people,elem=person,
                cond=person.age<16
```

It is easy to demonstrate that these specifications are sufficient for solving the problem

```
people -> children
```

i.e. for finding all children from a given set of people.

Actually the concept of subset specified above can be used for generating new sets which are not contained in any other set. Therefore we shall call this concept also a filter:

```
filter:subset
```

The following example demonstrates how a set of unitvectors can be specified by using a filter which takes points one by one (see the specification of a set) and computes the values for vector.mod and vector.arg which constitute a vector. These computations are initiated when the subproblem

```
of.selector -> cond
```

is solved for the relation R of the filter for unitvectors.

```
point:(x,y: num );
vector:(mod,arg: num );
vector.mod= sqrt (x^2 + y^2);
vector.arg= if x=0 & y>0 then 90 elif x=0 & y<0 then -90
elif x>0 then atan (y/x) elif x<0 then 180+
atan (y/x) fi;
points:set of=point;
unitvectors: filter of=points, elem=vector, cond=vector.mod=1
```

Operations with sets

Having two finite sets A and B represented by their components A.val and B.val it is possible to build a value of a new set, using set-theoretical operations: union, intersection, difference and direct product. The first operation is a partial operation, because we have a restriction that all elements of a set must have one and the same type. The specifications of operations can be very simple:

```
union:(copy set:
       vir A.B:set;
        R:A.val,B.val ->val(G));
intersection:(copy set;
              vir A,B:set;
               R:A.val,B.val -> val(H));
difference:(copy set;
            virA,B:set;
              R:A.val,B.val -> Val(K));
product:(copy set;
         virA,B:set;
           R:A.val,B.val -> val(L))
```

It may seem that the programs G,H,K,L depend very much on the representation of sets. But it is not necessarily so, because it is possible to use operations create and addelem for constructing new sets and the relation r1 for selecting elements of sets which are given as operands.

Quantifiers

In representing conditions like "there exists an element with the property p in the set S" or "all elements of the set S have the property p" we need quantifiers over sets. They can be specified analogically to the concept of subset, only the result will be a boolean value and not a set value. The specifications of quantifiers are as follows:

```
all:(S:set;
     cond:bool;
     result:bool;
    (S.select -> cond),S.val -> result(M));
exist:(S:set;
     cond:bool;
     result:bool;
     (S.select -> cond),S.val -> result(N))
```

Concepts of different data models

(1) The concept of set can be regarded also as a concept of a relation between the components of elements of a set. This enables us to represent relational data models immediately in terms of sets.

(2) We did not restrict the type of elements of sets in any way, hence, we can use sets as components of elements of other sets and build also hierarchial data models in terms of sets.

(3) Network data models (CODASYL data models) are based on a different set concept, which can be built from our sets. The set relation in CODASYL data model binds two types of records R1 and R2, called owners and members, in such a way that for any owner there is a set of members and any member has exactly one owner. This can be expressed by the following specification:

```
codaset:(member,owner:undefined;
        currentset:set of=member;
        setrelation:space;
        r1:owner,setrelation -> currentset(P);
        r2:member,setrelation -> owner(Q))
```

In order to implement this concept we must design an additional data structure for representing setrelation and have to program two functions P,Q which use this data structure retriving either a set of members (currentset) of a given owner or an owner of a given member.

(4) Finally, we need some concepts which bind the data models with actual files:

```
take:(set:set;
     filename:string;
     R:filename -> set.val(S));

keep:(set:set;
     filename:string;
     result:bool;
     R:set,val, filename -> result(T))
```

For implementing these concepts we must use global data in some catalogue of files, but on the logical level these concepts are very simple - they just enable us to take a set from somewhere if we know a name of a file and also to store a set permanently in a file.

Having implemented the concepts described above we get the possibility to use different data models in one and the same integrated data base.

7. Concluding remarks

We have described the complete semantics of a simple specification language which is an essential part of the UTOPIST language which is in practical use as the input language of the PRIZ system. We hope that this approach can be useful also for describing semantics of data descriptions of other high level languages. The description of the semantics relies on automatic deduction of formulas of the form X -> Y which express solvability of the problems. In this sense, the semantics is closely related to logic programming.

APPENDIX 1

If we agree that X, Y,... are predicate symbols such that X(t) means "t is a proper value for x", Y(t) means "t is a proper value of y" etc then instead of

$$X \rightarrow Y$$

we can write more precisely

$$(\exists s\ X(s)) \rightarrow \exists t\ Y(t),$$

or

$$\forall s\ (X(s) \rightarrow \exists t\ Y(t)),$$

The fact that the function f computes y from x we can express by

$$\forall s\ (X(s) \rightarrow Y(f(s))).$$

Actually this formula is abbreviated to $X \underset{f}{\rightarrow} Y$.

Continuing in the same manner, we can check that the formula

$$(U \underset{g}{\rightarrow} V) \rightarrow (X \underset{F(g)}{\longrightarrow} Y)$$

is an abbreviation for

$$\forall g(\forall u(U(u) \rightarrow V(g(u))) \rightarrow \forall x(X(x) \rightarrow Y(f(g,x)))).$$

A generalisation for the formulas

$$\underline{X} \rightarrow Y \text{ and } \underline{(\underline{U} \rightarrow V)} \rightarrow (\underline{X} \rightarrow Y)$$

is obvious.

APPENDIX 2

Inference rules for structural synthesis of programs (SSR)

$$\frac{\vdash \underline{X} \rightarrow V \quad \underline{\Gamma \vdash X}}{\Gamma \vdash V} \quad (\rightarrow -)$$

where $\underline{\Gamma \vdash X}$ is a set of sequents for all X in $\underline{X}$

$$\frac{\vdash (\underline{U} \to V) \to (\underline{X} \to Y) \quad \underline{\Gamma \vdash X} \quad \underline{\Sigma, U \vdash V}}{\underline{\Gamma}, \underline{\Sigma} \vdash Y} \quad (\to - -) .$$

where $\underline{\Gamma \vdash X}$ is a set of sequents for all X in $\underline{X}$ and $\underline{\Sigma, U \vdash V}$ is a set of sequents for all (U -> V), in $\underline{(U \to V)}$.

$$\frac{\Gamma, \underline{X} \vdash Y}{\Gamma \vdash \underline{X} \to Y} \quad (\to +)$$

APPENDIX 3

Taking into the account that

$$X \underset{f}{\to} Y \rightleftarrows \forall s (X(s) \to Y(f(s)))$$

and

$$(U \underset{g}{\to} V) \to (X \underset{F(g)}{\longrightarrow} Y) \rightleftarrows$$

$$\rightleftarrows \forall g \; (\forall u (U(u) \to V(g(u))) \to \forall x (X(x) \to Y(F(g,x))),$$

we can extend the inference rules SSR so that they will contain the rules for building new terms:

$$\frac{\vdash X \underset{f}{\to} V \qquad \Gamma \vdash X(t)}{\Gamma \vdash V\,(f(t))} \quad (\to -)$$

$$\frac{\vdash (U \underset{g}{\to} V) \to (X \underset{F(g)}{\longrightarrow} Y) \quad \Gamma \vdash X(s) \quad \Sigma, U \vdash V(t)}{\Gamma, \Sigma \vdash Y\,(F(\lambda ut, s))} \quad (\to - -)$$

$$\frac{\vdash \Gamma, X \vdash Y(t)}{\Gamma \vdash X \underset{\lambda xt}{\longrightarrow} Y} \quad (\to +)$$

These rules represent the method for constructing a program simultaneously with a proof.

REFERENCES

[1] Kahro, M. et al.: Programming system PRIZ for ES computers, "Finansy i Statistika", Moscow (1981) (Russian).

[2] Mints, G., Tyugu, E.: Justification of the Structural Synthesis of Programs, Science of Computer Programming No. 2 (1982), pp. 215-240.

INDUCTIVE INFERENCE HIERARCHIES: PROBABILISTIC VS PLURALISTIC STRATEGIES

Robert P. Daley

Department of Computer Science
University of Pittsburgh
Pittsburgh, PA 15260

Abstract

In this paper we will briefly survey the developments in hiearchy results in recursion theoretic inductive inference, especially with respect to trading off one feature of the inference process against another, and present some new results regarding trade-offs between probabilistic and pluralistic strategies.

§1 Introduction

In the last two decades a great deal of work has beer done in the area of recursion theoretic inductive inference, which s a machine independent theory of learning algorithms. An excellent review of work in this area is contained in the survey paper by Angluin and Smith [1].

The central concern of this work is, of course, the theoretical foundations of automated learning systems. We begin, therefore, with the archetype of the learning situation. The typical learning scenario can be expressed as follows: A *scientist*, presented with some *phenomenon*, gathers some *experimental data*, (perhaps by conducting experiments and thereby interacting with the phenomenon, or by passively making observations) and formulates some *theory*, which explains what was observed. This process is, naturally, an ongoing one with repeated gatherings of data and with repeated conjecturings of theories. Inference in this setting is, therefore, of a limiting nature, and successful inference will involve a *success criterion* and a *convergence criterion*. Thus we see that the system being explored by workers in inductive inference is a complex one consisting of several fundamental components. Moreover, the components are in no manner fixed, but rather possess several quite natural possible forms. For example, the *phenomena* investigated most by researchers in theoretic inductive inference have consisted in 1) computable functions, and 2) languages of the Chomsky hierarchy. The *observational data* for phenomena which are functions take the form of finite portions of the graphs of these functions, and for languages usually are instances from the language (positive data) and sometimes erroneous instances (i.e., words from the complement of the language) (negative data). The *learning algorithms* employed have been of various sorts including deterministic, probabilistic, and pluralistic (i.e., multiple algorithms). The *theories* which are produced by these learning algorithms are usually programs (for function identification) or grammars (for language identification). The *success criterion* has varied, for function identification, from absolutely correct programs for the function to some kind of approximation to the function. And, finally the *convergence criterion* has varied from first-order convergence, where the algorithm produces an eventually constant sequence of hypothesized theories, to second-order convergence, where the hypothesized theories are required to converge in behavior only and not in form.

Given the combinatorial universe of possible and plausible inference situations arising from ramified components of the inference process, it is not surprising that someone from outside the area might be bewildered by the number of hierarchy results. Actually, these hierarchies exist basically for two reasons: first, the inference problem in the strictest sense is in general unsolvable, and therefore it is natural to modify some part of system by either weakening the success or convergence criteria or by strengthening the inference algorithm; and second, the ability to infer something is strongly dependent on each of the components of the system, so that with each weakening of the success or convergence criteria or strengthening of the inference algorithm an increase in inference power is observed. The construction of new hierarchies is not the major goal in this area, but rather the exploration of the dependence of the inference process on any particular component in the system. Of particular importance are those results which relate one component to another in precise terms, i.e., results which allow one to trade off one feature of the inference process against another. Finally, the ultimate goal of inductive inference research is to provide a firm foundation for practical learning algorithms, such as encountered in Artificial Intelligence, by detailing the limited domains in which learning algorithms can feasibly operate, and by providing formal tools with which to measure the applicibility of heuristic approaches to learning.

We are particularly interested in this paper in questions relating the various features of the components involved in the inductive inference process. Although numerous researchers have worked in this area we will introduce a new notation here which is based on that used by Case and Smith [3] and which takes into account the combinatorial explosion produced by combining restrictions on numerous features of the inference process simultaneously. An inductive inference machine M will be chosen from an acceptable gödel numbering of the partial recursive functions, whose input-output behavior is the partial recursive function ϕ_M.

§2 *EX* Inference

In this section we consider the inductive inference of total recursive functions where the convergence criterion is first-order convergence, i.e., where an inductive inference machine M, when presented with successively larger initial segments $f|k$ of some total recursive function f, is required to converge in the limit to a particular program p for the function f. We will assume without loss of generality throughout that an IIM will also produce some response to any initial segment. Case and Smith have termed this type of inference EX-identification, where EX stands for "explanatory". Formally, given a total recursive function f we say that the IIM EX-identifies f, and write $f \in EX(M)$ if and only if $(\overset{\infty}{\forall} k)[\phi_M(f|k) = p]$ and $\phi_p = f$. We define $EX = \{S \mid (\exists M) S \subseteq EX(M)\}$, which the set of all sets of functions which can be EX-identified by determinsitic algorithms. This is the basic definition for EX identification. The hierarchies mentioned above arise by modifying this to some degree or other. We will attempt here to create a common framework for all the modifications by stipulating that an inductive inference machine M in response to some finite initial segment $f|k$ will enumerate a (finite) ordered set $S_{M,f|k}$ of hypothesized programs for f. For EX identification we simply have $card(S_{M,f|k}) = 1$. We now proceed to reformulate the other variants of

EX identification which we consider in this paper within this framework. The number of possible combinations of parameters for these modifications have grown too large to be expressed in terms of numerical subscripts and superscripts, so we will also adopt a new notation for combining them as well. We will indicate the particular combination by attaching to EX a formal parameter list, where some missing parameter entries will take on default values. For example, to define EX^m-identification, where the final program is allowed to disagree with the input function at up to m places, we define $f \in EX\langle \mathbf{E}:m\rangle(M)$ if and only if there is a program p such that $(\overset{\infty}{\forall} k)[S_{M,f|k} = \{p\}]$ and $\phi_p =^m f$, where $f =^m g$ means that $card\{x \mid f(x) \neq g(x)\} \leq m$. Throughout, we use m and n for integers, $*$ to mean an unbounded integer, and q and r for rational numbers. The default value for the parameter $\mathbf{E}$ is 0, i.e., $EX\langle \mathbf{E}:0\rangle = EX$. We will also use the parameters $\mathbf{O}$ to restrict the number of errors of omission (i.e., x such that $\phi_M(x)\uparrow$) and $\mathbf{C}$ to restrict the number of errors of commission (i.e., x such that $\phi_M(x)\downarrow \neq f(x)$). One can restrict also the number of mind changes made by an IIM as follows: $f \in EX\langle \mathbf{M}:m\rangle(M)$ if and only if $f \in EX(M)$ and $card\{k \mid S_{M,f|k} \neq S_{M,f|k+1}\} \leq m$. Team (or pluralistic) identification is defined by, $f \in EX\langle \mathbf{T}:n\rangle(M)$ if and only if $(\forall k)[card(S_{M,f|k}) = n]$ and there exists a $j \leq n$ and a program p such that $\phi_p = f$ and $(\overset{\infty}{\forall} k)[\pi_j(S_{M,f|k}) = p]$, where π_j is the jth projection function. The default value for the parameter $\mathbf{T}$ is 1. Frequency identification (see [6]) is defined by, $f \in EX\langle \mathbf{F}:q\rangle(M)$ if and only if $(\forall k)[S_{M,f|k} \subseteq S_{M,f|k+1}$ and $card(S_{M,f|k}) = k]$ and $(\overset{\infty}{\forall} k)[card\{i \in S_{M,f|k} \mid \phi_i = f\}/k \geq q]$. Finally, probabilistic inference (see [5,8]) is defined by, $f \in EX\langle \mathbf{P}:q\rangle(M)$ if and only if $(\forall k)[card(S_{M,f|k}) = 2^k]$ and the probability that a path through the (infinite) tree $T_{M,f}$ will converge to a correct program for f is at least q, where the nodes of $T_{M,f}$ are $\bigcup_{k \geq 0} S_{M,f|k}$ and for all k and all $j \leq 2^k$ there is an edge from $\pi_j(S_{M,f|k})$ to $\pi_{2\times j-1}(S_{M,f|k+1})$ and to $\pi_{2\times j}(S_{M,f|k+1})$. Team, frequency, and probabilistic inference can all be viewed as an attempt deal with the non-union property of inference, viz., there are sets $S_1 \in EX$ and $S_2 \in EX$ such that $S_1 \cup S_2 \notin EX$. Indeed, Pitt [5] has shown that for all $n \geq 1$ and $m \geq 0$ and $q \leq 1$, $EX\langle \mathbf{E}:m, \mathbf{T}:n\rangle = EX\langle \mathbf{E}:m, \mathbf{P}:q\rangle = EX\langle \mathbf{E}:m, \mathbf{F}:q\rangle$ if and only if

$q > 1/(n+1)$. This is a very nice characterization which in essence says that the uncertainty in a probabilistic algorithm which has a success ratio of $1/n$ is equivEOJ9t to the uncertainty of having a pluralistic algorithm which has a success ratio of 1 out of the n points of view entertained. Smith [7] has shown that one can trade-off errors for numbers of machines, $EX\langle \mathbf{E}:m, \mathbf{T}:n\rangle \subseteq EX\langle \mathbf{E}:u, \mathbf{T}:v\rangle$ if and only if $v \geq n \times (\lceil (m+1)/(u+1)\rceil)$. It is quite interesting that this same formula holds for the same trade-off for BC (i.e., second-order convergence) inference (see [4]), as well as for the trade-off between mind changes and number of machines for EX inference (see [2]). Wiehagen, Frievalds and Kinber [8] have shown that one can convert probabilistic strategies into deterministic ones by increasing the number of mind changes, e.g., $EX\langle \mathbf{P}:q, \mathbf{M}:0\rangle \subseteq EX$ if and only if $q > 2/3$, and $EX\langle \mathbf{P}:q, \mathbf{M}:0\rangle \subseteq EX\langle \mathbf{M}:1\rangle$, if and only if $q > 6/11$. A doctoral student at the Unviersity of Pittsburgh, Thomas Martinak, is currently extending these results involving mind changes, e.g., $EX\langle \mathbf{P}:q, \mathbf{M}:0\rangle \subseteq EX\langle \mathbf{M}:2\rangle$ if and only if $q \geq 15/32$, and $EX\langle \mathbf{P}:q, \mathbf{M}:0\rangle \subseteq EX\langle \mathbf{M}:3\rangle$ if and only if $q \geq 30/73$.

§3 *BC* Inference

In this section we deal with inference where the convergence criterion is second-order, i.e., the IIM is not required to converge to a fixed program, but rather is permitted to change its mind infinitely often, but from some point onward all of its hypotheses are required to be correct. Case and Smith termed this type of inference *BC*-identification, where *BC* stands for "behaviorally correct". We say that M *BC*-identifies f, and write $f \in BC(M)$, if and only if $(\overset{\infty}{\forall} k)[card(S_{M,f|k}) = 1 \text{ and } \phi_{\pi_1(S_{M,f|k})} = f]$ i.e., M produces an infinite sequence of prog··ams all but finitely many of which are programs for the function f. As for *EX*-identification we can define the parameters **E**, **O**, **C**, **F**, **P**, and **T** in a straightforward way. Pitt [5] showed that for all $n > 1$ and $q \leq 1$, $BC\langle \mathbf{P}:q\rangle = BC\langle \mathbf{F}:q\rangle = BC\langle \mathbf{T}:n\rangle$ if and only if $q > 1/(n+1)$. We present here some partial results for the $BC\langle \mathbf{E}:m\rangle$ case. The results are only partial since we do not as yet have lower bound results which show the exact correspondence. In dealing with probabilistic inference machines we will use a result from [5] that if $f \in BC\langle \mathbf{E}:m, \mathbf{P}:q\rangle(M)$, then $(\overset{\infty}{\forall} k)[card\{i \in S_{M,f|k} \mid \phi_i =^m f\} \geq q \times 2^k$, where of course $card(S_{M,f|k}) = 2^k$. The following result is cruicial in the constructions below and follows from the proof that $BC\langle \mathbf{E}:m, \mathbf{C}:k\rangle = BC\langle \mathbf{E}:k\rangle$ for all $k \le m$ given in [4] by observing that nowhere in that proof was the fact that the total number of errors (of all types) was bounded by m.

Lemma 1: *For all* $m \ge 0$, $BC\langle \mathbf{O}:\dot{*}, \mathbf{C}:m\rangle = BC\langle \mathbf{E}:m\rangle$.

We also mention the following result from [4] which shows that the number of errors can be decreased by adding more machines to the inference process.

Fact: *For all* m *and all* $k \le m$, $BC\langle \mathbf{E}:m\rangle \subseteq BC\langle \mathbf{E}:k, \mathbf{T}:\lceil (m+1)/(k+1)\rceil\rangle$.

The next result is proven in the same way as the analagous result in Pitt [5].

Lemma 2: *For all* $n \ge 1$ *and* $m \ge 0$, $BC\langle \mathbf{E}:m, \mathbf{T}:n\rangle \subseteq BC\langle \mathbf{E}:m, \mathbf{P}:1/n\rangle$.

Proof: The probabilistic machine simply tosses an n sided coin and then always selects the $j^{\underline{th}}$ program from the set $S_{M,f|k}$ of n programs, where j is the result of the coin toss. ■

Thus, the above lemma gives a lower bound for on the number of team members required of a pluralistic machine to simulate a particular probabilistic machine, i.e., since $BC\langle \mathbf{T}:n-1\rangle \subset BC\langle \mathbf{T}:n\rangle$, if $BC\langle \mathbf{P}:q\rangle \subseteq BC\langle \mathbf{T}:n\rangle$, then $q > 1/(n+1)$. To date, these are the only known lower bounds. Given a probabilistic inference machine M and a total recursive function $f \in BC\langle \mathbf{P}:q\rangle$, we classify programs in $S_{M,f|k}$ (see also [5]) as follows:

$$G_{M,f|k} = \{ i \in S_{M,f|k} \mid \phi_i =^m f \},$$
$$B_{M,f|k} = \{ i \in S_{M,f|k} \mid card\{ x \mid \phi_i(x) \ne f(x) \} > m \},$$
$$U_{M,f|k} = S_{M,f|k} - (G_{M,f|k} \cup B_{M,f|k}).$$

The set $G_{M,f|k}$ is the set of good (modulo m errors) programs in $S_{M,f|k}$, $B_{M,f|k}$ is the set of bad (> m errors of commission) programs in $S_{M,f|k}$, and $U_{M,f|k}$ is the set of programs with many undefined values (i.e., errors of omission) and which therefore are neither good nor bad (more whimsically, ugly). Pitt has termed these sets of programs good, wrong, and slow respectively. A key property in the constructions is that errors of commission are eventually detectable and therefore the programs belonging to $B_{M,f|k}$ can eventually be discovered. We will also denote the cardinalities of these sets by $g_{M,f|k}$, $b_{M,f|k}$, and $u_{M,f|k}$ respectively. The following two theorems show that it is always possible to replace a probabilistic machine by a team of deterministic machines.

Theorem 3: *For all* $m \geq 0$ *and* $q > (m+1)/(m+2)$, $BC\langle \mathbf{E}:m, \mathbf{P}:q\rangle \subseteq BC\langle \mathbf{E}:m\rangle$.
Proof: Given a probabilistic inference machine M, suppose that $f \in BC\langle \mathbf{E}:m, \mathbf{P}:q\rangle(M)$, where $q > (m+1)/(m+2)$. Then, for sufficiently large k, $g_{M,f|k} > ((m+1)/(m+2)) \times 2^k$. Our deterministic machine $\hat{M}$ operates as follows: On input $f|k$, $\hat{M}$ simulates M on $f|k$ and obtains the set $S_{M,f|k}$ of 2^k programs produced by M. Then $\hat{M}$ outputs the (set consisting of the single) program p_k, where

$$\phi_{p_k} = \begin{cases} y, & \text{if } \quad card\{i \in S_{M,f|k} \mid \phi_i(x) = y\} > ((m+1)/(m+2)) \times 2^k, \\ \uparrow, & \text{otherwise.} \end{cases}$$

Thus, p_k requires a plurality vote of $(m+1)/(m+2)$ of the programs in $S_{M,f|k}$. Clearly, p_k is well defined, since there can be at most one such y. We consider first only the maximum number of errors of commission in the worst case which can be made by p_k for sufficiently large k. In the worst case $B_{M,f|k} = S_{M,f|k} - G_{M,f|k}$, i.e., all the programs in $S_{M,f|k}$ which are not good are bad, and $g_{M,f|k} = ((m+1)/(m+2)) \times 2^k + 1$, since programs in $G_{M,f|k}$ can contribute to at most m errors of commission of p_k, while those in $B_{M,f|k}$ can contribute to an unlimited number. Each error of commission made by p_k requires that more than $((m+1)/(m+2)) \times 2^k$ programs agree on a wrong output. Since $b_{M,f|k} \leq (1/(m+2)) \times 2^k - 1$, the programs in $B_{M,f|k}$ can contribute jointly at most $(1/(m+2)) \times 2^k - 1$ votes to any error, so that each error of commission by p_k requires $(m/(m+2)) \times 2^k + 2$

votes from programs in $G_{M,f|k}$. Thus $m+1$ errors of commission by p_k would require $(m+1)\times((m/(m+2))\times 2^k+2)$ votes (i.e, errors of commission) by these good programs. But since these good programs make at most m errors of commission each, the total number of votes made by them is no more than $m\times(((m+1)/(m+2))\times 2^k+1)$. Thus, for sufficiently large k the programs p_k produced by $\hat{M}$ make at most m errors of commission. Considering the errors of omission made by p_k, we see that in the worst case all programs in $S_{M,f|k}-G_{M,f|k}$ would be everywhere undefined, so that each error of omission made by any member of $G_{M,f|k}$ would cause p_k to fail to find an appropriate plurality vote. Thus, the number of errors of omission made by p_k is at most $m(\times((m+1)/(m+2))\times 2^k+1)$, which clearly increases without bound with increasing values of k, but which is finite for each k. Therefore, $f\in BC\langle \mathbf{O}:*, \mathbf{C}:m\rangle(\hat{M})$, and by Lemma 1, $f\in BC\langle \mathbf{E}:m\rangle(\hat{M})$. ■

Theorem 4: *For all* $m\geq 0$, $n>1$, *and* $q>1/n$, $BC\langle \mathbf{E}:m, \mathbf{P}:q\rangle \subseteq BC\langle \mathbf{E}:m, \mathbf{T}:r\rangle$, *where* $r=(m+1)\times n^2/2$.

Proof: This proof is a combination of the technique used by Pitt [5] and the techniques used in Theorem 3 above. Given a probabilistic inference machine M and any $q>1/n$, we will construct $(m+1)\times(n-1)$ machines $\hat{M}_i$ such that for each $f\in BC\langle \mathbf{E}:m, \mathbf{P}:q\rangle(M)$, $f\in BC\langle \mathbf{E}:m+i\rangle(\hat{M}_i)$ for some $0\leq i<(m+1)\times(n-1)$. Then from the fact that $BC\langle \mathbf{E}:m+i\rangle \subseteq BC\langle \mathbf{E}:m, \mathbf{T}:\lceil(m+i+1)/(m+1)\rceil\rangle$, and by defining a machine $\hat{M}$ such that $S_{\hat{M},f|k} = \bigcup_{i=0}^{(m+1)\times(n-1)-1} S_{\hat{M}_i,f|k}$, we obtain the upper bound of $((m+1)\times n^2-(m-1)\times n-2\times m)/2$. We now describe the machines $\hat{M}_i$ for $0\leq i<(m+1)\times(n-1)$. Suppose $f\in BC\langle \mathbf{E}:m, \mathbf{P}:q\rangle(M)$. Since programs in $B_{M,f|k}$ can be detected eventually, the machine $\hat{M}_i$ first extracts from the sequence $\{S_{M,f|k}\}$ of programs produced by M on input f a subsequence (if one exists) of those $S_{M,f|k}$ such that $b_{M,f|k}\geq((m+1)\times(n+1)-(i+1))/((m+1)\times n)$, and then produces for each such k the set $\hat{S}_{\hat{M},f|k}$ derived from $S_{M,f|k}$ by eliminating $((m+1)\times(n+1)-(i+1))/((m+1)\times n)$ of the programs discovered to belong to $B_{M,f|k}$. Then, $\hat{M}_i$ produces a program $p_{i,k}$ which is analagous to the program constructed in Theorem 3 above, where $p_{i,k}$ requires a plurality vote of q from the programs in $\hat{S}_{\hat{M},f|k}$. As before we will estimate the maximum number of errors of commission made by $p_{i,k}$ for sufficiently large k. Since $f \in BC\langle \mathbf{E}:m, \mathbf{P}:q\rangle$, there must exist some integer i such that $0 \leq i < (m+1)\times(n-1)$ and

$$(\overset{\infty}{\forall} k)[b_{M,f|k} < ((m+1)\times(n+1)-(i+1))/((m+1)\times n)],$$

and

$$(\overset{\infty}{\exists} k)[b_{M,f|k} \geq ((m+1)\times(n+1)-(i+1))/((m+1)\times n)].$$

If $i = 0$, then $card(\hat{S}_{\hat{M},f|k} \cap (B_{M,f|k} \cup U_{M,f|k})) < 1/((m+1)\times n)$, so that this really is an instance of Theorem 3 above, and in this case $f \in BC\langle \mathbf{E}:m\rangle(\hat{M}_0)$. For $i > 0$, one can show that $card(\hat{S}_{\hat{M},f|k} \cap (B_{M,f|k} \cup U_{M,f|k})) < (i+1)/((m+1)\times n)$ and $card(\hat{S}_{\hat{M},f|k} \cap B_{M,f|k}) < 1/((m+1)\times n)$, since $((m+1)\times(n+1)-(i+1))/((m+1)\times n)$ programs were removed from $S_{M,f|k}$ in creating $\hat{S}_{\hat{M},f|k}$. As in the proof of Theorem 3 above, each error of commission created by $p_{i,k}$ requires $1/((m+1)\times n)+2$ votes from programs in $G_{M,f|k} \cup U_{M,f|k}$, and by an analysis similar to that used above we have that $p_{i,k}$ can make at most $m+i$ errors of commission and a finite but unbounded number of errors of omission, so that $f \in BC\langle \mathbf{E}:m+i\rangle(\hat{M}_i)$.
■

We remark that the above upper bound is not tight, since by Theorem 3 we have $BC\langle \mathbf{E}:1, \mathbf{P}:q\rangle \subseteq BC\langle \mathbf{E}:1\rangle$, for any $q > 1/2$, but it is also true for any $q > 8/17$.

References

1) Angluin, D. and Smith, C., *A survey of inductive inference: theory and methods*, **Computing Surveys 15** (1983), 237-269.
2) Case, J. and Ngo Manguelle, S., *Refinements of inductive inference by poperian machines*, **Technical Report, SUNY Buffalo, Computer Science Dept., (1979).,**
3) Case, J. and Smith, C., *Comparison of identification criteria for machine inductive inference*, **Theoretical Computer Science 25** (1983), 193-220.
4) Daley, R., *On the error correcting power of pluralism in BC-type inductive inference*, **Theoretical Computer Science 24** (1983), 95-104.
5) Pitt, L., *A characterization of probabilistic inference*, **Proceedings of FOCS Symposium (1984), 485-494.,**
6) Podniecks, K., *Comparing various concepts of function prediction*, **Lecture Notes, Latvian State University (1974), 68-81.,**
7) Smith, C., *The power of pluralism for automatic program synthesis*, **Journal ACM 29** 1144-1165.
8) Wiehagen, R., Freivalds, R., and Kinber, E., *On the power of probabilistic strategies in inductive inference*, **Theoretical Computer Science 28** (1984), 111-133.

NATURAL MATHEMATICAL TEXTS VS. PROGRAMS

T.Gergely[1] and K. P. Vershinin[2]

ABSTRACT

One of the main aims of research on future generation computer systems is to allows computer support a high level of logic which, at the same time, is friendly and familiar to its users.

This requirement means that the programming acitivity is to be lifted on the level of a discipline which proposes the problem to be solved. In the present paper an approach is proposed to satisfy this requirement. The approach suggests the PTL–language that is close enough to the natural language and, at the same time, its texts remind one to mathematical texts. Program synthesis replaced by manipulating mathemtatical like text, which is but the specification of the problem to be solved and some hints on its solution method to be chosen.
The text manipulation allowed by approptiate inference rules and the final text serves to extract the set of instructions and to design the program as to solve the given problem.

Here the PTL language and the methods of program extraction are observed.

[1] T. Gergely
Research Institute for Applied Computer Science, P.O.Box. 146. Budapest 1502, Hungary

[2] K.P. Vershinin
Institute of Cybernetic, Kijev 207, Prospekt 40-letija Oktjabrja 142/144, USSR

1. INTRODUCTION

Future generations of computer systems are expected to raise the level of reasoning in the computer based problem solving from dealing with fineness of transforming algorithms into programs to dealing directly with the appropriate problem domain.

Traditionally computer based problem solving processes requires the following stages: problem specification, formal model development, algorithm construction, programming and only after the latter computer is involved in running the obtained program. Raising the level of reasoning requires the problem specification be directly sent to the computer after on „expert" analysis in order to be solved.

The „expert" analysis establishes the problem as ordinary on specific. Int the latter case, of course, the above listed stages are inevitable.

The conversation between the user (who specifies the problem and provides hints about the possibilities of solution) and between the computer system (which is to solve the problem) is to be realized by using a sufficiently formalized language.

Mathematical texts are the most formalized tools still preserving natural language characters. Moreover well developed tools of mathematical logic may handle these texts.

When we aim to develop a new programming style for the new generation of computer systems a rational comromise would be, fruitful among the following approaches:

- pure deductive approach, which requires a priori formalization and proof of an existential theorem corresponding to the problem to be solved (see e.g. [5], [6] and [7],
- logic programming approach (in a strict sense) which demands the presentation of a family of possible actions and of the required result by using a set of formulas of special form (see e.g. [4])
- functional programming approach which requires a refined algorithmic style reasoning for developing the necessary programs (of. [1])

  In the present paper one possible compromise is provided allowing our main goal namely, to raise the level of computer use in problem solving process.

  One of the main tools to do this is the language which should satisfy the following requirements.

- It should be flexible and of high expressive power and close to natural language,
- It should reconcile declarative and inperative components,
- It should provide possibility for using the well developed tools of mathematical logic for text- handling and transformation,
- It should provide tools for introducing and using definitions of new language units analogously to mathematicians ans they do,
- It should be formal in the sense that

(1) texts of this language may be transformed into some formal objects (e.g. into a set of formulas, programs etc. depending on the problem to be solved) and consequently

(2) the notion of good and correct texts may be formally defined.

In the present paper we introduce the PTL (programming by texts) language which satisfies the above requirements. By using this language the problem specification and hints for the solution method can be described as a text. Then by using appropriate transformations a new text is obtained, which can be fulfilled to be detailed such that from it a set of instructions may be extracted necessary for the solution of the given problem. A text is said to be detailed if it contains the proof of all of its statements and the justification of all of its constructions. The tolls of automatic theorem proving play a significant role in our approach namely, they also provide the above mentioned text transofrmations. Moreover as it can be seen below it is not sufficient to use „standard" proof methods like the resolution type ones, but more powerful methods are required which realize meaningful steps of proofs or constructions (like e.g.analogy).

In the present paper we neglect proof construction and deal only with the language itself by the use of which the texts are represented and with the method which allows us to extract the instructions from an appropriate text and construct the algorithm. Basic methods of proof construction can be found in [3].

Note that the algorithm obtained by our approach reflects the structure of reasoning w.r.t. the problem solving, i.e. it reflects the structure of the text of the problem solving from which it is extracted.

The fundamental difference between the approach proposed here and between most of the logical and transformational methods is that the proposed PTL language allows to use texts in a quite natural form easily handable even for non-mathematicians.
This provides certain level of informal presentation in program synthesis (cf. [8]). Note that all the PTL–texts are in capital letters.

2. PTL–TEXTS

We wish to preserve the structure of natural texts. By text we mean a sequence of sentences and separators or a partially ordered set of sections. In PTL-texts the following sorts of separators are used.

a) Syntactical separators are used for punctuational purposes:

– (blank) , . (dot), , (comma) , (,) .

b) Structural separators point out the structure of the text such as division in chapters, sections, paragraphs and analogous items (e.g. CHAPTER 3.1, 2.7.4. etc.).

c) Logical separators point out the logical structure of the text. They are devided into three groups:

I. DEFINITION
THEOREM
LEMMA
PROOF
QED
IT IS EVIDENT
LET US SHOW THAT
THIS ITEM IS COMPLETED
CASE
THE CASE IS CONSIDERED
THE CASE IS IMPOSSIBLE

II. BY THE OPPOSITE
CONTRADICTION
INDUCTION ON
BASE
STEP
THE INDUCTION IS COMPLETED
LET US CONSTRUCT
THE CONSTRUCTION IS COMPLETED

III. ACCORDING TO
AS THE RESULT OF

SINCE
HENCE
THEREFORE.

Separators of the third group serve for reference. Separators of the second group mark the beginning and the end of text corresponding to a certain proof method. Some of the separators of the first and second groups are left side e.g. PROOF, LET US SHOW THAT and some of them are right side e.g. OED, THIS ITEM IS COMPLETED. They play the role of left and right side brackets.

Structural and logical separators turn PTL–text into an ordered set of sections. It turns out that many arguments are localised in their sections. For example every supposition ,,acts'' in all ,,subordinate'' sections and in the section where it is introduced. It provides restriction to the possible ,,field of discourse'' during logical analysis of a given text. Say if we are searching for ,,logical predecessors'' of a given statement in a structured text then we can restrict ourselves to sections which are, in a sense, ,,relevant'' to the statement. Thus we obtain an analogy with the localization of variables in programming languages.

From logical point of view some sections contain certain sentences called goal of the section in question and the latter is said to be a *goal-section,* all other sections are called *goal less* ones. E.g. sections PROOF. . .QED, LET US SHOW THAT. . . THIS ITEM IS COMPLETED are goal-sections while sections ,,chapter'', ,,paragraph,'' ,,definition'' are not.

Let us see the detailed structure of some goal sections corresponding in some sense to given steps of a proof.

a) ,,Case'' section

The family of case type sections directly connected to one another corresponds to proof with case separation. The goal of each of the sections within the same family coincides with the goal of the covering section (which is the minimal section containing this family).

The first sentence of a case section is required to be a so called *main sentence.* From syntactical point of view such type of sections begins with separator CASE <number > and ends either by the separator CASE < number > IS CONSIDERED or by the separator CASE < number> IS IMPOSSIBLE.

b) ,,Construction'' section

This type of sections begins with the separator LET US CONSTRUCT which is followed by a sentence (called main one) of the form < variable > SUCH THAT < statement > or <named notion> SUCH THAT < statement > and it ends with the separator of the form THE CONSTRUCTION IS COMPLETED. The goal of this type of section is a statement on the existence of the object to be constructed. This goal may be obtained formally by adding to the main sentence the word THERE EXISTS.

c) ,,Reduction ad absurda'' section

The section begins with the separator TO CONTRADICT which is followed by the sentence LET $\mathfrak{B}$ BE FALSE, Where $\mathfrak{B}$ is the goal of the covering section and it ends with separator CONTRADICTION. The aim of this type of sections is the ,,empty'' statement (which corresponds to empty clause of resolution theorem proving).

d) ,,Induction'' section

This type of sections begins with the separator INDUCTION ON which is followed by certain term T (X) and it consist of two subsections beginning respectively with separators BASE and STEP. In the same time separator STEP is the end separator for the section of BASE.

The induction type section ends with the separator INDUCTION IS COMPLETED. The goal of this type of sections coincides with the goal of the covering section.

As usual, induction is used to prove statements of the form FOR EVERY X IT IS TRUE THAT IF X IS K THEN $\mathfrak{B}$ (X), where K is a notion, $\mathfrak{B}$ (X) is a statement. Section BASE is to contain supposition LET T (X) = O, where O is the least element of the totally ordered set on which (w.r.t. the total ordering <) induction takes place. Section STEP is to contain supposition of the form LET T (X) > O. SUPPOSE THAT IF Y IS K AND T (Y) < T (X) THEN $\mathfrak{B}$ (Y) (inductive assertion) $\mathfrak{B}$ (X) is the goal of both sections BASE and STEP.

Sections corresponding to other methods of reasoning (like reasoning by analogy) may be described analogously. For this the necessary separators are to be introduced, the necesaary suppositions are to be fixed and the goal is to be defined.

3. FORMAL DESCRIPTION OF PTL

Now we describe the language more formally. The sentence is the main unit of PTL. Sentences are of three kinds: statements, suppositions and instructions. Suppositions are of the following forms: LET < statement > or SUPPOSE–THAT < statement > . PTL-units not used independently are notions, actions, attributes and symbolic terms. All units of PTL are obtained either by substitution into the so called formalizers or by concatenation. The formalizers are analogous to the usual predicate and function symbols.

According to the type of received units we distinguish:

n – formalizers that are of notions,
a1 – formalizers that are of left attributes,
ar_1 – foralizers that are of right attributes of first type,
ar_2 – formalizers that are of right attributes of second type,
r – formalizers that are of atomic statements (relations),
sf – formalizers that are usual function symbols,
sp – formalizers that are usual predicate symbols,
ac – formalizers that are of actions,
i – formalizers that are of instructions.

We connect with every n-ary formalizer f its sort σ (f) the n+1 tuple < $s_1, \ldots, s_n, s$ > , where $s_1, \ldots, s_r$ are sorts of objects, which may be placed into the corresponding argument places of f and s is the sort of obtained object. E.g. for f $\stackrel{d}{=}$ HOMOMORPHISM_IN_ σ (f) = < GROUP, GROUP, FUNCTION > . Semantically a sort is a class of objects (e.g. sets, natural numbers). Syntactically it corresponds to O-ary n-formalizers SET, GROUP, REAL.

Note that the sort of an attribute is the sort of that notion which the attribute can be attached to. Semantically the sort of attribute is the class of objects which can posses the property expressed by the attribute.

We also distinguish logical and non-logical formalizers. The latter may be definable or underfinable.

Logical formalizers are:
IF_THEN_, –AND_,_OR_, IT_IS_WRONG_THAT_, _IFF_, EVERY_ SOME_, THERE EXISTS_, _ IS UNIOUE, _SUCH–THAT_, LET_, SUPPOSE_, _WILL_BE_STAND_FOR_.

Non-logical undefinable formalizers are as follows.
r – formalizers: – ϵ _
– IS –, _ = _, _BELONGS_TO_ , _ CONSISTS_OF_,
n – formalizers: CLASS, SET, ELEMENT OF –, RESULT OF –, OBJECT OF_
sf–formalizers. { _ }, { _ : _ }.

ac-formalizers: COMPUTATION OF –, EXECUTION OF –, – AND –, – PARALLELLY –,

i-formalizers: TAKE –, – ; – , IF – THEN –
WHILE – REPEAT –, DO –, – □ –
□ – , – ‖ – , ‖ –

Now let us see how some of the above introduced formalizers connect the syntactic units of the language.

Let S stand for situations
P stand for statements
C stand for suppositions
N stand for notions
T stand for terms
A stand for actions
I stand for instractions
V stand for variables

Then we have

$P \xrightarrow{\text{LET\_}} C$

$P \xrightarrow{\text{SUPPOSE THAT\_}} C$

$I \xrightarrow{\text{EXECUTION OF\_}} A$

$A \xrightarrow{\text{DO\_}} I$

$A \xrightarrow{\text{RESULT OF\_}} N$

$A \xrightarrow{\text{OBJECT OF\_}} N$

$T \xrightarrow{\text{COMPUTATION OF\_}} A$

$T \times N \xrightarrow{\text{\_IS\_}} P$

$T \times T \xrightarrow{\text{\_=\_}} P$

$A \times A \xrightarrow{\text{\_AND\_}} A$

$A \times A \xrightarrow{\text{\_PARALLELLY\_}} A$

$P \times I \xrightarrow{\text{IF\_THEN\_}} I$

$P \times I \xrightarrow{\text{WHILE\_ REPEAT\_}} I$

$I \times I \xrightarrow{\text{\_,\_}} I$

$I \times I \xrightarrow{\text{\_||\_}} I$

$V \times T \xrightarrow{\text{TAKE\_=\_}} I$

$V \times N \xrightarrow{\text{TAKE\_ IS\_}} I$

Fig. 1. illustrates the above given interrelations among language units.

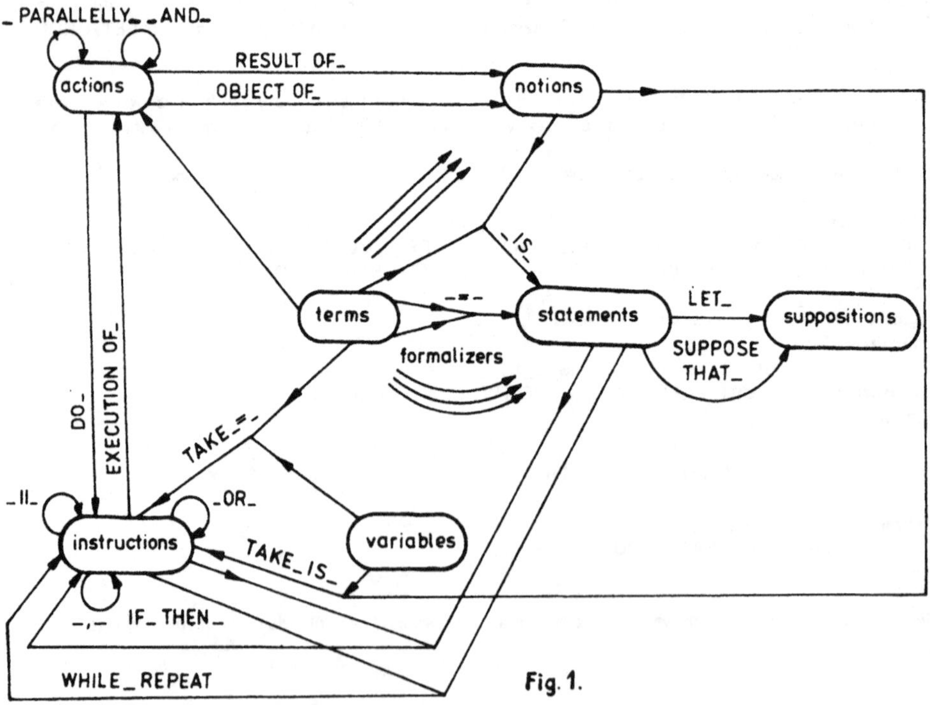

Fig. 1.

Formalizers of attributes are obtained from r-formalizers and unary c-formalizers in the following way.

From unary r-formalizers we obtain al-formalizers.
E.g.

$f_1 \overset{d}{=}$ _ IS_ABELIAN is r-formalizer,
$f_2 \overset{d}{=}$ ABELIAN is al-formalizer,
$f_1 \overset{d}{=}$ _ IS_MEROMORPHIC is r-formalizer,
$f_2 \overset{d}{=}$ MEROMORPHIC is al-formalizer.

From the r-formalizers of arity more than 1 we obtain
ar_1 — formalizers.

$f_1 \overset{d}{=}$ _DIVIDES _ is r -formalizer,
$f_2 \overset{d}{=}$ DIVIDING _ is ar_1-formalizer,
$f_1 \overset{d}{=}$ _IS_COMPARED_WITH _MODULO_ is r-formalizer,
$f_2 \overset{d}{=}$ COMPARED_WITH_ MODULO_ is ar_1-formalizer.

We obtain ar_2-formalizers from unary n-formalizers by the permutation of components in sort tuple. E.g.

$f_1 \overset{d}{=}$ LENGTH_OF _isn-formalizer,
$\sigma(f_1) = <$ WORD, NUMBER $>$;
$f_2 \overset{d}{=}$ OF_THE_LENGTH_ is ar_2-formalizer,
$\sigma(f_2) = <$ NUMBER, WORD $>$;
$f_1 \overset{d}{=}$ ORDER_OF_ is e-formalizer;
$\sigma(f_1) = <$ GROUP, NUMBER $>$;
$f_2 \overset{d}{=}$ OF_ORDER_ is ar_2 -formalizer,
$\sigma(f_2) = <$ NUMBER, GROUP $>$.

Besides substitution into formalizers there is one more way of forming attributes. We explain it by an example: from ar_2-formalizer OF_THE_ORDER_ and al-formalizer FINITE we may obtain the right attribute OF_ THE_FINITE ORDER.

Attributes are used as follows. Left attributes are attached to the left side of a whole construction e.g. SUBGROUP OF G, FINITE SUBGROUP OF G. Right attributes are attached to the right side of the first „meaningful" word of n-formalizers. This word is called the leader of the given formalizer. E.g. SUBGROUP OF INDEX 2 OF G is a construction obtained in this way; SUBGROUP is the leader of its formalizer SUBGROUP OF_; OF INDEX 2 is the right attribute obtained from the ar_2-formalizer OF INDEX_.

We call the units of PTL, obtained by attaching attributes to notions, attributed notions (a-notions).

Other non-logical formalizers are introduced by definitions. Admitted types of definitions are strictly fixed, which we consider circumstantially below.

Let us detail such an object as a notion. We noted above that a notion may be treated as a degisnation of a class. So it follows that we should indicate the meaning of each occurence of a notion which,

a) for declarative context, can be

(i) arbitrary element of the corresponding class;
(ii) some elements of the class;
(iii) earlier mentioned element of the class, and

b) for imperative context, can be

(i) execution of the given action for all elements of the corresponding class;
(ii) execution of the action for some element of this class (nondeterministic execution);
(iii) execution of the action for a given element mentioned earlier.

In the first case we add the word EVERY to the left side of the notion. In the second case we use the word SOME in the same way. We call these objects bounded notions. In the third case we add to leader of the corresponding n-formalizer the string ◊ N, where N is the designation (or name) of the given object (e. g. PARTITION ◊ S (R) OF SET ◊ M IS_COMPATIBLE_WITH H). The objects obtained in such a way are called *named notions.*

We consider bounded and named notions and the usual symbolic terms to be PTL-terms, and we permit to place them into the argument places of non-logical formalizers.

Finally let us make some remarks on the quantification. Remember that we use only restricted quantifiers in PTL and the quantifier on each variable X must be restricted by the formula of the type X IS T or $X \epsilon T$ where T is a PTL-term. The universal quantifier being restricted may be introduced either by using implication with X IS T $X \epsilon T$ as an antecedent or by using bounded notion (of the type EVERY K). The existential quantifier may be introduced either by means of bounded notions (of the type SOME K) or by means of substitution in formalizer THERE_EXISTS_.

4. REPRESENTATION OF PTL–STATEMENTS IN PREDICATE CALCULUS WITH INSTRUCTIONS

Let some sets of n–, r–, ac–, i–, sf–, sp-formalizers be fixed.

We show in this section how to translate a PTL-statement into a formula of ordinary predicate language to which instructions are added:

a) functional symbols coincide with n-formalizers and sf-formalizers;

b) predicate symbols are $=$, ϵ (both are binary) and all r-formalizers and sp-formalizers;

c) $\wedge$, $\vee$, $\supset$ iff, $\forall$, $\exists$ are the usual logical connectives and quantifiers;

d) variable symbols coincide with those of PTL;

e) formalizers of instructions.

Terms, atomic formulas, formulas and instructions are defined as usually.

Let $\mathfrak{B}$ be a statement or instruction of PTL. Let $T_{\mathfrak{B}}$ be the parse tree of $\mathfrak{B}$. Now we are interested in that case when the „main formalizer" f of $\mathfrak{B}$ is non-logical.

We call the node N of $T_{\mathfrak{B}}$ *term-like* (t-node) iff N corresponds to some occurence of a notation in $\mathfrak{B}$
We connect a tree $T^i_{\mathfrak{B}}$ with i-th argument place of. It is „growing" from this argument place and consists of t-nodes only. (Note, that some $T^i_{\mathfrak{B}}$ might be empty.)

We call an occurence of a notion in $\mathfrak{B}$ *term-like* (t-occurence) iff it corresponds to a t-node in some $T^i_{\mathfrak{B}}$ i.e. occurences in attributes are not term-like. We call the t-occurence of a notion in $\mathfrak{B}$ *unblocked* iff it corresponds to a „leaf" in some $T^i_{\mathfrak{B}}$.

The nodes of the tree $T_{\mathfrak{B}}$ are to be ordered by depth first from left to right.

We shall write $\mathfrak{B} = \mathfrak{B}(K)$ iff K is the first (according to the order mentioned above) unblocked t-occurence of the notion in $\mathfrak{B}$.

Let $\forall X_K\ \mathfrak{C}\ (\exists X_K\ \mathfrak{C})$ be an abbreviation for $X\ (X \epsilon K \supset \mathfrak{C})\ (\ X\ (X \epsilon K \supset \mathfrak{C})$ accordingly).

Let K_E denote the named notion K with the name E.

Now we form rules for the elimination of bounded and named notions (we coll them B-rules). First let us consider the occurence of these notions in declarative contexts, i.e. let P be a statement.

B_1 · $\mathfrak{C}$ (EVERY K) → IF X IS K THEN $\mathfrak{C}$(X), where X is a new variable symbol;
B_2 · $\mathfrak{C}$ (SOME K) → THERE–EXISTS K_X SUCH–THAT $\mathfrak{C}$(X), where X is a new variable symbol;
B_3 · $\mathfrak{C}$ (K_X SUCH–THAT $\mathfrak{B}$) → IF X IS K AND $\mathfrak{B}$ THEN $\mathfrak{C}$(X), where X was not mentioned earlier;
B_4 · $\mathfrak{C}$ (K_X) → IF X IS K THEN, where X was not mentioned earlier;
B_5 · $\mathfrak{C}$ (K_E) → $\mathfrak{C}$(E), where E is a symbolic term or variable symbol mentioned earlier.

Now let us consider the occurence of bounded end named notiones in imperative contexts, i.e. let $\mathfrak{J}$ be an instruction.
It is sufficient to consider the case when $\mathfrak{J}$ is of the form SUPPOSE THAT X IS THE RESULT OF $\mathfrak{A}$(K'), where $\mathfrak{A}$ is an action, K' is a bounded notion (as above we have choos the first unblocked t-occurence).

In the beginning let the argument place of the object of $\mathfrak{A}$ be occupied by T and not by K', i.e. $\mathfrak{A}$ = $\mathfrak{A}$ (K' T). Then we have B_6· SUPPOSE THAT X IS RESULT OF $\mathfrak{A}$ (ANY K,T) → TAKE X = T. TAKE Z = {V | V I S K}. WHILE Z IS NOT EMPTY IS NOT TRUE REPEAT SELECTION V FROM Z AND $\mathfrak{A}$ (V,X).

B_7 · SUPPOSE THAT X IS RESULT OF $\mathfrak{A}$ (SOME K,T) → TAKE X = T. TAKE Z = {V | V IS K }. DO (V∈Z) $\mathfrak{A}$ (V,X).

Let now K' stay in the argument place of the object of action $\mathfrak{A}$. Then:

B_8· SUPPOSE THAT X IS RESULT OF $\mathfrak{A}$ (ANY K) → TAKE X = {V | V IS K }. DO PARALLELY (V∈X) $\mathfrak{A}$ (V).

B_9· SUPPOSE X IS RESULT OF $\mathfrak{A}$ (SOME K) TAKE X = {V | V IS K}. DO (V∈X) $\mathfrak{A}$ (V).

Examples.

Let L, l, S and P be set of letters, a letter, a set of words and a word respectively and an action DELETION_FROM_ be defined. First argument of the latter is a letter and the second one is a word. This word is the objectof this action. Then

1. SUPPOSE THAT Q IS THE RESULT OF DELETION OF ANY ELEMENT OF L FROM P→TAKE Q = P. TAKE Z = L. WHILE Z IS EMPTY IS NOT TRUE REPEAT SELECTION OF V FROM Z AND DELECTION V FROM Q.

2. SUPPOSE THAT Q IS THE RESULT OF DELETION OF l FROM ANY ELEMENT OF S → TAKE Q = S. DO PARALLELY (V∈Q) DELETIN l FROM V.

Next we show how to eliminate the t-occurences of a-notions. Note that after applying B-rules a-notions may have t-occurence only in substatement of the form of „t IS K", where t is a symbolic term. Then it is sufficient to eliminate a-notions from such a statement. The rules T_1–T_4 below represent this.

T_1· Let K be an a-notion with the left attribute A, i.e. $K \overset{d}{=} A\ K'$.
t IS K→t IS K' AND t IS A.

Example
G IS FINITE GROUP → IS GROUP AND G IS FINITE.

T_2 · Let K be an a-notion with the right attribute A of the first type. Let L be the leader of K, i.e. $K \overset{d}{=} LAK'$.
t IS K→t IS L K' AND t IS A.

Example
P IS PARTITION COMPATIBLE WITH M OF G→P IS PARTITION OF G AND P IS COMPATIBLE WITH M.

□

T_3· Let K be an a-notion with the right attribute A of the second type. Let L be the leader of K. Let A be obtained by the substitution of term t in ar-formalizer F_,
i.e. $A \overset{d}{=} F\,t_1$; $K \overset{d}{=} L$ OF–Ft_1 K'.

t IS K → t IS LK' AND t_1 IS Ft.

□

Example

H IS SUBGROUP OF INDEX 2 OF G → H IS SUBGROUP OF G AND 2 IS INDEX OF H.

□

T4· Let a right attribute A be obtained from a left attribute A_1 by concatenating it to the leader L of ar_2-attribute R (i.e. $R \overset{d}{=} L\_$). Let K be an a-notion with the attribute A (i.e. $K \overset{d}{=} L_1$ OF AK' $\overset{d}{=}$ L_1 OF A_1 LK', where L_1 is the leader of K).
t IS K → t is L_1 K' AND L OF t IS A_1.

□

Example

H IS $\underbrace{\text{SUBGROUP}}_{L_1}$, OF $\underbrace{\text{FINITE}}_{A_1}$ $\underbrace{\text{ORDER}}_{L}$ $\underbrace{\text{OF G}}_{K'}$

H IS SUBGROUP OF G AND ORDER OF H IS FINITE.

□

Evidently after applying B-and T-rules we obtain a statement of PTL when it is possible and this does not contain bounded notions and attributes.

A notion is called *elementary* if it does not contain occurences of attributes and bounded notions. We call a statement literal that is obtained by substituting symbolic terms into a non-logical r-formalizer or a statement of the form „t IS K" where t is a symbolic term, K is an elementary notion.

Finally we form a number of rules, application of which completes the translation. Here $*[\mathfrak{R}]$ will denote the result of translation of a statement $\mathfrak{R}$.

- 1. If $\mathfrak{R}$ is a literal or an elementary instruction then $*[\mathfrak{R}] \overset{d}{=} \mathfrak{R}$
- 2. $*[t \text{ IS } K] \overset{d}{=} t \in K$, where K is an elementary construction.
- 3. $*[t_1 \in t_2] \overset{d}{=} t_1 \in t_2$.
- 4. $*[t_1$ IS–EOUAL–TO $t_2] \overset{d}{=} t_1 = t_2$.
- 5. $*[\mathfrak{R}_1 \text{ AND } \mathfrak{R}_2] \overset{d}{=} *[\mathfrak{R}_1]\ \&\ *[\mathfrak{R}_2]$.
- 6. $*[\mathfrak{R}_1 \text{ OR } \mathfrak{R}_2] \overset{d}{=} *[\mathfrak{R}_1] \vee *[\mathfrak{R}_2]$
- 7. $*$ [IT–IS–WRONG–THAT $\mathfrak{R}] \overset{d}{=} \neg *[\mathfrak{R}]$
- 8. If is a variable symbol which occures only in $\mathfrak{C}, \mathfrak{C}_1$ and $\mathfrak{C}, \mathfrak{C}_1$ are not instructions then
  $*$ [IF X IS K THEN $\mathfrak{C}] \overset{d}{=} \forall X_K\ *[\mathfrak{C}]$.
- 9. Under the same condition
  $*$ [IF X IS K AND $\mathfrak{C}_1$ THEN $\mathfrak{C}] \overset{d}{=} \forall X_K\ *$[IF $\mathfrak{C}_1$ THEN $\mathfrak{C}$]
- 10. Under the same condition
  $*$[IF $X \in t$ THEN $\mathfrak{C}] \overset{d}{=} \forall X_t\ *[\mathfrak{C}]$
- 11. Under the same condition
  $*$ IF $X \in t$ AND $\mathfrak{C}_1$ THEN $\mathfrak{C} \overset{d}{=} \forall X_t$
  $*$ [IF $\mathfrak{C}_1$ THEN $\mathfrak{C}$].

* 12. $*[\text{IF } \mathfrak{S}_1 \text{ THEN } \mathfrak{S}_2] \overset{d}{=} *[\mathfrak{S}_1] \supset *[\mathfrak{S}_2]$
* 13. Under the condition as in * 8.

  $*[\text{THERE–EXISTS } K_X \text{ SUCH–THAT } \mathfrak{S}] \overset{d}{=} \exists X_K \; *[\mathfrak{S}]$
* 14. $*[\text{THERE–EXISTS } K] \overset{d}{=} \exists X_{\sigma(K)} \; *[X \text{ IS } K]$, where $\sigma(K)$ is the sort of K, X is a new variable symbol.
* 15. If $\mathfrak{J}, \mathfrak{J}_2$ are instructions, σ is a statement then

  $*[\text{IF } \mathfrak{S} \text{ THEN } \mathfrak{J}_1] \overset{d}{=} \text{IF } *[\mathfrak{S}] \text{ THEN} *[\mathfrak{J}_1]$
* 16. Under the same condition

  $*[\mathfrak{J}_1 ; \mathfrak{J}_2] \overset{d}{=} *[\mathfrak{J}_1] ; *[\mathfrak{J}_2]$.
* 17. Under the same condition

  $*[\mathfrak{J}_1 \cap \mathfrak{J}_2] \quad *[\mathfrak{J}_1] \cap *[\mathfrak{J}_2]$
* 18. Under the same condition

  $*[\text{WHILE } \mathfrak{S} \text{ REPEAT } \mathfrak{J}_1] = \text{WHILE } *[\mathfrak{S}] \text{ REPEAT } *[\mathfrak{J}_1]$

Example

$\mathfrak{P} \overset{d}{=}$ EVERY SUBGROUP OF SOME GROUP IS–ABELIAN.

$\mathfrak{P} \xrightarrow{B2}$ THERE–EXISTS GROUP ◇ X SUCH–THAT EVERY SUBGROUP OF X IS–ABELIAN $\xrightarrow{B1}$ THERE–EXISTS GROUP ◇ X SUCH THAT IF Y IS SUBGROUP OF X THEN Y IS–ABELIAN $\xrightarrow{*13}$ $\exists$ X (X IS GROUP AND IF Y IS SUBGROUP OF X THEN Y IS–ABELIAN) $\xrightarrow{*2,\ *5}$ $\exists$ X (X ϵ GROUP & IF Y IS SUBGROUP OF X THEN Y IS–ABELIAN) $\xrightarrow{*8,\ *12}$ $\exists$ X (X ϵ GROUP & $\forall$ Y (Y ϵ SUBGROUP OF $\supset$ Y IS–ABELIAN))

Translation is completed.

5. WHAT TO EXTRACT FROM A TEXT AND HOW TO DO IT?

Let us now have a text in the above developed language which describes the conditions of some problems, which contains reasoning with respect to the solution of this problem, and may be it contains some fragments of the solution in the form of certain constructions and instructions. Our aim is to transform this text into the algorithm providing the solution of the formulated problem (if a solution exists at all). By an algorithm we mean a set of instructions of the above given form and a description of data which the algorithm is to work with.

As to reach this aim the following parts of a text are important supposing that all the above described necessary syntactical transformations have been done.

a) Suppositions of the form LET X BE K, where X is a variable and K is a notion. These suppositions are to be transformed into data description. We do not describe the mechanism of such transformations, since all notions, except the elementary ones (see above), are introduced by definition. The construction of the definitions is simple enough (see below). Therefore defined data types are to be put into correspondence with elementary notions. Further on an analogy of data refinement procedure can be used.

b) Instructions. According to our suppositions all instructions are of elementary form and they may be directly transfered into the algorithm.

c) Sections with an existential statement as a goal. Sections of ,,reduction ad absurdum'' and ,,induction'' play a significant role. It is natural to consider that if an existential statement is proved by ,,reduction ad absurdum'' then it is impossible to provide the algorithm to construct the object in question. Therefore texts with such section will be considered as incorrect. Section of type ,,induction'' is analysed in detail below.

d) Section of „theorem" or ‚lemma".

If the goal (conclusion) of this type of section is an existential statement, then each one of its use in the proof or in the construction is analogous with a procedure call in programming. Therefore this type of sections is to be considered as an independent text and a family of instructions is to be corresponded to it in such a way that those variables in the place . . of which concrete terms are to be substituted while a concrete usage takes place. This is an analogy with formal parameters.

If the conclusion of a theorem or a lemma is not an existential theorem then only its formulation is interesting for us and the text of the proof is not.

e) Section of „definition"

The defined formalizers and their sort can be extracted from the text of a definition. It is easy to formulate rules of application of definitions. During the parsing of PTL-text we have a possibility to deal with some restricted fragments of PTL-grammar and this fragment may be automatically changed after having analysed the corresponding definitions in the text.

Let us see some examples of definitions:

D1. Let M BE SET.
P IS PARTITION OF M IFF P IS SET SUCHTHAT (IF X ϵ P THEN X IS SUBSET OF M) AND (IF X, Y ϵ P THEN X $\cap$ Y = $\emptyset$) AND IF X ϵ M THEN X BELONGS–TO SOME ELEMENT OF P.

D2. LET M, N BE SETS. LET P BE PARTITION OF M. P IS–COMPATIBLE–WITH N IFF CARDINALITY OF EVERY ELEMENT OF P IS–EOUAL–TO CARDINALITY OF N.

D3. LET M BE SET. LET R BE EOUIVALENCE–RELATION ON M.
SUPPOSE S (R) IS SET SUCH–THAT IF X ϵ S (R) THEN THERE–EXISTS ELEMENT Y OF M SUCH-THAT X = { Z | Z R Y }.

D4. LET X BE A LETTER, LET P BE A WORD. DELETING X FROM P GIVES THE WORD P' SUCH THAT IF X DOES NOT OCCURED IN P THEN P' = P AND IF P = P_1 X P_2 AND X DOES NOT OCCURED IN P_1 AND P_2 THEN P' = P_1P_2.

Here D1 is the definition of the n-formalizer PARTITION OF _ its sort is < SET, SET >. D2 is the definition of the r-formalizer _ IS– COMDATIBLE–WITH _ of the sort < SET, SET, BOOLEAN >. D3 is the definition of the sf-formalizer S (_), its sort is < SET, SET > . D4 is the definition of the ac-formalizer DELETING_ FROM_.

6. WHAT „GOOD TEXT" MEANS AND HOW TO EXTRACT PROGRAM FROM IT?

Let us consider an elementary-section of a text (i.e. such a section which does not contain goalsection subordinated to it). For each sentence of this type it is easy to define and construct the family of its all logical antecedents (i.e. that is the family of such statements which can be used while proving the given statement).

A statement is said to be *correct* if it is either a supposition consistent with its logical antecedents or a statement which can be deduced from its logical antecedents by using the following inference rules, case separation, modus ponens, substitution of terms in the place of variables, usage of an auxiliary theorem or lemma, usage of special proof method like proof by induction.

Text is said to be *detailed* if it contains a proof for its each statement (i.e. all intermediate statements which are obtained by the above mentioned rules also belong to the text under consideration).

An elementary goal-section is said to be *correct* if

(i) its all statements are correct;
(ii) its text may be transformed into a detailed text which is the proof of its goal.

A non-elementary goal section is said to be correct if

(i) each directly subordinated to it section is correct
(ii) the elementary section obtained from the given one by replacing each subordinated to it section by the goal of the latter is also correct.

Therefor it is necessary to have a possibility

a) to check the correctness of a text,
b) to transoform the text into a detailed one,
c) to extract a family of instructions from the detailed text corresponding to the elementary section,
d) to collect an instruction family corresponding to the covering section from the above families of instructions.

As it is shown in Vershinin (1982) a) and b) may be realized by standard methods of automatic theorem proving (it is expecially true that a resolution type proof may be effectively transformed into a direct natural proof of the some statement, which uses only the above mentioned inference rules).

Requirement c) is trivial, since from an elementary section a sequence of instructions may be extracted. If among them there are some complex ones, then for their ,,recognition'' syntactic transformations B.7–B.9 are to be used.

Requirement d) has been widely discussed in the literature (see e.g. [2], [5], [6] and [7] except for transformation corresponding to inductive proof. Though the latter is concerned in [5] the formalism used there doesn't allow to consider texts near to natural and it isn't clear how to use the methods of automatic proving. In comparison with it our approach detailed below is more friendly to the user and it allows automatic proof construction due to consideration of the *entire* texts. Let us analyse circumstantially inductive proofs.

Let symbols $K_1, \ldots, K_n$ denote notions, $x, x_1, \ldots, x_n$ $y_1, \ldots y_n$ be individual variables, P, Q are statements, $f, g, t_1, \ldots, t_n$, r are functions and the values of function r are elements of a well ordered set.

Let us suppose that a theorem of the following form
LET x_1 BE K_1 . . . LET x_n BE K_n.
LET P $(x_1, \ldots, x_n)$.
THEN THERE EXISTS x SUCH THAT x IS K
AND Q $(x_1, \ldots, x_n, x)$.
is proved by induction.
The proof itself is of the following construction:

PROOF.
INDUCTION BY R $(x_1, \ldots, x_n)$
BASE. LET r $(x_1, \ldots, x_n) = 0$

SUPPOSE x = $(x_1, \ldots, x_n)$
SHOW Q $(x_1, \ldots, x_n, x)$. –– IT HAS BEEN SHOWN
STEP. LET r $(x_1, \ldots, x_n) > 0$
LET IF y_1 IS K_1 AND. . . AND y_n IS K_n AND r $(y_1, \ldots, y_n) <$ r $(x_1, \ldots, x_n)$ AND P $(y_1, \ldots, y_n)$.
THEN THERE EXISTS y SUCH THAT y is IS K AND Q $(y_1, \ldots, y_n, y)$.

SUPPOSE $y_1 = t_1 (x_1, \ldots, x_n)$
.
.
.
SUPPOSE $y_n = t_n (x_1, \ldots, x_n)$

----

y_1 IS $K_1 \ldots y_n$ IS K_n · $P(y_1, \ldots, y_n)$.

$r(y_1, \ldots y_n) < r(x_1, \ldots, x_n)$.

THERE EXISTS y SUCH THAT y IS K AND $Q(y_1, \ldots, y_n, y)$

SUPPOSE y IS K SUCH THAT $Q(y_1, \ldots, y_n, y)$.

SUPPOSE $x = g(x_1, \ldots, x_n, y)$

----

x IS K. _ _ _ $Q(x_1, \ldots, x_n, x)$.

INDUCTION IS COMPLETED

Here symbols _ _ _ denote an arbitrary text, the construction of which is not essential in our investigation.

Note that all natural proofs analysed by us can be easily represented within the above schema.

The above described schema defines some function $y(x_1, \ldots, x_n)$. In order to understand which operations are to be executed for its computation let us represent the actual situation in the way shown in Fig. 2.

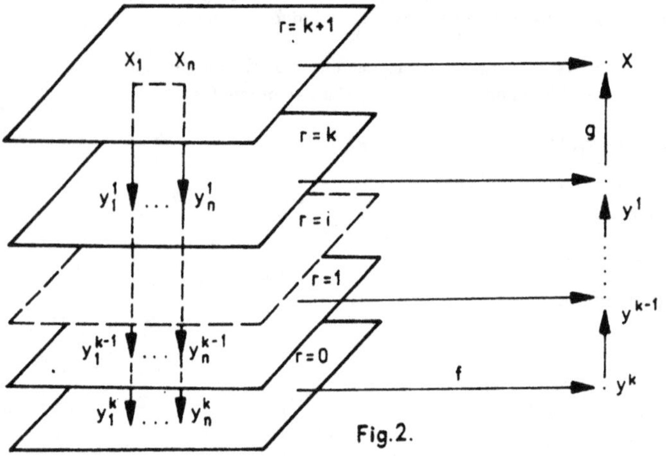

Fig.2.

The entire family of values of variables $x_1, \ldots, x_n$ is decomposed into layer-sets of level of function $r(x_1, \ldots, x_n)$ functions $t_1, \ldots, t_n$ get realized descending from the given layer to the layer corresponding to the lower value of r. Function f computes the necessary value on the lowest level. Function g provides lifting to the layer corresponding to greater value of r. Therefore computation of function q for given $x_1, \ldots, x_n$ is realized as follows:

$$r(x_1, \ldots, x_n) \stackrel{?}{=} 0$$

↓ no

$$y_1^1 = t_1(x_1, \ldots, x_n)$$

⋮

$$y_n^1 = t_n(x_1, \ldots, x_n)$$

$$\downarrow$$

$$r(y_1^1, \ldots, y_n^1) \stackrel{?}{=} 0$$

$$\downarrow \text{no}$$

$$y_1^2 = t_1(y_1^1, \ldots, y_n^1)$$

$$\vdots$$

$$y_n^2 = tn(y_1^1, \ldots, y_n^1)$$

$$\downarrow$$

$$\vdots$$

$$\downarrow$$

$$r(y_1^k, \ldots, y_n^k) \stackrel{?}{=} 0$$

$$\downarrow \text{yes}$$

$$y^k = f(y_1^k, \ldots, y_n^k)$$

$$y^{k-1} = g(y_1^{k-1}, \ldots, y_n^{k-1}, y^k)$$

$$\vdots$$

$$y^1 = g(y_1^1, \ldots, y_n^1, y_2)$$

$$x = g(x_1, \ldots, x_n, y^1)$$

Now let us correspond declaration of program variables to statements of the form x_i IS K_i; program terms F, G, T_i, R to functions f, g, t_i and r respectively where program terms are to compute the latters, conditions $\mathfrak{U}$ and $\mathfrak{Q}$ to statements U and Q respectively. Therefore by using an idealized programming language the following program (denoted by QI) with input variables $x_1, \ldots, x_n$ and output variable x can be obtained which computes the function q:

```
QI (X1, . . ., Xn, X):
    < declaration >
IF  R (X1, . . ., Xn) = O THEN TAKEX = F (X1, . . ., Xn) ; STOP FI;
TAKE Y1 = T1 (X1, . . ., Xn) = O;  . . .: TAKE Yn = Tn (X1, . . ., Xn);
CALL QI (Y1, .  ., Yn, Y) ,
TAKE X  = G (X1, . . ., Xn, Y);
END.
```

As we can see this program is recursive. With respect to this let us pay attention to the following important particular case when „lifting" function g is of the form g $(y_1, \ldots y_n, y) = y$ i.e. it doesn't depend on the previous values. In this case it is easy to transform OI into an interative one:

```
QI (X1, . . ., Xn, X):
  < declaration >
WHILE R (X1, . . ., Xn)    ≠ O REPEAT ;
TAKE  Y1 = T1 (X1, . . ., Xn); . . . ; TAKE Yn = Tn (X1, . . ., Xn) ;
TAKE  X1 = Y1 ; . . . ;  TAKE Xn = Yn  ;
TAKE  X = F (X1, . . ., Xn);
END;
```

By analysing the proposed computation schema many other cases can be found where recursive programs can be easily transformed into iterating ones.

Note that from the aboves immediately follows that if the text to be considered is really a proof then the obtained program is correct.

Example

Let us consider the following task:
construct a program which computes for given elements a and b of commutative Euclidean ring such elements x and y, that x a + y.b = GCD (a,b). (This is a particular case of Chinese remainder theorem.)
At the same time we obtain the program which computes the greates common devisor (GCD). So we suppose, that a text is given which contains the definition of commutative Euclidean ring R with operations + and. and definition of GCD. In these definitions the following functions take place: quat (x, y) which is equal to the quationt of x divided by y, and rem (x, y) which is but the residual of dividing x by y.

Moreover, we suppose that the function N(x) is also defined which computes the norm of element x. Suppose we have the following text fragment:

THEOREM

LET a, b BE ELEMENTS OF R. LET N (a) ⩾ N'(b), THEN THERE ARE d, x, y SUCH THAT d, x, y ARE ELEMENTS OF R AND d IS GCD (a, b) AND x.a+y.b = d.

PROOF

INDUCTION ON N (rem (a, b)).
BASIS. LET N (rem (a, b)) = O. THEN b DEVIDES a.
SUPPOSE d = b AND x = o AND y = 1.
(*) STEP. LET N (rem (a, b)) > O. LET US SUPPOSE THAT IF p, q ARE ELEMENTS OF R AND N (rem (p,q)) < N (rem (a, b)) AND N (p) ⩾ N (q) THEN THERE EXIST s,x;y' SUCH THAT s IS GCD (p,q) AND x' . p + y' · q = s.

a = b' quot (a, b) + rem (a,b) AND N (rem (a,b)) < N (b).
(**) b = rem (a,b) · quot (b, rem (a, b)) + rem (b, rem (a,b)) AND
N = (rem (b, rem (a,b))) < N (rem (a,b)).

THERE EXIST s,x'y' SUCH THAT s IS GCD (b;
rem (a, b)) AND x'. b+y' rem (a, b) = s.

(***) SUPPOSE d = s AND x = y' AND y = x − y' · quot (a, b).
INDUCTION IS COMPLETED.

Remarks

1. This text is represented in the described language and can be directly put into a computer and processed by formal methods.

2. The above proof may be generated automatically having formalized the theorem and all the necessary definitions. Thus, e.g. statements marked by (*) are obtained by solving the system of equations with unknown x and y:

$$\begin{cases} b = d \\ x \cdot a + y \cdot b = d \end{cases}$$

Inductive assertion can be also easily formalized automatically on basis of the formulation of the theorem.

Statements (**) are results of duble use of the definition of Euclidean ring (since here none of the other steps of searching proof take to new statements).

Statements (***) can be obtained by solving the following system of equations:

$$\begin{cases} x \cdot a + y \cdot b = d \\ s = d \\ x' \cdot b + y' \cdot \text{rem}(a, b) = s \\ a = b \cdot \text{quot}(a, b) + \text{rem}(a, b) \end{cases}$$

with unknown x and y.

From the above text of proof by using our method two program can be obtained.

One for computing

```
CRT (A, B, X, Y):
     < declaration >
IF   N (REM(A,B)) = O THEN TAKE X = O; TAKE Y = 1; STOP FI;
TAKE A1 = B; TAKE B1 = REM (A, B);
CALL CRT (A1, B1, X1, Y1);
TAKE X = Y1; TAKE Y = X1 – Y1 . OUOT (A,B);

END
```

Another one for computing greatest common devisor.

```
And GCD (A,B,D):
          < declaration >
IF N (REM(A,B)) = O THEN TAKE D = B; STOP FI;
TAKE A1 = B; TAKE B1 = REM (A, B);
CALL GCD (A1, B1, D1);
TAKE D = D1; END.
```

According to our remark the last program can be rewritten into an iterative one:

```
G6 D (A, B, D);
     < declaration >
WHILE N (REM (A;B)) ≠ O REPEAT
TAKE X = B: TAKE Y = REM (A, B);
TAKE A = X;  TAKE B = Y
TAKE D = B;  END;
```

7. CONCLUSION

The approach developed here opens an attractive way of program synthesis namely, it replaces program writing by mathematical text assembly. This text is but the specification of the problem to be solved together with some hints on the solution method to be chosen. After this we hope to prove the statements in the text automatically and the program can be extracted from the proof without any difficulty. However, by the use of this method various difficulties arise. One of the main difficulties beyond automatic theorem proving itself is that the methods of automatic theorem proving work only when the theory of appropriate problem domain is well developed. Otherwise the problem cannot possibly be described adequately even if such a liberal language PTL is used. Therefore it is very important to develop the conceptual means and the appropriate theory for the problem domain which we intend to work within.

REFERENCES

[1] Bachus, J.; Can programming be literated from von Neumann style? A functional style and its algebra of programs, Comm. ACM. 21(1978), pp. 613–641.

[2] Constable R.L., A constructive programming logic, Information Processing'77, North-Holland, 1977.

[3] Gergely, T. and Vershinin, K. P. ; Concept sensitive formal language for task specification, in Mathematical Logic in Computer Science, North-Holland, 1981, pp. 429–470.

[4] Kowalski, R.; Logic for Problem solving, North Holland, 1979.

[5] Manna, Z. and Waldinger, R.; A deductive approach program synthesis, SRI Technical Note 177, 1978.

[6] Nepeivoda, N.N.; The logical approach to programming, in LNCS, vol 122, Springer Verlag, 1981, pp. 261–289.

[7] Sato, M.; Toward a mathematical theory of program synthesis, Proceedings of 6-th IJCAI. 1979, pp. 757–762.

[8] Scherlis, W.L. and Scott, D.L.; First steps towards inferential programming, Information Processing 83, North-Holland, 1983, pp. 199–212.

[9] Vershinin, K.P., On the correctness of mathematical texts and its computer based checking, ph. D. thesis, Kijev, 1982.

AN ALGEBRAIC FRAMEWORK FOR INDUCTIVE PROGRAM SYNTHESIS

Klaus P. Jantke +)

Software development is a serious bottleneck of current information processing practice. Consequently, mathematically based attempts to widen this bottleneck form a main stream of theoretical computer science. Among them abstract data type theory plays a leading role, as it is widely accepted that during a complex software design process particular decisions about implementation details should be postponed as long as possible. Instead, properties of and relations between software modules should be specified in an abstract manner emphasizing machine independent features. Algebraic semantics so has set the stage for languages and systems like CLEAR , LARCH , ASL , ACT ONE , and others (cf. [04], [10], [22], and [06], resp.).

The intentions of the authors of software design systems and related approaches range from faking a rational design process (cf. [20]) to guiding the programmers intuition by means of formal tools [18]. The formal approach developed in the present paper is aimed at the development of algorithmic tools which will free the programmer from the burden of stupidly implementing simple algorithms and trivial structures. Thus he/she becomes free for the creative work of designing sophisticated structures and programming tricky algorithms.

The key idea of the present approach already sketched in [12] and [13] consists in incorporating inductive inference methods into abstract data type investigations. The ultimate goal is to improve the power of concerning algebraically based design systems by additionally providing a facility for synthesizing programs in processing incomplete specifications.

+) Humboldt University Berlin, Computing Center
1086 Berlin, P.O.Box 1297
German Democratic Republic

This approach is basically motivated by the authors research work in inductive inference. Inductive inference (cf. [01], [17]) is a mathematical theory of synthesizing (or learning/identifying, alternatively) objects from incomplete information. Since Gold's seminal paper [08] some inductive inference approaches led to exciting applications like Shapiro's program synthesis method and Nix's intelligent text processing system [19] . Now the time seems to be ripe for extensively using inductive inference results for automatic programming.

The present paper is purely mathematical in spirit. It is devoted to outlining a mathematical approach for joining abstract data type investigations and inductive inference approaches. The resulting concept is intended to form a formal framework for the author's applied work and, moreover, to exhibit some ways for combining methods and results belonging to different mathematical disciplines.

1. Algebraic Specifications

We direct the reader to the basic text books [06], [16], and [21] for careful and comprehensive discussions of the underlying concepts. Syntactically, we will follow Ehrig's and Mahr's notation in [06], mainly, as it leads from theoretical investigations to applications (by means of ACT ONE). Our approach is characterized by confining ourselves to total algebras only. Thus it is more restricted than the general approach investigated by Reichel in [21],e.g. However, in the author's opinion it is powerful enough for a wide class of applications, in particular under final algebra semantics (cf. [15]). Throughout the first chapter we restrict our introduction to the basic notions and to those concepts which will be used later.

Signatures are triples **SIG** = (S,O,ar), where S and O are nonempty sets of sort names and operator names, respectively, and ar is an arity function assigning to every operator name F a nonempty sequence ar(F) = s1 ... sn s (n=0) of sort names s1, ... , sn , s. The meaning is that F is the name of a function mapping from the cartesian product of the sets named by s1 , ... , sn into the set named by s. In case n equals zero, F is understood to be a constant of the sort s. Usually, we write F: s1 ... sn ---> s instead of ar(F) = s1 ... sn s . The following example implicitly explains a style of notation which is widely used. The sort names of S are listed following the key word sorts. This is possible, as we assume finite signatures, i.e. the sets S and O are assumed to be finite. The key word opns precedes the list of operator names, which is enriched by a description of their arity as described above. Now, the syntax will be exemplified by means of some very simple specifications, which will be used in the sequel.

```
def boole is
    sorts boole
    opns TRUE:  --->  boole
         FALSE:  --->  boole
end of def
```

In fact, this defines a signature **SIG** = (S,O,ar), where S contains the only sort name boole and O contains two operator names TRUE and FALSE of the same arity. More precisely, both operators are constants of the sort boole, i.e. ar(TRUE) = ar(FALSE) = boole . Operators of the same arity may be written in one line indicating the arity only once, e.g.

```
opns TRUE, FALSE:  --->  boole
```

The following examples are almost self-explaining. The last of them provides more information than the preceding, as it consists of a signature enriched by an equational axiom describing a desired property.

Equations of that type are headed by the key word eqns.

```
def alpha is
    sorts letters
    opns  A,B,C,D,E,F,G,H,I,J,K,L,M:  --->  letters
          N,O,P,Q,R,S,T,U,V,W,X,Y,Z:  --->  letters
end of def

def nat is
    sorts nat
    opns  0:  --->  nat
    S: nat  --->  nat
end of def

def nat' is
    sorts nat
    opns  0,ERROR:  --->  nat
    S: nat  --->  nat
    eqns of sort nat
    S(ERROR)  =  ERROR
end of def
```

As the specification named by **nat'** is a proper extension of the preceding specification **nat** we can use a corresponding notation as follows.

```
def nat' is
    nat and
        opns ERROR: --->  nat
        eqns of sort nat
        S(ERROR)  =  ERROR                                        (1)
end of def
```

We suppress almost all further details of the underlying specification language and direct the reader to [06] in this regard. The concepts above are basic. Additionally, we will need parametrized specifications. They will be introduced implicitly. Moreover, it turns out that pure equational specifications are not expressive enough. [02] contains a very impressive example of a reasonable data type which requires conditional term equations for its specification. The existence of a lot of similar examples is the key reason for permitting conditional equations. Thus we take an approach being a little bit more general than the concept offered by [06]. This concept and all others will be introduced implicitly, too.

2. Initial and Final Algebra Semantics

The present chapter is aimed at giving a sketch only, for the sake of completeness of our introduction. For deeper insights we refer to the fundamental paper [07], to Wand's paper [24] on final algebra semantics or to one of the text books mentioned above.

We assume any specification as described above. All parameter specifications are assumed to be instantiated. We permit specifications with conditional equations probably containing variables. For explaining the meaning of such a specification we take into account all finitely generated algebras of the signature given by the specification. Recall that the signature is defined by the text following the key words sorts and opns. An algebra of a given signature contains for every sort name a carrier set and for every operator name a total function (therefore, we should speak about total algebra semantics, correctly) which maps in correspondence with the arity indicated in the specification. Such an algebra is said to be finitely generated over some signature, if for every element there exists some term build from constants and operators, which describes the concerning element.

The class of finitely generated algebras forms the model class taken into consideration. For every non-trivial specification, like the single axiom S(ERROR) = ERROR above, there are finitely generated algebras, in which the specification is valid, and others which do not satisfy the axioms presented. For every finite, heterogeneous and finitary signature SIG and for every set E of conditional equations probably containing variables from some suitable effectively enumerable collection we denote by **ALG(SIG,E)** the class of all finitely generated models of E, i.e. the class of all finitely generated algebras over the given signature in which the axioms of E are satisfied.

Unfortunately, this concept does not yield for every specification a meaning being uniquely defined up to isomorphism. Therefore, we try to choose some model of E (up to isomorphism) which can be easily characterized by useful mathematical properties. There are two basic approaches being opposite to one another. /1/ E is understood as a description of the "largest" possible model of E. This concept is well-known as the initial algebra approach. In fact, the algebra specified by some specification E over some signature SIG may be imagined as the algebra of all variable-free terms over SIG factorized by the congruence relation induced by E. The final algebra specified by E on SIG will be dentoted by **Ainit(SIG,E)** . /2/ E is understood as the "smallest" non-trivial model of E, in case it exists. This approach, which plays a minor role in the area of algebraic semantics, is called the final (or terminal) algebra approach. For the final algebra approach we take into account the model class which results from **ALG(SIG,E)** , if we eliminate the unit algebra of the signature SIG (and every isomorphic structure). The resulting model class is denoted by **ALG+(SIG,E)** . By **Afin(SIG,E)** we denote (up to isomorphism) the final model in **ALG+(SIG,E)**.

As the final algebra approach is less popular than the initial one, we add some information for illuminating some of its basic features. The reader should consult the author's paper [15] in this regard.

First of all, as we exclude the unit algebra, i.e. we take into account only those algebraic structures containing at least one carrier set which consists of more than one element, it is possible to use conditional equations for expressing inequalities. For instance, we consider the signature **nat'** introduced above . The implication

```
S(x) = 0  ===>  y = z
```

implies that S(x) and 0 are different for every instantiation of x provided that the unit algebra is excluded . Consequently, by

```
def nat* is
    nat' and
    eqns of sort nat
    for all x,y,z in
    S(x) = S(y)  ===>  x = y                                  (2)
    S(x) = 0  ===>  y = z                                     (3)
end of def
```

we define the algebra of the natural numbers generated by one constant zero and the successor function and containing an exception element under final algebra semantics.

In [15] the author proved that within the framework of total algebras the final algebra approach is more expressive than the initial one. It is possible to specify each partial recursive function possessing a recursively decidable graph under final semantics, whereas every function specified under initial semantics has a recursively decidable domain. We confine ourselves to a sketch of the kernel formalism, only. For simplicity, let us consider unary recursive functions. Such a function f is said to be specified by some operator F and by some set E of axioms under initial or final semantics, respectively, if and only if in the initial resp. final algebra the following equivalences are valid for arbitrary natural numbers m and n :

$$F(\ S^m(0)\ ) = S^n(0) \quad \text{, in case } f(m) = n \text{ holds.} \qquad (C1)$$

$$F(\ S^m(0)\ ) = \text{ERROR} \quad \text{, in case } f(m) \text{ is undefined.} \qquad (C2)$$

This is the basic convention for the result mentioned above. It is an immediate result of Godel's completeness theorem that for every specification E on any given signature each term equation being valid under initial algebra semantics is provable from the underlying specification E. Similarly, under initial algebra semantics it turns out that each term inequality which is valid can be derived from the given specification and from some formula expressing that the unit algebra is excluded. If we take the properties (C1) and (C2) above as a fundamental convention for specifying computable functions, this implies that a searching procedure can be specified under initial algebra semantics if and only if its halting problem is (effectively) known to be decidable in advance. Such a strong assumption is not necessary for specifying searching procedures under final algebra semantics.

For illustrating specific features of final algebra semantics, this will do.

3. A Peep at Inductive Inference

This chapter is aimed at sketching some fundamentals of inductive inference. The author's basic idea is to join inductive inference research work and abstract data type investigations for the development of new tools supporting the process of software development. It is not claimed that inductive inference methods should be utilized for automatically synthesizing arbitrary software systems. But there is some evidence that within programming support systems certain problems are easily solvable by inductive inference strategies, i.e. inductive inference methods seem to be particularly tailored to specific subtasks as illustrated in chapter 4 of the present paper. We direct the reader to similar discussions in [12] and [14].

First we will give a brief introduction into the theory of inductive inference, for which [01] and [17] are appropriate surveys. Every inductive inference concept assumes some class of objects of interest. The problem under consideration consists in synthesizing any given object of this class. Objects are presented in an incomplete way. This refers to one more parameter of every inductive inference concepts. There must be a specification language for presenting information about objects to be identified. Every particular information may be incomplete with respect to the object to be described. In case the presented information is to weak, an identification may be impossible. Therefore, it is necessary to investigate information sequences describing an object to be synthesized in the limit. The semantics of sequences of admissible information units form one more parameter, i.e. we have to explain what does it mean that a sequence describes an object in the limit. Inductive inference algorithms have to process information about objects to be identified. They generate hypotheses intended to describe a given target object. Thus in working up information sequences they generate sequences of hypotheses. It is necessary to explain how such a sequence of hypotheses describes a learning process, i.e. in which cases such a sequence describes a unique object which is finally guessed by the inductive inference algorithm. The space of possible hypotheses and the mentioned concept of convergency form two more parameters of every inductive inference concept. Moreover, every hypothesis is assigned its semantics. The following figure summarizes this abstract concept as a whole.

The central problem of inductive inference research work consists in the incompleteness of information to be processed. As initially announced, it is the author's intent to introduce this point of view into the investigations dealt with algebraic specifications. This seems to be quite natural, as it is impossible to decide, in general, whether or not some intermediate specification designed by some user describes the desired software system correctly. If algebraic specifications are

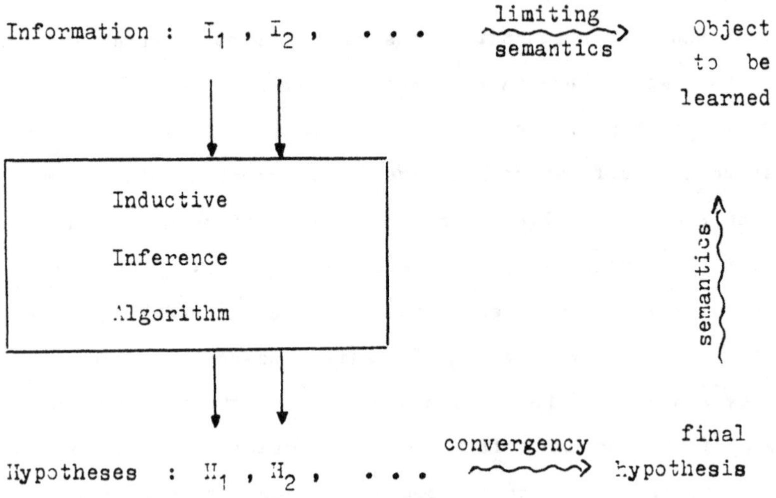

Figure 1

intended to be processed, it may happen that they describe the software system to be synthesized incompletely. Usually, a stepwise design process yields a sequence of incomplete specifications intended to approach a target system somehow in the limit. Therefore, we claim that the inductive inference philosophy reflects inherent features of every real software design process. Consequently, there must be (at least some sub-)tasks which can be solved be means of inductive inference techniques. Let us have a closer look at some introductory examples.

4. Basic Examples

4.1. A Lucid Toy Example

The main intent of the present example is to illuminate the importance of the underlying syntactical concepts, i.e. to exhibit that the algebraic framework is of some importance for inductive inference considerations, as it yields some hints what assumptions are of importance for the performed inductive inference process.

Let us consider rectangular tables consisting of three rows and four columns as shown in the following figures. Each cell contains some item which is a black or white symbol of a certain shape. Figure 2 shows two tables of that kind. In the right table two cells remained open. The task is to complete this rectangular in analogy to the other rectangular given in the same figure. The meaning of the phrase "in analogy to" is unspecified up to now. However, many readers would probably proceed as follows. They have a closer look at the complete rectangular for detecting some regularities. After recognizing certain regularities they try to complete the second table in such a way that the rules recognized before are satisfied by the completed table, too.

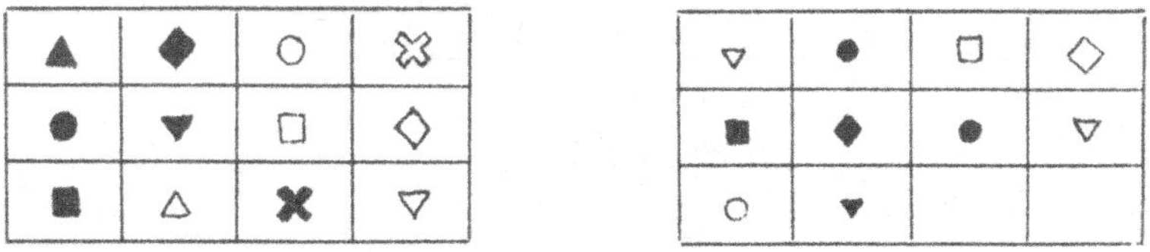

Figure 2

We propose some regularities in the sequel.

(R1) For every shape of symbols there is the same number of entries of this shape in the table.

(R2) For every colour of symbols there is the same number of entries of this colour in the table.

(R3) In each row there are not two different entries of the same shape.

(R4) In each column there are not two different entries of the same shape.

(R5) Different colums contain differently many white entries.

For formulating these rules we have used concepts like "shape", "colour", "row", "column", and (for counting the number of white entries) "cardinality". The rules above may be understood as first order formulae of some language containing syntactical expressions for the concepts mentioned. In fact, we have assumed some signature.

Unfortunately, there is no way to complete the second table of figure 2 such that every rule is satisfied. Consequently, it is necessary to cancel at least one of the regularities detected. But which one? Let us continue the game by presenting one more table which is intended to provide more information.

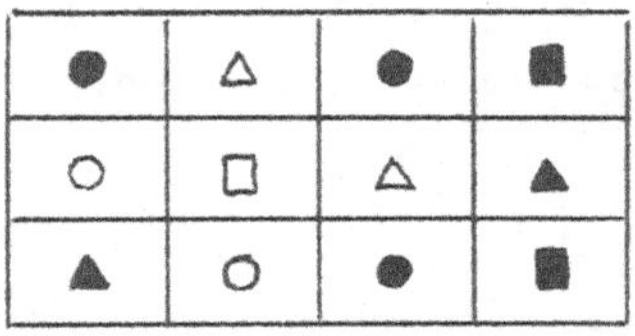

Figure 3

The reader will easily recognize that the last table shown in figure 3 violates every rule above. Therefore, solving the presented problem requires new efforts of learning regularities. This seems to be considerably difficult, if we have to use only the syntactical concepts introduced above. Instead, we propose another syntactical concept which enables to recognize one more regularity which can be expressed without difficulties. The concerning concept is known as the knight move on a chess board. Thus we get

(R6) All cells containing symbols of the same shape can be ordered along a sequence of knight moves such that the colour of symbols alternates.

With respect to (R6) there are different possibilities to complete the second table of figure 2.

The discussed principle of solving the present problem consists of two subtasks, namely learning an analogy concept (first order formulae over some signature) and constructing a solution which is a model of the set of axioms learned before. We direct the reader to [14] for a more detailed investigation.

For exhibiting the essentials of our investigation above let us consider the tables under consideration as finite relations. In fact, we have studied the problem of inductively inferring data dependencies. The availability of the concept of knight moves may be understood as the accessibility of some more finite relation describing which cells are reachable from one another by one knight move. Then (R6) represents a simple interrelational functional dependency. Whether such a new relation is accessible or not essentially influences the considered process of inductively inferring data dependencies. This illuminates the importance of the underlying syntactical knowledge (let us say: the underlying signature) for inductive inference processes.

4.2. A Classical Example

In [23] Trakhtenbrot and Barzdin investigated the problem of learning finite deterministic automata with an initial state from finite samples of their input/output behavior. These investigations reflect some instantiation of the general inductive inference approach shown in figure 1 of the present paper.

Finite deterministic initial automata can be easily understood as algebraic structures of the signature

```
def automaton(input,output) is
    formal sorts input
                 output
    sorts        state
    opns         Z0 :  --->  state
                 DELTA :  state x input  --->  state
                 LAMBDA :  state x input  --->  output
end of def
```

input and **output** are parameter structures and may be instantiated by **alpha** , e.g. Presenting the input/output behavior of some automaton over fixed input and output alphabets means giving pairs (x,y) of words of the corresponding input and output sets, respectively. More formally, this may be understood as giving equations describing the input/outout behavior as exemplified in the sequel. Let us assume that the parameters of the specification above are instantiated by **alpha** . Suppose that x is a word ab of the length 2 which, if fed into some given automaton, yields the output word y = uv . Here, a,b,u, and v are variables for constants of **alpha** , i.e. they vary on A,B, ... , Z . The knowledge that the input of x = ab results in the output of y = uv may be written as:

LAMBDA(Z0,a) = u (AUT1)

LAMBDA(Z0,DELTA(Z0,a),b) = v (AUT2)

Adding the equations (AUT1) and (AUT2) to the specification of **automaton** yields a new specification **automaton/ex2** . Synthesizing a finite deterministic initial automaton means constructing a particular model, i.e. a **fixed data type** which may be understood as an implementation of the abstract data type **automaton/ex2** . It is implicitly assumed that the constants of the parameter specification **output** must be different from one another. This me interpreted as the presence of some conditional equations which imply the concerning inequalities under final algebra semantics, as explained above.

It turns out that Trakthenbrot's and Barzdin's inductive inference algorithm yields the final algebra semantics, in case it exists. Otherwise, the algorithm yields some model which is minimal in the model class under consideration.

4.3. A Program Synthesis Example

The example we are dealt with is investigated in detail by Lange in his paper in the present volume. So it is sufficient to sketch the basic idea in the present chapter.

We are interested in iterative sorting algorithms SORT which can be described in an abstract manner by

SORT(f) = IF ORD(f) = TRUE THEN f ELSE SORT(NEXT (f)) ,

where f is a variable for the file to be sorted. ORD names a supposed standard predicate testing whether any given file is ordered or not. NEXT is a procedure which describes the core of the work performed by the sorting algorithm named SORT.

The inductive inference problem consists in synthesizing the procedure NEXT from examples of its behavior. We assume that lists to be sorted are build on the data structure introduced by the name **alpha** above. In doing so we need some ordering relation on the assumed alphabet. This will be introduced as follows.

```
def alpha* is
    alpha and boole and
    opns LESS : letters x letters  --->  boole
    eqns of sort boole
    for all x,y,z in letters
    LESS(x,x) = FALSE
    LESS(A,B) = TRUE
    LESS(B,C) = TRUE
    . . .
    LESS(Y,Z) = TRUE
    LESS(x,y) = TRUE  &  LESS(y,z) = TRUE  ===>  LESS(x,z) = TRUE
    LESS(x,y) = TRUE  ===>  LESS(y,x) = FALSE
end of def
```

On **alpha*** we can define lists as usual. There is no difficulty to define on the resulting data structure a predicate which tests whether or not any given list is ordered with respect to the properties of LESS defined above. We omit all these technical details in the sequel. Suppose that the defined predicate checking a file for being ordered is named by ORD. For lucidity, lists will be written without explicitly mentioning the constructor function appending elements to sublists.

A possible input/output example describing the behavior of a particular procedure NEXT we have in mind may be

```
in  =  X M N V S T A Q C D B U W K Z Y
out =  X Y Z S T U C Q D B A W V N M K
```

in and out are names for abbreviating these lists in the sequel. The example above, if presented in a more formal way, is some term equation as follows, where in and out are only used for shortening the presentation.

NEXT(in) = out

I.e. giving an input/output example means presenting an axiom which enriches an underlying specification. This specification represents basic knowledge like available syntactical concepts and properties of functions which may be used for a description of the target procedure to be synthesized.

A quite general program synthesis method is based on the idea to decompose every input and every output with respect to so-called selectors and constructors, respectively, for "expressing the output in terms of the input". In our example under consideration this principle can be sketched as follows. If a selector function IN is available which computes for every given file its longest ordered initial segment, and if a similar selector function FIN computes for every given file its longest final segment which is a reversed ordered list, then it is possible to detect that the output abbreviated by out may be expressed as

out = / IN(in) , INV(FIN (in)) , list /

where / ... , ... , ... / is used as a notation for the concatenation of the corresponding lists. INV denotes one more assumed basic function which reverses every list. The concatenation of list may be considered as a constructor function. list names some remaining list.

Note that the choice of the corresponding selectors and constructors essentially influences the way of expressing the output in terms of the corresponding input. Thus it controls the inductive inference process. This is completely similar to the problem discussed in chapter 4.1.
For more details we refer to Lange's paper in the present volume.

5. The Algebraic Framework of Inductive Inference Problems

We assume that there is some signature **SIG** of interest . Software systems to be synthesized are understood as algebraic structures of this signature. For representing information about a target software system it may be necessary to use auxiliary concepts which do not belong explicitly to the signature of interest. Therefore, we consider a signature **SIG'** which is an enrichment of **SIG** , i.e. the set of sort names and the set of operator names of **SIG'** cover the corresponding sets in the signature of interest, and the arity function of the smaller signature is exactly the restriction of the arity function of **SIG'** to the names of operators under consideration.

It is assumed that **boole** occurs as a substructure, for expressing tests, if necessary. The set O' of operators names of **SIG'** is assumed to be devided into three subsets B' , C' , and S'. B' contains exactly the boolean-valued operator names. The operators in C' and S' are called constructors and selectors, respectively. They are related to one another by some properties described by conditional term equations collected in BK . We refer to BK as the basic knowledge about the standard functions being available. Note that we do not require that C' and S' are disjoint, although this is desirable, in general. Constructors and selectors shall satisfy the following conditions.

(CONSTR) For every variable-free term t build on **SIG'** , in case t is not boolean-valued, there exists some term t', which consists of constructors only, such that the equation t = t' is valid in the initial resp. final model of BK.

(SELECT) For every s-sorted term t (where s is different from boole) and for every variable x occurring in t there exists some term t', which is build from selectors only and which contains a variable y of the sort s, such that the term equation x = t'(y<-t) is valid in the initial resp. final model of BK.

Note that the approach proposed works for initial and final algebra semantics as well. But the basic knowledge necessary for achieving the properties expressed by (CONSTR) and (SELECT) depends essentially on the chosen semantics, in general. For every assumed pair of signatures SIG and **SIG'**, the choice of constructors and selectors, i.e. the definition of C' resp. S', and the decision about the basic knowledge BK assumed essentially controls every inductive inference process.

Suppose that F is some new operator name. For simplicity, we consider F as being unary. We investigate the inductive inference problem of synthesizing a program for the function specified by F in the limit provided that there is presented step by step a limiting specification of F. In general, a limiting specification is a sequence E1 , E2 , ... of finite sets of conditional term equations build on **SIG'** and probably containing F, additionally. (In the example of chapter 4.3., instead of F we have used the name NEXT.) By **SIG*** we denote the signature **SIG'** enriched by F. E* will abbreviate the union of all intermediate specifications E1 , E2 , ... Some function is said to be specified in the limit by E* under initial or final algebra semantics if and only if it is defined up to isomorphism by the interpretation of F in **Ainit(SIG***,E*) or **Afin(SIG***,E*), respectively. Note that we do not require the effective accessibility of infinitely many specifications. It is only required the potentially infinte specification process approaches a uniquely defined meaning. Each intermediate specification is allowed to be incomplete. In particular, it's possible that for every intermediate specification En the final algebra does not exist.

There are two different inference goals, in general. /1/ The space of hypotheses consists of sets of conditional axioms, i.e. the ultimate goal of any inductive inference process is a complete specification. /2/ Hypotheses are effective descriptions of algebraic structures, i.e. the ultimate goal is a correct implementation. Because of the lack of space we have to suppress all further discussions.

Within the general framework above it is possible to describe a large variety of known inductive inference algorithm and to develop new families of algorithms, as exemplified by Lange's paper already mentioned. We confine ourselves to a sketch of a family of algorithms which strongly depend on some basic knowledge and a corresponding assumption about constructors and selectors. We assume the final algebra approach, as explained in [12].

Intermediate specifications are finite sets of input/output examples for F, i.e. finite sets of equations like NEXT(in) = out or LAMBDA(ZO,a) = u above. By composing the presented outputs step by step using constructors, and by decomposing the corresponding inputs step by step using selectors, the inductive inference algorithm searches for some term t as follows: a) Its outermost operators are constructors and its innermost operators are selectors, and it contains exactly one variable x. Therefore, we write t(x), for short. b) For every pair (in,out) , which describes an input/output example, i.e. which is presented by an equation F(in) = out , the equation t(x<-in) = out can not be rejected by proving the corresponding inequality from BK, the input/output examples and the fact that the unit algebra is excluded. Note that exactly this is the work performed by Trakhtenbrot's and Barzdin's tree matching procedure. The simplest term t is used as a description of the target algorithm. It remains to detect repetitions in t for constructing recursive calls. To sum up the situation, program synthesis is understood as synthesizing terms being consistent with the information processed.

References

[01] Angluin, Dana / Smith, C.H. A survey of inductive inference: theory and methods, Computing Surveys 15 (1983) 3, 238 - 269

[02] Bergstra, Jan A. / Meyer, J.-J.Ch. On specifying sets of integers, EIK 20 (1984) 10/11, 531 - 541

[03] Bergstra, Jan / Tucker, J.V. A natural data type with finite equational final semantics specification but no effective equational initial semantics specification, Bull. EATCS 11 (1980), 23 - 33

[04] Burstall, Rod / Goguen, J. The semantics of CLEAR , a specification language, in: Abstract Software Specifications (D. Bjorner, ed.), Springer-Verlag, Berlin-Heidelberg-New York-Tokyo, 1979 (Lecture Notes in Computer Science 86),

[05] CIP Language Group The Munich Project CIP, Volume 1: The Wide Spectrum Language CIP-L, Springer - Verlag, Berlin-Heidelberg-New York-Tokyo, 1985 (Lecture Notes in Computer Science 183)

[06] Ehrig, Hartmut / Mahr, B. Fundamentals of Algebraic Specification 1, Springer-Verlag, Berlin-Heidelberg-New York-Tokyo, 1985 (EATCS Monographs on Theoretical Computer Science 6)

[07] Goguen, J.A. / Thatcher, J.W. / Wagner, E.G. An initial algebra approach to the specification, correctness, and implementation of abstract data types, in: Current Trends in Programming Methodology, R.T. Yeh (ed.), Prentice-Hall, 1978, 80 - 149

[08] Gold, E. Mark Language identification in the limit, Inf. and Control 10 (1967), 447 - 474

[09] Guttag, John V. The specification and application to programming of abstract data types, Ph. D. Thesis, Univ. of Toronto, 1975

[10] Horning, J.J. Combining algebraic specifications in LARCH, in: Formal Methods and Software Development, Vol. 2, H. Ehrig / Ch. Floyd / M. Nivat / J. Thatcher (eds.), Springer-Verlag, Berlin - Heidelberg-New York-Tokyo, 1985 (Lecture Notes in Computer Science 186), 12 - 26

[11] Jantke, Klaus P. A characterization theorem on partial recursive functions and abstract data types, Bull. EATCS 15 (1981), 40 - 46

[12] Jantke, Klaus P. A generalized approach to inductive inference in: Artificial intelligence and information - control system of robots, I. Plander (ed.), North-Holland, 1984, 189 - 192

[13] Jantke, Klaus P. The main proof theoretic problems in inductive inference, in: Frege Conference 1984, G. Wechsung (ed.), Akademie-Verlag Berlin, 1984, 321 - 330

[14] Jantke, Klaus P. Program synthesis by analogy - a two-phased approach, in: Proc. AIMSA'84, W. Bibel / B. Petkoff (eds.), North-Holland, 1985

[15] Jantke, Klaus P. The recursive power of algebraic semantics, submitted to EIK

[16] Klaeren, Herbert A. Algebraische Spezifikationen - Eine Einfuehrung, Springer-Verlag, Berlin-Heidelberg-New York-Tokyo, 1983

[17] Klette, Reinhard / Wiehagen, R. Research in the theory of inductive inference by GDR mathematicians - a survey, Inf. Sciences 22 (1980), 149 - 169

[18] Naur, P. Intuition in software development, in: Formal Methods and Software Development, Vol. 2, H. Ehrig / Ch. Floyd / M. Nivat / J. Thatcher (eds.), Springer-Verlag, Berlin-Heidelberg-New York -Tokyo, 1985 (Lecture Notes in Computer Science 186), 60 - 79

[19] Nix, Robert P. Editing by example, Yale University, New Haven, Dep. Comp. Sci., Techn. Report 280, 1983

[20] Parnas, D.L. / Clements, P.C. A rational design process: how and why to fake it, in: Formal Methods and Software Development, Vol. 2, H. Ehrig / Ch. Floyd / M. Nivat / J. Thatcher (eds.), Springer-Verlag, Berlin-Heidelberg-New York-Tokyo, 1985 (Lecture Notes in Computer Science 186), 80 - 100

[21] Reichel, Horst Structural induction on partial algebras Akademie-Verlag, Berlin, 1984 (Mathematical Research 18)

[22] Sannella, Don / Wirsing, M. A kernel language for algebraic specification and implementation, Proc. FCT 1983, Bergholm

[23] Trakhtenbrot, B.A. / Barzdin, J.M. Finite Automata: Behaviour and Synthesis, North-Holland, 1974

[24] Wand, Mitchel Final algebra semantics and data type extensions, J. Computer Syst. Sci. 19 (1979), 27 - 44

APPROXIMATION LOGIC

Helena Rasiowa and Andrzej Skowron
Institute of Mathematics
University of Warsaw
PKiN 9th floor, 00-901 Warsaw

Introduction

In many branches of computer science there is a need of approximation methods. Rough sets theory due to Pawlak [4] may be taken as a starting point to develop an approximation logic. This logic should be a tool to deal with different problems of approximation in computer science.

The first step to construct an approximation logic was given in [6]. In this paper the rough concepts logic based on the first order predicate calculus was formulated.

The present paper is a continuation of [6]. The rough concepts logic is here extended to a family of approximation logics by introducing decreasing sequences (finite or infinite of order $\omega+1$) of indescernibility relations and various kinds of approximation operators determined by these relations. All considered operators have properties of the modal operators in S5 modal logic [1]. If the sequence of indescernibility relations is infinite then the $(\omega+1)$-th indescernibility relation is the intersection of relations in that sequence.

An axiomatization for approximation logics is given and the theorem establishing the completeness of that axiomatization is proved.

An extension of approximation logics with new approximation operators defined by finite sequences of indescernibility relations is also presented.

The second part of the paper contains different examples ilustrating usefulness of approximation logic in formulation of basic approximation problems. In particular a notion of an approximating translation based on two special kinds of approximation theories is formulated.

At the end of the paper a notion of an approximate program and its semantics is introduced. This is the main step in constructing a programming logic with programs and their approximations. Properties of such a logic will be presented in [7].

1. Fundamental concepts

An approximation space of any order ξ, $1 \leq \xi \leq \omega+1$, is a system

$$A = (U, (I_j)_{0 \leq j < \xi}),$$

where $U \neq \emptyset$, $I_j \subset U \times U$ are equivalence relations (indescernibility relations) and $I_{j+1} \subset I_j$ for $0 \leq j < j+1 < \xi$.
If $\xi = \omega+1$, then we assume that

$$(1) \qquad I_\omega = \bigcap_{0 \leq j < \omega} I_j .$$

Let N and N_o be in the sequel the set of all positive integers and the set of all non-negative integers, respectively. For any $n \in N$ let

$$A^n = (U^n, (I_j^n)_{0 \leq j < \xi}),$$

where $I_j^n \subset U^n \times U^n$ is an equivalence relation in U^n defined thus

(2) $((u_1,\ldots,u_n),(u_1',\ldots,u_n')) \in I_j^n$ iff $(u_i,u_i') \in I_j$ for each $i = 1,\ldots,n$.

Observe, that A^n is also an approximation space. The order of A^n is the same as that of the space A.

Equivalence classes $[(u_1,\ldots,u_n)]_j$ of the relations I_j^n, $0 \leq j < \xi$ and the empty set $\emptyset$ will be said to be I_j-elementary n-ary relations in A and unions of I_j-elementary n-ary relations will be said to be n-ary I_j-definable relations in A.

Let $Def(A_j^n)$ be the family of all n-ary relations I_j-definable in A. Clearly, $Def(A_j^n) \subset Def(A_{j+1}^n)$.

For any $R \subset U^n$ let $\overline{A}_j R$ be the least n-ary relation I_j-definable in A and containing R - to be called an upper j-th approximation of R in A - and let $\underline{A}_j R$ be the greatest n-ary relation I_j-definable in A and contained in R - to be called a lower j-th approximation of R in A.

It follows that

(3) $(u_1,\ldots,u_n) \in \overline{A}_j R$ iff there are $u_1',\ldots,u_n' \in U$ such that

$(u_i,u_i') \in I_j$ for $i = 1,\ldots,n$

and $(u_1',\ldots,u_n') \in R$.

(4) $(u_1,\dots u_n) \in \underline{A}_j R$ iff for all $u_1^-,\dots,u_n^- \in U$, if $(u_i,u_i^-) \in I_j$ for $i = 1,\dots,n$, then $(u_1^-,\dots,u_n^-) \in R$.

Moreover,

(5) $\bar{A}_{j+1}R \subset \bar{A}_j R$ and $\underline{A}_j R \subset \underline{A}_{j+1}R$ for $0 \leqslant j < j+1 < \xi$.

Clearly $R \subset U^n$ is I_j-definable iff $\underline{A}_j R = \bar{A}_j R$.
It follows from (4) and (5) that for any $R \subset U^n$, if R is I_j-definable then R is I_{j+1}-definable, but not conversely.

Four classes of I_j-undefinable n-ary relations in A are considered:

(6) $R \subset U^n$ is said to be roughly I_j-definable in A if $\bar{A}_j R \neq U^n$ and $\underline{A}_j R \neq \emptyset$,

(7) $R \subset U^n$ is said to be externally I_j-undefinable if $\bar{A}_j R = U^n$ and $\underline{A}_j R \neq \emptyset$,

(8) $R \subset U^n$ is said to be internally I_j-undefinable if $\underline{A}_j R = \emptyset$ and $\bar{A}_j R \neq U^n$,

(9) $R \subset U^n$ is said to be totally I_j-undefinable if $\underline{A}_j R = \emptyset$ and $\bar{A}_j R = U^n$.

Observe that if $R \subset U^n$ is roughly I_j-definable, then it is also roughly I_{j+1}-definable. If $R \subset U^n$ is totally I_{j+1}-undefinable, then it is totally I_j-undefinable.

Example 1. Let R^+ be the set of all non-negative real numbers. For each $0 \leqslant j < \omega$, $0 \leqslant m < 2^j$, $n \in N_o$ let us set

$$P_{j,m,n} = \left\{x \in R^+ \middle| n + \frac{m}{2^j} \leqslant x < n + \frac{m+1}{2^j}\right\}.$$

Let us define equivalence relations I_j, $0 \leqslant j < \omega$, in R^+ thus:

$(x,y) \in I_j$ iff ($x \in P_{j,m,n}$ is equivalent with $y \in P_{j,m,n}$) for each $0 \leqslant m < 2^j$ and $n \in N_o$,

$$I_\omega = \bigcap_{0 \leqslant j < \omega} I_j.$$

Then $A = (R^+, (I_j)_{0 \leqslant j \leqslant \omega})$ is an approximation space. It is easy to see that in particular

$(x,y) \in I_o$ iff Entier x = Entier y.

Moreover $(x,y) \in I_\omega$ iff $(x,y) \in I_j$ for each $0 \leqslant j < \omega$. This holds iff $x=y$. Thus I_ω is the identity relation in R^+.
Note that $\underline{A}_0(\leqslant) \neq \emptyset$ and $\bar{A}_0(\leqslant) \neq R^2$. Thus the relation $\leqslant$ is roughly I_0-definable and consequently roughly I_j-definable for each $0 \leqslant j < \omega$. Since for the identity relation $Id \subset R^+ \times R^+$, we have

$$\underline{A}_j Id = \emptyset,\ \bar{A}_j Id \neq R^+ \times R^+$$

Id is I_j-internally undefinable for $0 \leqslant j < \omega$.
The set $Z = \{(x,y) \mid x \in N_0, y \in N_0\}$ is totally I_0-undefinable.
The set $S = \{(x,y) \mid 0 \leqslant x < 1,\ 0 \leqslant y < 1\} \cup Z$ is externally I_0-undefinable.

2. Approximation languages

For any ξ, $1 \leqslant \xi \leqslant \omega+1$, let $\underline{L}_\xi = (Alph_\xi, T, F_\xi)$ be a countable first order predicate language such that:

(i) $Alph_\xi = Var \cup \{\pi_j \mid 0 \leqslant j < \xi\} \cup \{\varrho_1, \ldots, \varrho_m\} \cup$
$\cup \{\varphi_1, \ldots, \varphi_k\} \cup \{\vee, \wedge, \rightarrow, \neg, \forall, \exists\} \cup \{\underline{A}_j \mid 0 \leqslant j < \xi\} \cup$
$\cup \{(,)\}$,

where Var is a countable set of individual variables,

π_j for $0 \leqslant j < \xi$ are binary predicates to be interpreted as equivalence relations,

ϱ_i for $i = 1, \ldots, m$ are $\nu(i)$-ary predicates, $\nu: \{1, \ldots, m\} \rightarrow N$,

φ_i for $i = 1, \ldots, k$ are $\varkappa(i)$-argument functors, $\varkappa: \{1, \ldots, k\} \rightarrow N_0$,

$\underline{A}_j$ for $0 \leqslant j < \xi$ are unary propositional connectives.

(ii) The set T of all terms is defined as usually.

(iii) The set $F_{\xi at}$ of atomic formulas is the least set containing $\pi_j(\tau_1, \tau_2)$ for $\tau_1, \tau_2 \in T$ and $0 \leqslant j < \xi$, and $\varrho_i(\tau_1, \ldots, \tau_{\nu(i)})$ for $\tau_1, \ldots, \tau_{\nu(i)} \in T$ and $i = 1, \ldots, m$.

The set F_ξ of all formulas is then defined as usually.

We set $\bar{A}_j \alpha \overset{df}{=\!=} \neg \underline{A}_j \neg \alpha$ for each $\alpha \in F_\xi$ and $0 \leqslant j < \xi$.

A semantics of $\underline{L}_\xi$ is defined by means of notions of a model and of a valuation.

By a model of $\underline{L}_\xi$ we mean any relational system

$$M = (U, (I_j)_{0 \leq j < \xi}, R_1, \ldots, R_m, f_1, \ldots, f_k)$$

such that

$A = (U, (I_j)_{0 \leq j < \xi})$ is an approximation space of order ξ,

R_i is $\nu(i)$-ary relation in U for any $1 \leq i \leq m$,

f_i is $\varkappa(i)$-argument function in U for any $1 \leq i \leq k$.

Let $Val = U^{Var}$ be the set of all valuations in U.
For each $\tau \in T$, let $\tau(M,v)$ be the realization of τ in M by a valuation $v \in Val$. We remind that

(t1) $x(M,v) = v(x)$,

(t2) $\varphi_i(\tau_1, \ldots, \tau_{\varkappa(i)})(M,v) = f_i(\tau_1(M,v), \ldots, \tau_{\varkappa(i)}(M,v))$.

By induction with respect to a structure of a formula we define the notion of satisfiability of formulas in M. We say that a valuation $v \in Val$ satisfies a formula α in M, in symbols

$$M, v \models \alpha,$$

if the following conditions are satisfied:

$M, v \models \pi_j(\tau_1, \tau_2)$ iff $(\tau_1(M,v), \tau_2(M,v)) \in I_j$, $0 \leq j < \xi$,

$M, v \models \varrho_i(\tau_1, \ldots, \tau_{\nu(i)})$ iff $(\tau_1(M,v), \ldots, \tau_{\nu(i)}(M,v)) \in R_i$, $i = 1, \ldots, m$,

$M, v \models \neg \alpha$ iff non $M, v \models \alpha$,

$M, v \models \alpha \vee \beta$ iff $M, v \models \alpha$ or $M, v \models \beta$,

$M, v \models \alpha \wedge \beta$ iff $M, v \models \alpha$ and $M, v \models \beta$,

$M, v \models \alpha \rightarrow \beta$ iff non $M, v \models \alpha$ or $M, v \models \beta$,

$M, v \models (\forall x)\alpha$ iff $M, v_u \models \alpha$ for each $u \in U$, where $v_u(x) = u$ and $v_u(y) = v(y)$ for every $y \in Var$, $y \neq x$,

$M, v \models (\exists x)\alpha$ iff non $M, v \models (\forall x)\neg \alpha$,

$M, v \models \underline{A}_j \alpha(x_1, \ldots, x_n)$, where $x_1, \ldots, x_n$ are all free individual variables in α, iff for all $u_1, \ldots, u_n \in U$ if $(v(x_i), u_i) \in I_j$ for $i = 1, \ldots, n$, then $M, v_{u_1, \ldots, u_n} \models \alpha(x_1, \ldots, x_n)$,

where $v_{u_1, \ldots, u_n}(x_i) = u_i$ for $i = 1, \ldots, n$ and

$v_{u_1, \ldots, u_n}(y) = v(y)$ for $y \neq x_1, \ldots, x_n, y \in Var$.

Observe, that by (1) in Sec. 1, if $\xi = \omega+1$, then

$$M,v \models \pi_\omega(\tau_1,\tau_2) \text{ iff } (\tau_1(M,v),\tau_2(M,v)) \in I_j \text{ for each } 0 \leq j < \omega.$$

A formula α is said to be satisfiable in M iff there is a valuation v such that $M,v \models \alpha$. A formula α is said to be valid in M iff for each valuation v, $M,v \models \alpha$. For any set $\mathcal{A} \subset F$ let $Cn(\mathcal{A}) = \{\alpha \in F_\xi \mid$ for every model M, α is valid in M whenever all formulas in $\mathcal{A}$ are valid in M$\}$.

To each $\alpha \in F_\xi$ we assign a set α_M of all valuations $v \in Val$ which satisfy α in M. Thus

$$\alpha_M = \{v \in Val \mid M,v \models \alpha\}.$$

Clearly, a formula α is satisfiable in M iff $\alpha_M \neq \emptyset$.
A formula α is valid in M, iff $\alpha_M = Val$. A formula α is said to be valid provided α is valid in every model M.

For any formula $\alpha \in F_\xi$ let $Var\alpha$ be the set of all free individual variables in α.

For any $\alpha(x_1,\ldots,x_n)$, where $Var\alpha = \{x_1,\ldots,x_n\}$ let us set

$$\alpha_M\!\downarrow\ = \{(u_1,\ldots,u_n) \in U^n \mid u_1=v(x_1) \wedge \ldots \wedge u_n=v(x_n) \text{ for some } v \in \alpha_M\}.$$

3. Examples of properties definable in approximation languages

Example 1

Let $U \neq \emptyset$ be a set of patients and consider subsets $P_j \subset U$ for $0 \leq j < \xi$, where $\xi < \omega$. If $u \in P_j$, then we say that u has the j-th symptom. Let $1,\ldots,m$ be names of some illnesses, and let $R_i \subset U$, for $i = 1,\ldots,m$ be subsets of U such that $u \in U$ iff u has illness i. Define the equivalence relation I_j, for $0 \leq j < \xi$ thus:

$$(u_1,u_2) \in I_j \text{ iff } ((u_1 \in P_0 \text{ iff } u_2 \in P_0) \text{ and} \ldots \text{and } (u_1 \in P_j \text{ iff } u_2 \in P_j)).$$

Then $M = (U,(I_j)_{0 \leq j < \xi}, R_1,\ldots,R_m)$ is a model of a language L_ξ in which $T = Var$ and $\nu(i)=1$ for $i = 1,\ldots,m$.

The set $(\underline{A}_j \varrho_i)_M\!\downarrow$ for any $0 \leq j < \xi$ is the greatest subset of all patients with illness i definable by symptoms $P_0,\ldots,P_j$.

The set $(\bar{A}_j \varrho_i)_M\!\downarrow$ for any $0 \leq s < \xi$ is the least set of patients containing the set of all patients with illness i and definable by symptoms $P_0,\ldots,P_j$.

Clearly $(\underline{A}_o \varrho_i)_M \downarrow \subset \ldots \subset (\underline{A}_{\xi-1} \varrho_i)_M \downarrow$

and $(\bar{A}_o \varrho_i)_M \downarrow \supset \ldots \supset (\bar{A}_{\xi-1} \varrho_i)_M \downarrow$.

If $(\underline{A}_j \varrho_i)_M \downarrow = R_i$, then illness i is definable by symptoms $P_o, \ldots, P_j$.

Example 2

Observe that for any formula $\alpha(x_1,\ldots,x_n) \in F_\xi$, such that $\mathrm{Var}\,\alpha(x_1,\ldots,x_n) = \{x_1,\ldots,x_n\}$ and a model $M =$ $= (U,(I_j)_{0 \leq j < \xi}, R_1,\ldots,R_m, f_1,\ldots,f_k)$ we have

$$\alpha(x_1,\ldots,x_n)_M \downarrow \subset U^n.$$

Let $A = (U,(I_j)_{0 \leq j < \xi})$. According to the terminology adopted in Sec. 1 (cf. also [4]) we have the following definitions:

$\alpha(x_1,\ldots,x_n)_M \downarrow$ is I_j-definable iff $\underline{A}_j \alpha(x_1,\ldots,x_n)_M \downarrow =$ $\bar{A}_j \alpha(x_1,\ldots,x_n)_M \downarrow$

$\alpha(x_1,\ldots,x_n)_M \downarrow$ is roughly I_j-definable in A iff

$\underline{A}_j \alpha(x_1,\ldots,x_n)$ is satisfiable in M, and

$\neg\, \bar{A}_j \alpha(x_1,\ldots,x_n)$ is satisfiable in M,

$\alpha(x_1,\ldots,x_n)_M \downarrow$ is externally I_j-undefinable in A iff

$\underline{A}_j \alpha(x_1,\ldots,x_n)$ is satisfiable in M and

$\bar{A}_j \alpha(x_1,\ldots,x_n)$ is valid in M,

$\alpha(x_1,\ldots,x_n)_M \downarrow$ is internally I_j-undefinable in A iff

$\neg\, \underline{A}_j \alpha(x_1,\ldots,x_n)$ is valid in M and

$\neg\, \bar{A}_j \alpha(x_1,\ldots,x_n)$ is satisfiable in M,

$\alpha(x_1,\ldots,x_n)_M \downarrow$ is totally I_j-undefinable in A iff

$\neg\, \underline{A}_j \alpha(x_1,\ldots,x_n)$ is valid in M and

$\bar{A}_j \alpha(x_1,\ldots,x_n)$ is valid in M.

Let us note the following:

Fact:

(i) $\alpha(x_1,\ldots,x_n)_M \downarrow$ is I_j-definable in A iff $M \models \underline{A}_j \alpha(x_1,\ldots,x_n) \leftrightarrow$ $\bar{A}_j \alpha(x_1,\ldots,x_n)$,

(ii) $\alpha(x_1,\ldots,x_n)_M\downarrow$ is roughly I_j-definable in A iff

$$M \models \exists x_1 \ldots \exists x_n \underline{A}_j\alpha(x_1,\ldots,x_n) \wedge \exists x_1 \ldots \exists x_n \underline{A}_j \neg \alpha(x_1,\ldots,x_n),$$

(iii) $\alpha(x_1,\ldots,x_n)_M\downarrow$ is externally I_j-undefinable in A iff

$$M \models \exists x_1 \ldots \exists x_n \underline{A}_j\alpha(x_1,\ldots,x_n) \wedge \forall x_1 \ldots \forall x_n \bar{A}_j\alpha(x_1,\ldots,x_n),$$

(iv) $\alpha(x_1,\ldots,x_n)_M\downarrow$ is internally I_j-undefinable in A iff

$$M \models \forall x_1 \ldots \forall x_n \neg \underline{A}_j\alpha(x_1,\ldots,x_n) \wedge \exists x_1 \ldots \exists x_n \underline{A}_j\neg\alpha(x_1,\ldots,x_n),$$

(v) $\alpha(x_1,\ldots,x_n)_M\downarrow$ is totally I_j-undefinable in A iff

$$M \models \forall x_1 \ldots \forall x_n \neg \underline{A}_j\alpha(x_1,\ldots,x_n) \wedge \forall x_1 \ldots \forall x_n \bar{A}_j\alpha(x_1,\ldots,x_n).$$

4. Deductive system of approximation logic L_ξ

The following axiom schemes are adopted:

[Ax1] Axiom schemes for classical propositional calculus,

[Ax2] $\underline{A}_j(\alpha \to \beta) \to (\underline{A}_j\alpha \to \underline{A}_j\beta)$,

[Ax3] $\underline{A}_j\alpha \to \alpha$,

[Ax4] $\pi_j(x,x)$,

[Ax5] $\pi_j(x,y) \to (\pi_j(z,y) \to \pi_j(x,z))$,

[Ax6] $\pi_j(x,y) \to (\underline{A}_j\alpha(x) \to \underline{A}_j\alpha(y))$,

[Ax7] $\forall y_1 \ldots \forall y_n ((\pi_j(x_1,y_1) \wedge \ldots \wedge \pi_j(x_n,y_n)) \to \alpha(y_1,\ldots,y_n))$
$\to \underline{A}_j\alpha(x_1,\ldots,x_n)$, where $\mathrm{Var}\alpha = \{x_1,\ldots,x_n\}$,

[Ax8] $\alpha \to \underline{A}_j\alpha$, if $\mathrm{Var}\alpha = \emptyset$,

[Ax9] $\pi_{j'}(x,y) \to \pi_j(x,y)$ for $0 \leq j \leq j' < \xi$,

Rules of inference

(MP) $\dfrac{\alpha, \alpha \to \beta}{\beta}$,

(G) $\dfrac{\alpha}{\underline{A}_j\alpha}$ for each $0 \leq j < \xi$,

(ω) $\dfrac{\{\alpha \to \pi_j(\tau_1,\tau_2)\}_{0 \leq j < \omega}}{\alpha \to \pi_\omega(\tau_1,\tau_2)}$ in the case $\xi = \omega+1$

- rule of substitution for free individual variables
- rules of introduction and elimination of quantifiers.

$\mathcal{A} \vdash \alpha$ denotes that α is provable from the set $\mathcal{A} \subset F_\xi$.

Observe that we have the following:

Lemma 1

(i) If $\mathcal{A} \vdash \alpha \to \beta$ then $\mathcal{A} \vdash \underline{A}_j\alpha \to \underline{A}_j\beta$,

(ii) $\vdash (\pi_j(x_1,y_1) \to \ldots \to (\pi_j(x_n,y_n) \to (\underline{A}_j\alpha(x_1,\ldots,x_n) \leftrightarrow \underline{A}_j\alpha(y_1,\ldots,y_n))\ldots)$

(iii) $\vdash \underline{A}_j\alpha(x_1,\ldots,x_n) \to \forall y_1\ldots\forall y_n(\pi_j(x_1,y_1) \wedge \ldots \wedge \pi_j(x_n,y_n)) \to \alpha(y_1,\ldots,y_n))$,

(iv) $\vdash \underline{A}_j\alpha \to \underline{A}_j\underline{A}_j\ \alpha$,

(v) $\vdash \alpha \to \underline{A}_j \neg \underline{A}_j \neg \alpha$,

(vi) $\vdash \underline{A}_j\alpha \to \underline{A}_{j'}\ \alpha$, for $0 \leqslant j \leqslant j' < \xi$,

(vii) $\vdash \underline{A}_j\underline{A}_{j'}\ \alpha \leftrightarrow \underline{A}_j\ \alpha$ for $0 \leqslant j \leqslant j' < \xi$,

(viii) $\vdash \underline{A}_{j'}\underline{A}_j\ \alpha \leftrightarrow \underline{A}_j\ \alpha$ for $0 \leqslant j \leqslant j' < \xi$,

(ix) $\vdash (\forall x)\underline{A}_j\alpha(x) \leftrightarrow \underline{A}_j(\forall x)\alpha(x)$,

(x) $\vdash (\exists x)\ \underline{A}_j\alpha(x) \to \underline{A}_j(\exists x)\alpha(x)$,

(xi) $\vdash (\underline{A}_j\alpha \vee \underline{A}_j\beta) \to \underline{A}_j(\alpha \vee \beta)$,

(xii) $\vdash \underline{A}_j(\alpha \wedge \beta) \leftrightarrow (\underline{A}_j\alpha \wedge \underline{A}_j\beta)$.

It follows from Ax2, Ax3 and properties (iv), (v) that operators $\underline{A}_j$ have properties of the modal operators in S5 modal logic.

Soundness theorem. If $\mathcal{A} \vdash \alpha$, then $\mathcal{A} \models \alpha$.

Proof by an easy verification. For instance in the case of rule (ω). Suppose $M,v \models \alpha \to \pi_j(\tau_1,\tau_2)$ for each $0 \leqslant j < \omega$. Then $M,v \models \neg\alpha$ or $(\tau_1(M,v),\tau_2(M,v)) \in I_j$ for each $0 \leqslant j < \omega$. If $M,v \models \neg\alpha$ then $M,v \models \alpha \to \pi_\omega(\tau_1,\tau_2)$. In the opposite case, since $I_\omega = \bigcap_{0 \leqslant j<\omega} I_j$, we have $(\tau_1(M,v),\tau_2(M,v)) \in I_\omega$. Thus $M,v \models \alpha \to \pi_\omega(\tau_1,\tau_2)$ holds too.

Theorem on the existence of a model. If non $\mathcal{A} \vdash \alpha_o$, then there exists a model M such that each $\beta \in \mathcal{A}$ is valid in M, but for some valuation v, non $M,v \models \alpha_o$.

Sketch of the proof

Assume non($\mathcal{A} \vdash \alpha_o$). We define $\approx_{\mathcal{A}}$ as follows:

$$\alpha \approx_{\mathcal{A}} \beta \quad \text{iff} \quad \mathcal{A} \vdash \alpha \to \beta \quad \text{and} \quad \mathcal{A} \vdash \beta \to \alpha .$$

The relation $\approx_{\mathcal{A}}$ is a congruence relation in the algebra of formulas. Let

$$\mathfrak{A} = (F/_{\approx}, \cup, \cap, \Rightarrow, -, (\underline{A}_j)_{0 \leqslant j < \xi}).$$

This algebra has the reduct

$$\mathfrak{L} = (F/_{\approx}, \cup, \cap, \Rightarrow, -)$$

being a Boolean algebra in which $|\alpha| = V$ iff $\mathcal{A} \vdash \alpha$. Let us note, that in the Boolean algebra $\mathfrak{L}$ we have

$$|(\exists x)\alpha(x)| = \bigcup_{\tau \in T} |\alpha(x/\tau)|,$$

(Q) $$|(\forall x)\alpha(x)| = \bigcap_{\tau \in T} |\alpha(x/\tau)|,$$

$$|\pi_\omega(\tau_1, \tau_2)| = \bigcap_{0 \leqslant j < \omega} |\pi_j(\tau_1, \tau_2)| \qquad \text{([Ax9] and rule } (\omega)).$$

Let $\mathfrak{F}$ be the set of all Q-filters in $\mathfrak{L}$, i.e. of maximal filters ∇ such that:

(i) $|(\exists x)\alpha(x)| \in \nabla$ iff there is $\tau \in T$ such that $|\alpha(x/\tau)| \in \nabla$,

(ii) $|(\forall x)\alpha(x)| \in \nabla$ iff for each $\tau \in T$, $|\alpha(x/\tau)| \in \nabla$,

(iii) $|\pi_\omega(\tau_1, \tau_2)| \in \nabla$ iff for each $0 \leqslant j < \omega$ $|\pi_j(\tau_1, \tau_2)| \in \nabla$.

Each $\nabla \in \mathfrak{F}$ determines a model M_∇ in the set T as follows

$M_\nabla = (T, (I_{j\nabla})_{0 \leqslant j < \xi}, R_{1\nabla}, \ldots, R_{m\nabla}, f_{1\nabla}, \ldots, f_{k\nabla})$, where

$(\tau_1, \tau_2) \in I_{j\nabla}$ iff $|\pi_j(\tau_1, \tau_2)| \in \nabla$,

$(\tau_1, \ldots, \tau_{\nu(i)}) \in R_i$ iff $|\varrho_i(\tau_1, \ldots, \tau_{\nu(i)})| \in \nabla$ for $i = 1, \ldots, m$,

$f_{i\nabla}(\tau_1, \ldots, \tau_{\varkappa(i)}) = \varphi_i(\tau_1, \ldots, \tau_{\varkappa(i)})$, $i = 1, \ldots, k$.

Indeed, by [Ax4] and [Ax5], it follows that $I_{j\nabla}$ are equivalence relations, and by [Ax9], that $I_{j'\nabla} \subset I_{j\nabla}$ for $0 \leqslant j < j' < \xi$. On the other hand, suppose that $(\tau_1, \tau_2) \in I_{j\nabla}$, $0 \leqslant j < \omega$. Then $|\pi_j(\tau_1, \tau_2)| \in \nabla$ for $0 \leqslant j < \omega$. Since ∇ is a Q-filter, it follows that $\bigcap_{0 \leqslant j < \omega} |\pi_j(\tau_1, \tau_2)| \in \nabla$. Consequently $|\pi_\omega(\tau_1, \tau_2)| \in \nabla$. Thus $(\tau_1, \tau_2) \in I_\omega$ i.e. $I_\omega = \bigcap_{0 \leqslant j < \omega} I_j$. So, M is a model.

<u>Lemma 2.</u> For each $\alpha \in F$ and $v \in Val = T^{Var}$

$$M_\nabla, v \models \alpha \quad \text{iff} \quad |v\alpha| \in \nabla,$$

where $v\alpha$ is a formula obtained from α by the simultaneous substituting of $v(x)$ for each free occurrence in α of any variable $x \in \mathrm{Var}$.

Proof - by inductive argument with respect to the length of α. For atomic formulas - by the definition of M_∇. For α in forms $(\exists x)\beta(x), (\forall x)\beta(x)$ - the assumption that ∇ is a Q-filter is applied.

Suppose α is $\underline{A}_j\beta(x_1,\ldots,x_n)$. Assume

$$M_\nabla, v \models \underline{A}_j\beta(x_1,\ldots,x_n) \quad \text{and} \quad \mathrm{Var}\,\beta = \{x_1,\ldots,x_n\}.$$

Then for all $\tau_1,\ldots,\tau_n \in T$:

if $|\pi_j(v(x_i),\tau_i)| \in \nabla$ for $i=1,\ldots,n$, then $|v_{\tau_1\ldots\tau_n}\beta(x_1,\ldots,x_n)| \in \nabla$.

Since ∇ is maximal, this holds iff for all $\tau_1,\ldots,\tau_n \in T$

$$|\pi_j(v(x_1),\tau_1) \wedge \ldots \wedge \pi_j(v(x_n),\tau_n) \to v_{\tau_1\ldots\tau_n}\beta(x_1,\ldots,x_n)| \in \nabla \quad .$$

Since ∇ is a Q-filter, this holds iff

$$|(\forall z_1) \ldots (\forall z_n)(\pi_j(v(x_1),z_1) \wedge \ldots \wedge \pi_j(v(x_n),z_n) \to \beta(z_1,\ldots,z_n))| \in \nabla$$

where $z_1,\ldots,z_n$ are new variables i.e. not occurring in β.

Hence by [Ax7] $|v\underline{A}_j\beta(x_1,\ldots,x_n)| \in \nabla$.

Now assume that

$|v\underline{A}_j\beta(x_1,\ldots,x_n)| \in \nabla$ and that $|\pi_j(v(x_i),\tau_i)| \in \nabla$ for $i = 1,\ldots,n$.

By Lemma 1 (ii)

$$|\underline{A}_j\ v\,\beta(x_1,\ldots,x_n) \to \underline{A}_j\ v_{\tau_1\ldots\tau_n}\beta(x_1,\ldots,x_n)| \in \nabla \quad .$$

Hence and by the assumption

$$|\underline{A}_j\ v_{\tau_1\ldots\tau_n}\beta(x_1,\ldots,x_n)| \in \nabla \quad .$$

This and [Ax3] yield

$$|v_{\tau_1\ldots\tau_n}\beta(x_1,\ldots,x_n)| \in \nabla \quad .$$

By the inductive hypothesis

$$M_\nabla,\ v_{\tau_1\ldots\tau_n} \models \beta(x_1,\ldots,x_n).$$

Hence $M_\nabla, v \models \underline{A}_j\beta(x_1,\ldots,x_n)$.

To complete the proof of our theorem observe that since $\mathrm{non}(\mathcal{A} \vdash \alpha_o)$, $|\alpha_o| \neq V$. Thus $|\neg\,\alpha_o| \neq \Lambda$. Hence there exists a

Q-filter ∇ such that $|\neg\alpha_o| \in \nabla$. This yields $M_\nabla, v_o \models \neg\alpha_o$, i.e. non($M_\nabla, v_o \models \alpha_o$), where $v_o \in Val$, $v_o(x) = x$ for each $x \in Var$. On the other hand for each $\alpha \in \mathcal{A}$, we have $M_\nabla, v \models \alpha$ for $v \in Val$, which completes the proof.

5. An extension of L_ξ logic

In this section we suggest an extension of the logic L_ξ by adjoining the following formation rule to the definition of the syntax of that logic:

(*) if $\alpha(\bar{x})$ is a formula and $\bar{x} = (x_1,\dots,x_k)$ are all free individual variables in α then

$$\underline{A}_{\underline{i}}\alpha(\bar{x}) \quad \text{and} \quad \bar{A}_{\underline{i}}\alpha(\bar{x})$$

are formulas, where $\underline{i} = (i_1,\dots,i_k)$ and $0 \leq i_j < \xi$ for $j = 1,\dots,k$.

The extension of the satisfiability relation $\models$ is defined as follows

$M,v \models \underline{A}_{\underline{i}}\alpha(\bar{x})$ iff for any v' such that $v'(y) = v(y)$ for $y \notin \{x_1,\dots,x_k\}$ and $(v(x_j),v'(x_j)) \in I_{i_j}$, for $j = 1,\dots,k$ we have

$$M,v' \models \alpha(\bar{x}),$$

$M,v \models \bar{A}_{\underline{i}}\alpha(\bar{x})$ iff there exists v' such that $v'(y) = v(y)$ for $y \notin \{x_1,\dots,x_k\}$ and $(v(x_j),v'(x_j)) \in I_{i_j}$ for $j = 1,\dots,k$ and

$$M,v' \models \alpha(\bar{x}).$$

The operators $\underline{A}_j$ and $\bar{A}_j$ as introduced in Sec. 2 are special cases of the operators $\underline{A}_{\underline{i}}$ and $\bar{A}_{\underline{i}}$ e.g. $\underline{A}_j\alpha(x_1,\dots,x_k)$ is defined by $\underline{A}_{\underline{i}}\alpha(x_1,\dots,x_k)$ where $\underline{i} = \underbrace{(j,\dots,j)}_{k\text{-times}}$ and $Var\ \alpha = \{x_1,\dots,x_k\}$.

The reader can obtain a complete axiomatization of the new logic modifying the axiom schemes of the L_ξ logic.

6. Approximations in theories

Let us consider a theory T in $\underline{L}_1$ with the following set $\mathcal{A}$ of specific axioms: (S0) axioms for equality predicate $=$.

(S1) $\neg(E(x) \wedge C(x))$,

(S2) $E(x) \vee C(x)$,

(S3) $In(x,y) \rightarrow (E(x) \wedge C(y))$,

(S4) $E(x) \rightarrow (\exists y!) In(x,y)$,

(S5) $\pi_o(x,x^-) \rightarrow (In(x) = In(x^-))$,

where $y = In(x)$ denotes $In(x,y)$,

(S6) $\rho_i(x_1,\dots,x_{\nu(i)}) \rightarrow (E(x_1) \wedge \dots \wedge E(x_{\nu(i)}))$,

(S6$^-$) $x_o = \varphi_i(x_1,\dots,x_{\varkappa(i)}) \rightarrow (E(x_o) \wedge \dots \wedge E(x_{\varkappa(i)}))$,

[(S7) some additional axioms about π_o].

The intuitive meaning for $E(x)$, $C(x)$, $In(x,y)$ is following

$E(x)$ iff "x is an element (object)",

$C(x)$ iff "x is an information corresponding to an equivalence class of π_o",

$In(x,y)$ iff "y is the information corresponding to the equivalence class $[x]_o$".

By $\mathcal{F}_E$ we denote the set of all formulas in $\underline{L}_1$ built without symbols In, C, E. The elements of F_E are called E-formulas.

A formula $\alpha(\bar{x})$, where $\bar{x} = (x_1,\dots,x_k)$ and $Var\ \alpha = \{x_1,\dots,x_k\}$ is called C-formula iff each variable x_i for $i=1,\dots,k$ appears in α only in subformulas of the form

$$x_i = In(x_i^-).$$

The set of C-formulas we denote by F_C.

<u>Example</u>

The following formulas are examples of C-formulas:

(i) $(\exists x_i^-)\dots(\exists x_{\nu(i)}^-)(x_1=In(x_1^-)\wedge\dots\wedge x_{\nu(i)} = In(x_{\nu(i)}^-)\wedge\rho_i(x_1^-,\dots,x_{\nu(i)}^-))$,

(ii) $(\forall x_1^-)\dots(\forall x_{\nu(i)}^-)(x_1=In(x_i^-)\wedge\dots\wedge x_{\nu(i)} = In(x_{\nu(i)}^-)\rightarrow\rho_i(x_1^-,\dots,x_{\nu(i)}^-))$,

(iii) $(\exists x_o^-)\dots(\exists x_{\varkappa(i)}^-)(x_o=In(x_o^-)\wedge\dots\wedge x_{\varkappa(i)} = In(x_{\varkappa(i)}^-)\wedge x_o^-=\varphi_i(x_1^-,\dots,x_{\varkappa(i)}^-))$,

(iv) $(\forall x_o^-)\dots(\forall x_{\varkappa(i)}^-)(x_o=In(x_o^-)\wedge\dots\wedge x_{\varkappa(i)} =In(x_{\varkappa(i)}^-)\rightarrow x_o^-=\varphi_i(x_1^-,\dots,x_{\varkappa(i)}^-))$.

By F_C^o we denote the set of all F_C formulas built from the formulas of the form (i) - (iv) using only logical connectives $\wedge,\vee,\neg,\rightarrow$ and quantifiers.

The formulas of the form (i) - (iv) represent approximations of primitive notions i.e. predicates and functors. Approximative properties are defined by formulas in the set F_C^o.

The central problem in an approximate reasoning is the construction of approximations for given properties. A notion of approximating translation in T which we present here seems to be a good tool to deal with that problem.

A partial function $t : F_E \multimap F_C^o$ is called an approximating translation in a model M for T if

$t(\alpha) = \beta$ iff $In_M(\alpha_M\downarrow) = \beta_M\downarrow$,

where $\alpha \in F_E$, $\beta \in F_C^o$ and

$In_M(\alpha_M\downarrow) = \{(In_M(a_1),\ldots,In_M(a_k)) \mid (a_1,\ldots,a_k) \in \alpha_M\downarrow\}$.

A partial function $t : F_E \multimap F_C^o$ is called an approximating translation in T iff for every model M of T the function t is an approximating translation in M for T.

Now we can formulate problems which we investigate in [7].

Problem 1. Characterize theories T in which there exist computable approximating translations in T.

Problem 2. Assuming the existence of computable approximating translation in T find bounds on the computational complexity of those translations.

Problem 3. Let M be a finite model for T and let $\alpha(\bar{x}) \in F_F$, $\beta(\bar{x}) \in F_C^o$. By $diff_M(\alpha,\beta)$ we denote the set

$$(\alpha_M\downarrow - In_M^{-1}(\beta_M\downarrow)) \cup (In_M^{-1}(\beta_M\downarrow) - \alpha_M\downarrow).$$

For a given $0 < p < 1$ characterize properties of the set X of E-formulas such that

$$\alpha \in X \quad \text{iff for some } \beta \in F_C \quad \frac{|diff_M(\alpha,\beta)|}{|\alpha_M|} < p$$

where by $|Z|$ we denote the cardinality of the set Z.

Let us consider now a theory*) T* in $\underline{L}_{\omega+1}$ with the following specific axioms:

*) The completeness theorem for L_ξ logics holds also in the case when we have a countable set of predicates.

(S0), (S1$^-$) $\neg(E(x) \wedge C_j(x))$ for $j \leqslant \omega$,

(S2$^-$) $\neg(C_i(x) \wedge C_j(x))$ for $i \neq j,\ i \leqslant \omega$ and $j \leqslant \omega$,

(S3$^-$) $In_j(x,y) \rightarrow (E(x) \wedge C_j(y))$ for $j \leqslant \omega$,

(S4$^-$) $\pi_j(x,x^-) \rightarrow (In_j(x) = In_j(x^-))$ for $j \leqslant \omega$,

(S5$^-$) $E(x) \rightarrow (\exists y!)\, In_j(x,y)$ for $j \leqslant \omega$,

(S6$^-$) $\varrho_i(x_1,\ldots,x_{\nu(i)}) \rightarrow (E(x_1) \wedge \ \ldots \ \wedge E(x_{\nu(i)}))$ for all predicate letters different from $E, C_1, C_2, \ldots, C_\omega, In_1, \ldots, In_\omega, \leqslant, =$,

(S7$^-$) " $<$ is a partial order in the set of elements which are not objects i.e. which are informations about objects"

(S8$^-$) $In_i(x) < In_j(x)$ for $j \geqslant i$,

(S9$^-$) "$In_\omega(x) = \text{l.u.b.}\{ In_j(x) : j \neq \omega\}$."

It is possible to write expressions in S7$^-$ and S9$^-$ using formulas from $F_{\omega+1}$ and an additional ω-rule.

The axiom (S9$^-$) describes the fact that the limit information (i.e. total information) about any object is the least upper bound of the set of partial informations ($In_j(x)$ for $j \neq \omega$) about that objects.

Now we can reformulate the definition of approximating translation. In the case of T^* it is enough to change the condition $I_M(\alpha_M\!\downarrow) = \beta_M\!\downarrow$ in the previous definition by

$$In_{\underline{j}M}(\alpha_M\!\downarrow) = \beta_M\!\downarrow \qquad \text{where} \quad \underline{j} = (j_1,\ldots,j_k)$$

is a parameter for the translation and

$$In_{\underline{j}M}(\alpha_M\!\downarrow) = \{ (In_{j_1}(a_1),\ldots,In_{j_k}(a_k)) \mid (a_1,\ldots,a_k) \in \alpha_M\!\downarrow \}.$$

To the list of problems we can now adjoin the problem of a characterization of properties of the translations hierarchy (we have different translations for different parameters $\underline{j}$).

Let us denote the approximating translation determined by $\underline{j}$ by $t_{\underline{j}}$. Up to now we have no results about the computational complexity of the following, important from the practical point of view, problem:

Problem 4. For a given $\alpha \in F_E$ find a minimal $\underline{j}$ such that $\alpha \in \text{Dom}\ t_{\underline{j}}$, assuming that $\alpha \in \text{Dom}\ t_{\underline{\omega}}$, where $\underline{\omega} = (\omega,\ldots,\omega)$.

At the end of this section we would like to suggest an approach to the problem of approximation of sets of sentences (see [8]).

Let S_C^j be the family of maximal consistent sets of sentences in F_C^o which are built without C_i, In_i for $i \neq j$.

We define the binary relations $<_{i,j}$ in $S_C^i \times S_C^j$, where $i,j < \xi$ in the following way

$X <_{i,j} Y$ iff there exists $Y' \subset Y$ s.t. for every model M if $M \models T$ then $M \models Y'$ iff $M \models X$.

If $X <_{i,j} Y$ then Y on "the level j is an approximation of X on the level i".

If $\{X \in S_C^i : \exists Y \in S_C^j \; X <_{i,j} Y\} = S_C^i$ then every "possible world of knowledge" on the level i can be approximated on the level j.

7. Approximate programs

The basic notion which we formulate in this section is a notion of approximation of programs.

The atomic programs are expressions of the form

$$p(\bar{x};\bar{y})$$

where p is a predicate symbol (from a given set of predicate symbols Φ_o)

$\bar{x} = (x_1,\dots,x_k)$ is the vector of input variables of p

$\bar{y} = (y_1,\dots,y_l)$ is the vector of output variables of p.

We construct the set $\mathcal{P}$ of programs as the least set with the following properties:

(P1) all atomic programs are in $\mathcal{P}$

(P2) if $\alpha \in F_E$ then $(\alpha?)$ is in $\mathcal{P}$

(P3) if $P,Q \in \mathcal{P}$ then $(P \cup Q)$, $(P;Q)$, P^* are programs in $\mathcal{P}$.

In a model M an atomic program $p(\bar{x};\bar{y})$ is interpreted as $k+l$-ary relation $p_M{\downarrow}$ in U. This relation defines the binary relation p_M in Val as follows

$$v \; p_M \; v' \quad \text{iff} \quad v'(z) = v(z) \quad \text{for} \quad z \notin \{y_1,\dots,y_l\}$$
$$\text{and} \quad (v(\bar{x}), v'(\bar{y})) \in p_M{\downarrow}.$$

The meaning of the other programs we define as usually.

Every atomic program $p(\bar{x};\bar{y})$ defines atomic approximate programs of the form (i) or (ii) (see Sec. 6), where instead of ϱ_i we substitute p.

The set of approximate programs $\mathcal{P}_{ap}$ is the least set such that:

(AP1) every atomic approximate program is in $\mathcal{P}_{ap}$

(AP2) if $\alpha \in F_C^O$ then $(\alpha ?) \in \mathcal{P}_{ap}$

(AP3) if $P, Q \in \mathcal{P}_{ap}$ then $(P;Q), (P \cup Q), P^*$ are in $\mathcal{P}_{ap}$.

The meaning of any atomic approximate program P in a given model is defined as previously taking instead of $p(\bar{x};\bar{y})$ corresponding atomic approximate program. Next we define the meaning of the other approximate programs using the standard definition of the semantics of programs in dynamic logic. From $\mathcal{P}(\mathcal{P}_{at})$ and F_E (F_C^O) we can built as usually the formulas of dynamic logic (dynamic logic with approximate programs). The properties of such logics will be discussed in [7]. Here we restrict ourselves to explain a notion of an approximation of one program by another. Let $P \in \mathcal{P}$ and $P' \in \mathcal{P}_{ap}$. P' is an approximation of P in a model M iff there exists j such that

$$In_j(P_M\downarrow) = P'_M\downarrow ,$$

where $P_M\downarrow$ and $P'_M\downarrow$ are defined for programs in an analogous way to that for formulas.

References

[1] Cresswell, M.J. and Hughes, G.E. (1968). An introduction to modal logic. London: Methuen and Co Ltd.

[2] Gabbay, D.M. (1976). Investigations in modal and tense logics with applications to problems in philosophy and linguistics. Reidel Synthese Library, 92.

[3] Orłowska, E. and Pawlak, Z. (1984). Expressive power of knowledge representation systems. International Journal of Man-Machine Studies 20, 485-500.

[4] Pawlak, Z. (1982). Rough sets. International Journal of Computer and Information Sciences, 11(5), 341-356.

[5] Rasiowa, H. and Sikorski, R. (1970). Mathematics of metamathematics. Warsaw: PWN.

[6] Rasiowa, H. and Skowron, A. (1984). Rough concepts logic. Lectures Notes in Computer Science (to appear).

[7] Rasiowa, H. and Skowron, A. (1985). Approximate reasoning (in preparation).

[8] Scott, D. Domains for denotational semantics. A corrected and expanded version of a paper prepared for ICALP'82, Aarhus, Denmark, July 1982.

LEARNING ON THE BASIS OF A POLYNOMIAL PATTERN SYNTHESIS ALGORITHM

Ognian Botusharov[1)]

Introduction

A considerable ammount of research work in AI has been dedicated to learning since it is obviously an integral part of any intelligent behaviour. Learning from samples of information is a major approach to this issue (cf./6/).

In the present paper we describe an application that synthesizes structures from positive data, i.e. data samples known to be consistent with the structure to be learnt. It is a system that performs automatic restructuring of a relational data base on the basis of samples of structurized information which is to be recorded in the data base. In addition, it allows intelligent data entry, once the data-base structure has been generated.

The backbone of the system's learning component is a pattern synthesis algorithm known from theoretical computer science (cf./2/).

Since it works in polynomial time, the system should be fast.

Patterns could be described as strings over a finite alphabet of constants and a disjoint alphabet of variables. The latter can be substituted by words over the alphabet of constants, thus generating a pattern language. We describe the structure of file records by patterns and synthesize it from record samples interpreted as words of the corresponding pattern language.

It should be said that off-line intelligent data entry system has already been developed (cf./5/). However it synthesizes simpler structures interpreted by subclass of the pattern family and uses another type of algorithm, based on MINL-computations (cf./4/).

Next we sketch the basic ideas of pattern synthesis.

Synthesis of Patterns from Positive Data

The problem of inductive inference of pattern languages (synthesis of patterns) was for the first time discussed in /1/.

Let us assume tha A is a finite alphabet of at least two different constants and X_n is a disjoint set of n variables. For any set Y let Y^+ denote the set of all non-empty words over Y. We define the class of all

1) Laboratory of Mathematical Linguistics, Institute of Mathematics, Sofia P.O.B. 373

patterns over A and X_n and denote it by P_n : $P_n = (A \cup X_n)^+$. Any mapping $s: X_n \rightarrow A^+$ shall be considered a substitution of the pattern variables. For an arbitrary pattern $p \in P_n$ the corresponding pattern language L(p) is defined as follows:

$L(p) = \{w/\text{there exists a substitution } s \text{ such that } s(p) = w\}$.

We shall call any finite set of non-empty words over A a sample.
Further a pattern p of a given class shall be called descriptive of a sample S if:

(1) $S \subseteq L(p)$

(2) There is no pattern $q \neq p$ within the same class with $S \subseteq L(q) \subsetneq L(p)$.

In other words p is descriptive of S if it is consistent with it and fits to it best.

Suppose that a pattern language is presented stepwise by samples which should exhaust it in the limit. Then the pattern synthesis problem can be stated as follows: Construct a recursive device device (algorithm) which works in steps, producing a consistent pattern for each sample and stabilizing in a finite number of steps on a correct pattern that is descriptive of the presented language. Formally, for any sequence of samples $S_1, S_2, \ldots$ with $S_1 \subseteq S_2 \subseteq \ldots$ and $\cup S_i = L$ (L is a pattern language) it should hold :

(1) For each input S_i the algorithm gives out a pattern-output p_i

(2) There is an index m such that $p_m = p_{m+k}$ for all natural numbers k and $L(p_m) = L$.

The main result used in our application is presented in /2/:

Theorem: Let n be any positive integer. There is a pattern synthesis algorithm (PSA_n) which for any sample S generates a pattern of maximal length that is descriptive of S within P_n. The number of steps, required by the PSA_n is polynomially bounded depending on /S/.

The proof is constructive and based on pattern-automata-like structures, which in /2/ are called parallelepipeds.

In the following we give a description of our system and motivate its development.

A System for Automatic Data-Base Restructuring and Intelligent Data Entry

Data bases are a wide spread means for storing large bodies of diverse information in a structured way. Through a relevant data-base management system (DBMS) it is made possible to retrieve, up-date, restructure the stored information and add new data to it, using a high level language. Often though it is necessary to alter the logical structure of the data carriers, i.e. new logical structures have to be generated and physically implemented, which is normal procedure when new files are to be included in an existing data base. Two typical restructuring examples are offered by the task to adapt existing data bases to new applications using the same DBMS (the new-generations problem) and by the so-called rapidly changing data bases, as those used by police headquarters to store information about crimes in big cities like New York (cf./3/).

The data-base restructuring tasks described above are performed by the system's manager who normally has to write appropriate programs in the high-level DBMS-language or even use low-level code.

Therefore we find it quite useful to develop a system for automatic data-base restructuring.

Another point of our interest is the data entry process. We consider it important to make it as natural as possible. One approach would be to reduce it to a simple procedure, analogous to the one used by man while typing data or filling in a form. This would be possible if a certain degree of intelligence characterized the data entry system.

In the following we briefly describe a system that performs automatic data-base restructuring and allows natural data entry.

The system's main component, the pattern synthesis block, is based on the mathematical background that was described in the previous section. It is intended for a relational data base with a corresponding DBMS. The data structures are homogeneous files with linear-structure records containing symbolic information. We restrict ourselves to symbolic information, since it is universal in the sense that any other type of information can be represented in symbolic form. Since files are homogeneous it is sufficient to consider the structure of a single record. It can be described as an array of fields with corresponding indentifiers (names) and length. Following the data entry process they are instantialized, i.e. filled in with symbol strings.We assume that the latter can be comprized of any symbols which are admitted by the DBMS. In addition we allow a more complex structure of the symbol strings: they could contain the so-called procedural attachments. A procedural attachment is given by the name of a procedure which can be addressed and executed on instantilized arguments, the latter being file names and/or instantializations of fields from the same record. Procedural attachments are used with the purpose to avoid storing large bodies of relatively seldom used information and eliminate complicated requests for retrieving them when necessary.

There are two tasks to complete if the structure of such a record is to be synthesized:

- the field names and those of the procedural attachments have to be determined and ordered;
- field format has to be fixed.

Our system performs those tasks automatically, learning the record structure from samples of instantialized records, which are known to have the desired structure. Here it makes use of the PSA_n mentioned in the previous section. The system's learning component works independently from the DBMS and could be applied to any relational data base.
The process of implementation of the learned file structure is carried out on the basis of structure manipulation techniques made available by the particular DBMS through a monitor. The intelligent data entry system uses the learnt structure to determine the destination of the input data, which is then recorded on the data carriers. The system is universal in the sense that it can operate with any type of data and relational record structure.
We give two examples of record structure, followed by instantialized record samples, from a particular application that will be used to illustrate the system's operation.

Personal Records File (Ia)

⟨NAME:X_1 CHR.NAME:X_2 SEX:X_3 DATE OF BIRTH:$X_4$19X_5 FAMILY STATUS:X_6 PASSPORT NR.:X_7 JOB:X_8 ORGANIZATION:X_9 POSITION:X_{10} JOB CHARACTERISTICS:SEARCH (JOBSCHEME,X_{10},X_9) AREAS OF INTEREST:X_{11} KEYWORDS FOR SCIENTIFIC RESULTS: X_{12}⟩

Publications File (Ib)

⟨AUTHOR-NAME:X_1 AUTHOR-CHR.NAME:X_2 TITLE:X_3 SOURCE NAME:X_4 VOL.:X_5 NR.:X_6 YEAR:X_7 PAGES:X_8-X_9 KEYWORDS:X_{10} AUTHOR'S ADDRESS:X_{11}⟩

These record structures are synthesized from the following type:
Input Samples for the Personal Records File: (IIa)

1. NAME: IVANOV CHR.NAME: PETER SEX: MALE DATE OF BIRTH: 19.02.1947 FAMILY STATUS: MARRIED PASSPORT NR.: B0385066 JOB: MATHEMATICIAN ORGANIZATION: ECOLOGY INSTITUTE POSITION: HEAD OF DEPT. OF STATISTICS JOB CHARACTERISTICS: SEARCH(JOBSCHEME, HEAD OF DEPT. OF STATISTICS, ECOLOGY INSTITUTE) AREAS OF INTEREST: STATISTICS, ARTIFICIAL INTELLIGENCE KEYWORDS FOR SCIENTIFIC RESULTS: CLUSTER ANALYSIS, FUZZY SETS, PATTERN RECOGNITION
2. NAME: PETKOV .....

   ⋮

Input Samples for the Publications File: (IIb)

1. AUTHOR-NAME: LEVESQUE AUTHOR-CHR.NAME: H.J. TITLE: FOUNDATIONS OF A FUNCTIONAL APPROACH TO KNOWLEDGE REPRESENTATION SOURCE NAME: AI VOL.: 23 NR.: 2 YEAR: 1984 PAGES: 155-212 KEYWORDS: KNOWLEDGE REPRESENTATION, KNOWLEDGE BASES, FIRST-ORDER LOGICS, ABSTRACT DATA TYPES, FUNCTIONAL CHARACTERIZATION AUTHOR'S ADDRESS: FAIRCHILD LABORATORY FOR AI RESEARCH, PALO ALTO, CA 94304, USA
2. AUTHOR-NAME: LEE .....

⋮

Here we make direct interpretation of the pattern formalism, described in the previous section . The finite alphabet A includes the whole Latin and Cyrillic alphabets, and all the service characters which are available on a terminal keyboard.

The input samples (IIa) and (IIb) are regarded as words over A and the structures (Ia) and (Ib), as patterns where field names like AUTHOR-NAME TITLE, as well as parenthesized procedural attachment names like SEARCH (JOBSCHEME, ... are strings of constants in the pattern. Constants can be separated inside the fields as well. Variables are denoted as indexed letters X which comprise the X_n.

As one can see a relatively simple frame structure (Ia, Ib), eventually with procedural attachments, has to be inferred from samples in which the slots named X_1, X_2, ... have been filled in. In example (Ia) the procedural attachment SEARCH retrieves and summarizes information about a particular position, occupied in a particular organization, which is kept in the JOBSCHEME-file. SEARCH is triggered any time the JOBCHARACTERISTICS-field is referred to. The block-diagram of the system is presented on Fig.1. We shall briefly describe its work.

The system's operation is supervised by the MONITOR. At the begining of a working session it requires specifications for the file whose structure is to be generated. Then it checks whether this file is already available in the data base, i.e. a restructuring process is to be started or it has to be generated for the first time. In the former case copy-procedures would have to be activated when the FILE RESTRUCTURING BLOCK is reached, in order to avoid loss of information.

Input samples are demanded from the user next. They are entered via terminal and following the second entry, each time a pattern hypothesis is produced by the PATTERN SYNTHESIS BLOCK. Constant strings are considered field indentifiers, if they begin with a letter and end with colon. Only the different patterns are put on display and each time the pattern hypothesis is changed the comentary 'CHANGE OF PATTERN' appears on the screen. If required, a list of the strings of constants, suggested as field indentifiers,can be put on the screen. After a number of input samples are

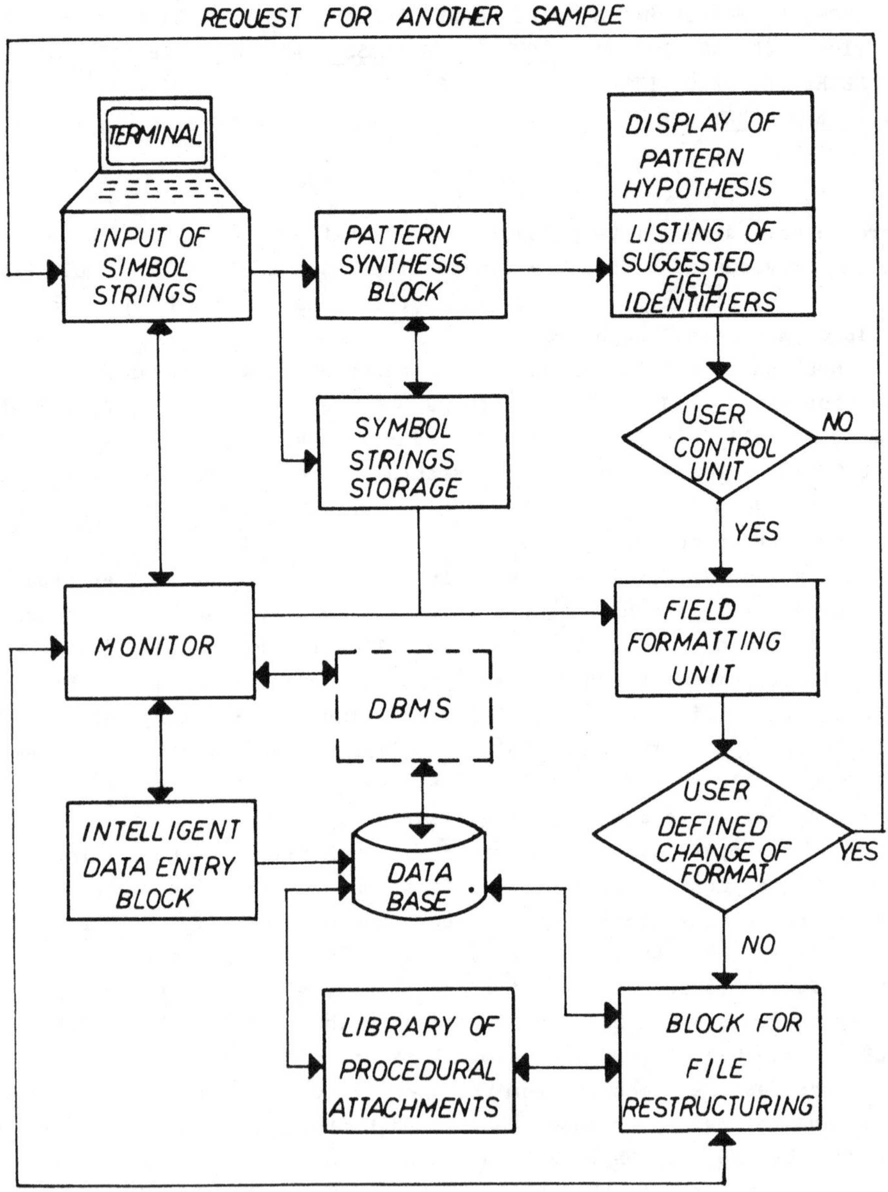
REQUEST FOR ANOTHER SAMPLE
TERMINAL
INPUT OF SIMBOL STRINGS
PATTERN SYNTHESIS BLOCK
DISPLAY OF PATTERN HYPOTHESIS
LISTING OF SUGGESTED FIELD IDENTIFIERS
SYMBOL STRINGS STORAGE
USER CONTROL UNIT
NO
YES
MONITOR
FIELD FORMATTING UNIT
DBMS
USER DEFINED CHANGE OF FORMAT
YES
NO
INTELLIGENT DATA ENTRY BLOCK
DATA BASE
LIBRARY OF PROCEDURAL ATTACHMENTS
BLOCK FOR FILE RESTRUCTURING

Fig. 1

fed in, the synthesis algorithm stabilizes on a given pattern. Then the user is asked whether this pattern is a sufficiently complete representation of the structure which underlies the input samples. At this place we should like to remember that all the synthesized patterns are consistent with the samples but not all are representations of the record structure. If the answer is negative, then the new input samples are required until the record structure is synthesized. Otherwise the FIELD-FORMATTING UNIT is activated, using a CHANGE FORMAT OF FIELD ... TO ... command or just entering a new sample of the same structure whose data have the desired format. The latter is comfortable when most of the formats have to be changed. It does not trigger the PATTERN SYNTHESIS BLOCK, since the system processes the samples using the last pattern as a mask for separating and estimating the field instantializations.
Once this operation is finished and the BLOCK FOR FILE RESTRUCTIRING begins its work. We would not like to go into details here. It should though be mentioned that each procedural attachment name is looked for in the LIBRARY OF PROCEDURAL ATTACHMENTS. If it is not found there, the user is required to define a procedure of his own and include it into the library under this name.
After the structure generation process is completed one can use the INTELLIGENT DATA ENTRY BLOCK. The data entry process is reduced to filling in the slots of the learnt structure. Hence the only requirement would be to enter data successively in the order, determined by the indexing of the pattern variables. Neither format specifications have to be met (with the exception of an upper bound to the length of the input symbol string), nor operators used.
An example of a data entry for the (Ib) structure is given on Fig. 2.

```
LEE
T.T
A STATE APPROACH TO ...
INT.J.COMPUTER AND ...
12
5
:
```

Fig. 2

author-name	LEE
author-sirname	T.T.
title	A STATE APPROACH ...
source name	INT.J.COMPUTER ...
volume	12
number	5
:	:

Fig. 3

It is obvious that the data entry process is as natural as the preparation of a bibliography on a sheet of paper. Another faciliation would be given if data is entered into the system the way a form is filled in, as illustrated on Fig.3, where the required inputs are given in capital letters.

Conclusions

The proposed system may be used as an intelligent component of any relational DBMS. It should be quite useful in restructuring rapidly changing data bases and in the entry process of large bodies of information, some of it possibly not exactly specified before.

It should be possible to speed up the work of the system by using an enconding procedure for the inputs (cf./5/). In this case changes are to be made in the PSA_n, since it would operate with a potentially infinite alphabet.

The system is currently been implemented on a SM-4 minicomputer (PDP-11 compatible) in LISP with the prospect to carry it over to a more powerful minicomputer, thus increasing speed and attractivity.

References

/1/ Angluin, D.: "Finding Patterns Common to a Set of Strings", J. of Computer and System Sciences 21(1980) 1

/2/ Jantke, K.P.: "Polynomial Time Inference of General Pattern Languages", Proceedings of STACS '84, Paris, LINCS 166

/3/ Martin, J.: "Computer Data-Base Organization", Prentice-Hall, 1977

/4/ Shapiro, E.: "Inductive Inference of Theories from Facts", Res. Report 192, Dept. Comp. Sci., Yale University, 1981

/5/ Shinohara, T.: Polynomial Time Inference of Extended Regular Pattern Languages", RIMS Symposia on Software Science and Engineering, Kyoto, 1982, LINCS 147

/6/ Winston, P.: "Artificial Intelligence", Addison-Wesley, 1977

THE PROOF-CHECKING COMPONENT FOR THE PLEATS PROGRAMMING SYSTEM ENABLING SPECIFICATION OF THEORIES

Jolanta Cybulka, Jerzy Bartoszek [1)]

1. INTRODUCTION

The basic aim of the presented paper is to point out the main ideas connected with a certain proof-checker building project. This proof-checker is to be a part of the already existing PLEATS programming system ([2]). The name PLEATS stands for the Programming Language Enabling Algorithmic Theories Specification, so the main and most interesting property of the system is that its user is allowed to create different algorithmic theories ([1], [6]) and "store" them in the computer. These theories can be built by means of the execution of certain operations on existing theories /i.e. primitive theories predeclared in the system or theories being previously specified by the user himself/. Except the theories' specification ability the PLEATS programming system enables its user to "work" within the specified theory by means of running programs written in this theory's language /the notion of a "program" is understood as it is provided with the algorithmic logic/. That is why the PLEATS system may be regarded as "a programming system". This feature of the PLEATS system is especially important to computer scientists. In section 3 we give a short algorithmic theory specification example.

We want to achieve one more interesting goal connected with the considered programming system. Namely we suggest, it will be useful for the user to have an ability to express facts /on the ground of the specified algorithmic theories/ and then to validate them. This leads us to a project of a certain sybsystem being an "automated deduction" component of the PLEATS system. We decided to develop this component as a proof-checker. Thinking about a proof-checker we were highly influenced by the LCF proof-checking system ([3], [4]).

The presentation of our proof-checking project goes as follows. At first the logical basis of a system is shortly described /section 2/, then we lead the reader through a theory specification and a proof verification example /section 3/, where the proposed "style" of deduction is illustrated. In the end, we make some remarks on the language

1) Technical University of Poznań
pl. Skłodowska-Curie 5
60-965 Poznań, Poland

suitable for conducting proofs /section 4/ and some final remarks /section 5/.

2. LOGICAL BASIS

It is very important to computer scientists to have a tool enabling to do some theoretical works about data structures and programs. A convenient way to express different properties of data structures and, especially, programs is to use algorithmic logic. As a logical basis of the proof-checker we take Gentzen-type formalisation of algorithmic logic ([5]). The adopted set of 'sequential rules" allows to conduct proofs both in natural deduction and goal-directed style /the "goal-directed style of proving" notion comes from the LCF system/.

In the natural deduction style a single sequential rule can be treated as an inference rule which, when applied to a theorem gives a new theorem. On the other hand, the same sequential rule serves as a primitive "deductive procedure" /or a "tactic"/ which, when applied to a formula being "a goal" of a deduction, produces a list of subgoals /maybe empty/ to be proved and a proof itself. We want our proof-checker to follow the mentioned above styles of conducting proofs.

Now, let us look at some sequential rules which are defined to deduce about algorithmic logic programs, such as conditional instruction and iteration instruction. In every rule the $\Vdash$-sign stands for the sequential derivability relation between sets of formulas. Sets of formulas are denoted $S_1, S_2, S_3, \ldots$, etc., α, β stand for single formulas and K, M denote arbitrary programs. Let us consider the conditional instruction rule first:

$$\frac{S_1 \Vdash \{(\beta \wedge K\alpha) \vee (\neg \beta \wedge M\alpha)\} \cup S_2 \cup S_3}{S_1 \Vdash S_2 \cup \{[\underline{\text{if}}\ \beta\ \underline{\text{then}}\ K\ \underline{\text{else}}\ M]\alpha\} \cup S_3}$$

In the natural deduction style of proving we can think about the above scheme as if it was the if-then-else program connective introduction rule /we called it IFI rule - see the example in section 3/. In the goal directed manner of proving, the mentioned rule is a basis to create a tactic for goals of the form:

$$S_1 \Vdash [\underline{\text{if}}\ \beta\ \underline{\text{then}}\ K\ \underline{\text{else}}\ M]\alpha$$

This tactic produces the subgoal:

$$S_1 \Vdash (\beta \wedge K\alpha) \vee (\neg \beta \wedge M\alpha)$$

to be proved. If this is done, the main goal is achieved.

The application and implementation of the above scheme causes no problems, but here arises one when we consider the scheme to deduce about iteration instruction:

$$\frac{S_1 \Vdash \{[\underline{if}\ \beta\ \underline{then}\ K\ \underline{else}]^i(\neg\beta \wedge \alpha) : i \in \mathcal{N}\} \cup S_2 \cup S_3}{S_1 \Vdash S_2 \cup \{[\underline{while}\ \beta\ \underline{do}\ K]\alpha\} \cup S_3}$$

The scheme has infinitiary many premises and the question, how to implement it effectively is still open.

3. A SPECIFICATION AND VERIFICATION EXAMPLE

The aim of this section is to show how an algorithmic theory can be specified using the PLEATS programming system and how one can work within this theory in the sense of running programs and doing proofs.

PLEATS is an interactive system, where " _ " is its prompt sign and every sentence written by it is preceded by "****" .

The interaction while specifying a theory goes as follows:

```
**** BEGINNING OF SESSION
_    AFFIX T1 AS LTH ENRICHED BY
_    VAR N,M,K,L;
_    FUN S;
_    AXIOMS
_    A1    (N = 0 v N > 0) => S(N) = [IF  N = 0
_                                       THEN M := 1
_                                       ELSE M := M + 1 ] M .
```

The theory named T1 is introduced as a basic LTH theory /a simplified version of LISP-like lists theory/ enriched by adding some individual variàbles N,M,L,K, the functor S and the axiom A1 /defining the meaning of the functor S/.

Now, we can run a program using the defined variables, functor and axiom:

```
_  USING T1 EXECUTE
_  BEGIN
_  K := 4;
_  L := S(K)
_  END.
```

The program running results can be displayed using the command:

```
_  USING T1 DISPLAY VALUE K,L.
**** VALUE OF K
 4
**** VALUE OF L
 5
```

Suppose that having specified the T1 theory we want to prove on its ground the following formula:

$$(M > 0) \wedge ([M := S(M-1)]\ TRUE) \wedge ([M := M*5]\ TRUE) \Longrightarrow$$
$$[IF\ \ M > 0\ \ THEN\ M := S(M-1)\ \ ELSE\ \ M := M*5]\ TRUE$$

which expresses the stop property of a certain program being a conditional instruction, under some assumptions.

Let us illustrate the natural deduction style of proving [1]. At first we assign to free variables [2] values being formulas and then we assume these formulas are true, assigning their values to some bound /to types/ variables:

```
_ USING T1 CHANGE TO PROOFCHECKER .
_ FREEVARS  F1 = "[M := S(M - 1)] TRUE",
            F2 = "[M := M*5] TRUE",
            P  = "M > 0"; ;

**** F1 = "[M := S(M - 1)] TRUE"  : FORM .
**** F2 = "[M := M*5] TRUE"       : FORM
**** P  = "M > 0" : FORM
_ BOUNDVARS TH1 = ASSUME (F1), TH2 = ASSUME (F2), TH3 = ASSUME (P) ;;
**** TH1 = "([M := S(M - 1)] TRUE) ⊩ ([M := S(M - 1)] TRUE)" : THM
**** TH2 = "([M := M*5] TRUE) ⊩  ([M := M*5] TRUE)" : THM
**** TH3 = "(M > 0) ⊩ (M > 0)" : THM
```

Note, that having assumed a formula α we obtain a theorem α⊩α. Now, we can construct the premise of the IFI rule /see section 2/, using rules to introduce ∧, ∨, ¬ logical connectives. We use bound variables to make sure that every formula obtained is a theorem.

```
_ BOUNDVARS TH4 = ANDI (TH3,TH1) ;;
**** TH4 = "(M > 0), ([M := S(M - 1)] TRUE)
               ⊩ (M > 0) ∧ ([M := S(M - 1)] TRUE)" : THM
_ BOUNDVARS F3 = "FALSE" ;;
**** F3 = "FALSE" : FORM
_ BOUNDVARS TH5 = NOTI (TH3,F3) ;;
**** TH5 = "¬(M > 0)" : THM
_ BOUNDVARS TH6 = ANDI (TH5,TH2) ;;
**** TH6 = "([M := M*5] TRUE) ⊩ ¬(M > 0) ∧ ([M := M*5] TRUE)" : THM
_ BOUNDVARS TH7 = ORI (TH4,TH6) ;;
**** TH7 = "(M > 0),([M := S(M)] TRUE),([M := M*5] TRUE)
          ⊩ ((M > 0) ∧ ([M := S(M - 1)] TRUE)) ∨ (¬(M > 0) ∧ ([M := M*5]
                                                    TRUE))" : THM
```

The application of the IFI rule to the theorem TH7 ends the proof:

```
_ BOUNDVARS TH8 = IFI (TH7) ;;
**** TH8 = "(M > 0),([M := S(M - 1)] TRUE),([M := M*5] TRUE)
          ⊩ [IF M > 0  THEN M := S(M - 1) ELSE M := M*5] TRUE" : THM
```

---

[1] We use a special language to conduct proofs, shortly described in section 4.

[2] i.e. variables not assigned to any type /sort/.

The main disadvantage of the above style of proving is that proofs are long and all the steps must be repeated in every case while proving a formula "similar" in the shape to the above one. So, following the ideas of the LCF system, we allow the user to "program" proofs in the sense of building special proving procedures to deal with certain kind of formulas. Thus, the proof is programmed once and then it may be applied many times.

Our examplary formula expresses the stop property of a certain conditional instruction. It is a case of more general problem, i.e. a stop property of an arbitrary program. As it was mentioned in section 2, proving properties of programs containing iteration instruction causes problems, so let us program /for simplicity/ a tactic to deal with the stop property of arbitrary programs without iteration instruction.

Let us assume that we have defined a primitive tactics IFITAC, BEGITAC, SUBTAC on the basis of adequate sequential rules /for conditional instruction, compound instruction and substitution instruction respectively/. Every tactic is considered to be a function with a parameter being a goal. The goal in our example is defined as follows:

```
_ TYPEDEC GOAL = LIST (FORM) # (PROGRAM # FORM);;
```

Thus the goal is a pair with the first component being a list of formulas /assumptions/ and the second one being a formula to be proved /in the shape of generalized formula/. As a result, the function being a tactic produces a pair containing a list of subgoals to be proved and a proof itself, both defined as follows:

```
_ TYPEDEC PROOF = LIST (THM) ⟶ THM ;;
_ TYPEDEC RESULT = LIST (GOAL) # PROOF ;;
```

The proof is a function which, having a list of theorems produces a theorem. Let us suppose, additionally, that we have special functions /so-called "tacticals" / which arguments are tactics. These functions define operations enabling to create complicated tactics /or "strategies"/ from existing ones. Let us adopt REPEAT and ORELSE tacticals from LCF /see [3] for details/. Now we are ready to define PROGSTOPTAC:

```
_ BOUNDVARS  X:GOAL ;;
****X = ? : GOAL
_ FUNCTION PROGSTOPTAC (X) DEFINED
_ BOUNDVARS  R:RESULT ;;
_ BEGIN
_ R:= REPEAT (IFITAC (X) ORELSE BEGITAC (X) ORELSE SUBSTAC (X))
_ END R ;;
****PROGSTOPTAC : - GOAL ⟶ RESULT
```

We can prove our examplary formula using PROGSTOPTAC:

```
_ BOUNDVARS FORMULA = "(M>0),([M := S(M - 1)] TRUE),([M := M*5] TRUE)
            ⊩ [IF  M>0  THEN M := S(M - 1) ELSE M := M*5] TRUE",
            STOPPROOF : RESULT ;;
****FORMULA = "(M>0),([M := S(M - 1)] TRUE),([M := M*5] TRUE)
              ⊩ [IF M>0 THEN M := S(M - 1) ELSE M := M*5] TRUE":FORM
****STOPPROOF = ? : RESULT
```

A proof is initialized by a program running:

```
_ STOPPROOF := PROGSTOPTAC (FORMULA) ;;
****STOPPROOF = "(M>0),([M := S(M - 1)] TRUE),([M := M*5] TRUE)
              ⊩ [IF M>0 THEN M := S(M - 1) ELSE M := M*5] TRUE": THM
```

Then, the session is ended:

```
_ EXIT.
****END OF SESSION
```

4. LANGUAGE OF THE PROOF-CHECKER

In the former section we gave a look at the language suggested to conduct proofs. Let us summarize its properties. There exist two basic kinds of expressions: declaration sentences and programs.

Among declarations one can: declare variables, types and functions. Variables can be bound to types /in that case typechecking holds while assigning values to bound variables/ or not /in such a case the variables are considered to be free/.

Types declarations enable to define sorts in the sense of Pascal-like programming languages. Some types are predeclared in the language /for instance FORM, THM, PROGRAM/ and some operations on types are admissible /i.e. the operation of pairing, of making a list of elements of arbitrary types and of defining a type being a set of functions from one type to another etc./.

Function declaration consists of the heading /name and a formal parameters list/, local variables declarations and a body being a generalized term /program and term/. A program defines the meaning of a function while a term represents function result.

Programs can appear not only in functions' definitions, but separately as well. They may be then regarded as "proving actions". The notion of a program is common to algorithmic logic and to Pascal-like languages and includes: substitution instruction, conditional instruction and iteration instruction.

5. FINAL REMARKS

To end with the proof-checker project presentation we emphasize some important problems that have not been solved yet.

The first is connected with the way of treating and implementation deduction rules about recursively defined functions and iteration programs /ω-rules/.

The second problem concerns the way of syntactic and semantic simplification of formulas and terms during a proof.

Another problem to deal with at present is a proof-checker implementation in the PLEATS programming system environment.

REFERENCES

[1] Banachowski, L., A. Kreczmar and others: An Introduction to Algorithmic Logic, Mathem. Investig. in the Theory of Programs, Banach Center Pub., vol. 2, 1977.

[2] Bartoszek, J.: The Programming Language with the Specifications of Algorithmic Theories. Ph. D. Thesis, 1983 /in Polish/.

[3] Gordon, M. J., A. J. Milner and Ch. P. Wadsworth: Edinburgh LCF, LNCS, Springer-Verlag 1979.

[4] Milner, R.: Logic for Computable Functions - Description of A Machine Implementation. Stanf. Univ. Reports, 1972.

[5] Mirkowska, G.: Algorithmic Logic and its Applications in the Theory of Programs I & II, Annales Societatis Mathematicae Polonae, Ser. IV, Fundamenta Informaticae, vol. I, nr. 1 & 2 (1977), 1-17 & 147-165.

[6] Rasiowa, H.: Algorithmic Logic, ICS PAS Reports, No 281, 1977.

THE METANET. A KNOWLEDGE REPRESENTATION TOOL BASED ON ABSTRACT DATA TYPES

Werner Dilger [1]
Wolfgang Womann [2]

ABSTRACT

The schema METANET is the specification of some kind of generalized semantic network as abstract data type. The theoretical basis of this work, namely Σ-termalgebras and rewrite rule systems, is introduced. It is described how the axiom schemas of the METANET arise by abstraction from real axioms and how axioms can be derived from axiom schemas by instantiation in turn, yielding a specification of a concrete sort of semantic networks. Some remarks on the properties and the use of METANET are passed.

INTRODUCTION

The concept of abstract data type is a well-defined means for the specification of data structures in large software systems. In the last ten years, large software systems have been developed in the area of AI and have become more and more important. It seems therefore a good idea to adopt mathematically well founded software engineering principles to such systems. We have made a step in this direction, defining one of the main data structures in AI, the semantic networks, which are closely related to frames, as abstract data types. In addition to the advantages that can be gained from such a definition in general, our approach has yielded a tool for testing and developing representation languages based on semantic networks. Our paper is divided in three sections. In the first and second ones, the theoretical basis of our work is given, namely Σ-termalgebras and rewrite rule systems. These parts are based on the work of Goguen, Thatcher, and Wagner [6], Dershowitz and Manna [3], Manna and Ness [10], Huet [8], and Knuth and Bendix [9].
In the last section the schema METANET is introduced as a generalized version of semantic networks, its specification as abstract data type is given, and some of its properties are described. This part is oriented on the type of networks introduced by Hendrix [7]. For other types see Findler [11], Barr and Feigenbaum [1], and Brachman [2]. More extended presentations of the METANET are given in Dilger and Womann [4 , 5].

---

1) Institut für Informations- und Datenverarbeitung D-7500 Karlsruhe 1
Sebastian-Kneipp-Str. 12

2) Nixdorf Computer AG, Berlinerstrasse 95, D-8000 München 40

Σ-TERMALGEBRAS

A *signature* is a pair (S,Σ) of sorts and operation symbols respectively. To each operation symbol f a *functionality* is assigned, specifying its domain and range. It is denoted by $f\colon s1\cdot\ldots\cdot sk \to s$ or by $f \in \Sigma_{w,s}$ where $w \in S^*$, $s \in S$, $w = s1\cdot\ldots\cdot sk$. An example is the signature nat, consisting of the sort nat and the zero-element and the successor-function as operations. Thus we could write nat = ({nat},{O,SUCC}) , but we prefer to denote it in another form, including the functionalities of the operation symbols:

nat

sorts: nat

operation symbols: O: → nat

SUCC: nat → nat

A signature can be regarded as a framework for algebras which all have in some sense the same structure. For algebras, however, we need real data and real operations on these data, not only abstract symbols. Thus, given a signature (S,Σ), an *algebra* is a pair (A,Σ_A), where $A = \{A_s \mid s \in S\}$ is a set of data sets and Σ_A is a set of k-ary operations ($k \geq 0$) $f_A\colon A_{s1} \times \ldots \times A_{sk} \to A_s$ with $f \in \Sigma_{s1\ldots sk,s}$, si, $s \in S$ ($i = 1,\ldots,k$). It is immediately clear in which way an algebra "fits" to the underlying signature. Take as an example the algebra $NAT = (\{N\}, \{O_{NAT}, SUCC_{NAT}\})$.

From the operation symbols in Σ we can build terms in the usual way. For each sort s the set $T_{\Sigma,s}$ of Σ-*terms* is defined by $\Sigma_{\lambda,s} \subseteq T_{\Sigma,s}$ and if $f \in \Sigma_{s1\ldots sk,s}$ and $ti \in T_{\Sigma,si}$ ($i = 1,\ldots,k$), then $f(t1,\ldots,tk) \in T_{\Sigma,s}$. The nat-terms e.g. are O, SUCC(O), SUCC(SUCC(O)),... . Now for the "fitting" of an algebra to the underlying signature it is required that the objects of the algebra have the same structure as the terms. This leads to the idea, that the terms could be themselves used as data sets for algebras.

Given a signature (S,Σ), the Σ-*termalgebra* T_Σ is defined by (1) $\{T_{\Sigma,s} \mid s \in S\}$ is the set of data sets, (2) the operations are $f_{T_\Sigma}\colon T_{\Sigma,s1} \times \ldots \times T_{\Sigma,sk} \to T_{\Sigma,s}$ with $f_{T_\Sigma}(t1,\ldots,tk) = f(t1,\ldots,tk)$, where $f \in \Sigma_{s1\ldots sk,s}$, $ti \in T_{\Sigma,si}$, $si,s \in S$ ($i = 1,\ldots,k$).

A Σ-termalgebra for a signature (S,Σ) is an initial algebra, and that means, it has two nice properties: It is unique except for isomorphic algebras, and for each other algebra A there is exactly one homomorphism leading from the Σ-termalgebra to A. Thus, the Σ-termalgebra can be taken as a representant of the class of algebras fitting to the signature, it describes the whole class in a *representation independent* way. In addition, all data of the Σ-termalgebra can be produced by operations, starting with the O-ary operations. These two properties are also the main properties that we claim for the abstract data types, and this justifies the definition: An *abstract data type* is a Σ-termalgebra.

We want to define the semantics of the operations of an abstract data type by axioms. For this purpose, we extend the Σ-termalgebras by variables. From the signature (S,Σ) we get the signature with variables (S,Σ(Var)) augmenting the set $\Sigma_{\lambda,s}$ of constants by the set Var_s of variables for each sort s. This yields a Σ(Var)-termalgebra or a Σ-termalgebra with variables. A pair e = (L,R), where L,R are Σ(Var)-terms of the same sort s, is called a *Σ(Var)-equation* of sort s. Let E_s be a set of Σ(Var)-equations of sort s and $E = \{E_s | s \in S\}$. Then a *specification* of an algebra or an abstract data type is a triple SPEC = (S,Σ(Var),E).

An example is the specification of the data type int.

int

sorts: int

operation symbols:	O:		→ int
	SUCC:	int	→ int
	PRED:	int	→ int

equations: SUCC(PRED(x)) = x
PRED(SUCC(x)) = x

REWRITE RULE SYSTEMS

Let (S,Σ(Var)) be a signature with variables. A *rewrite rule* is a triple p{c} → q, where $p,c,q \in T_{\Sigma(Var)}$, $Var(c) \subseteq Var(p)$ and $Var(q) \subseteq Var(p)$, Sort(c) = boole and Sort(p) = Sort(q). A *rewrite rule system* for (S,Σ(Var)) is a set of rewrite rules. We define rewrite rules as conditioned rules, c stands for the condition. Such a rule can be applied to a term t only if t satisfies the condition. Substitution and unification are defined in the usual way.

A rewrite rule system $T = \{p_i\{c_i\} \rightarrow q_i | i = 1,\dots,n\}$ induces an *inference relation* $\Rightarrow \subseteq T_{\Sigma(Var)} \times T_{\Sigma(Var)}$ on the set of Σ(Var)-terms by application of the rules on terms in the usual way.

T is called *noetherian* or *finitely terminating* iff there are no infinite inferences with respect to ⇒. T is called *confluent* iff for all $t,v,w \in T_{\Sigma(Var)}$ with t ⇒ v and t ⇒ w there is a $z \in T_{\Sigma(Var)}$ such that v ⇒ z and w ⇒ z. These two properties are important for the use of rewrite rule systems in practice. Noetheriaty guarantees that every inference stops after a finite number of steps, and due to confluence the result does not depend on the way the inference has taken, in other words: For each term t there is exactly one terminating element, called its *normalform*, denoted $\bar{t}$. In order to prove noetheriaty, a *weighting function* g is defined that assigns to each operation symbol of

$\Sigma(Var)$ a weight, i.e. an element of a well founded set. This is a well-ordered set that contains no infinite decreasing sequences with respect to its ordering. An example is the set of positive integers with the <-relation. The weighting function g is then extended to the terms in $T_{\Sigma(Var)}$. g should have the property that for all $s, t \in T_{\Sigma(Var)}$ with $s \rightarrow t$ it holds that $g(s) > g(t)$. Then each inference according to $\rightarrow$ stops, because there are no infinite sequences in the well founded set with respect to >. In a rewrite rule system for each rule $p(c) \rightarrow q$ $g(p) > g(q)$ must hold and g must be monotone in each operand such that application of the rule does not disturb the gradient from left to right.

For the proof of confluence, the *superposition algorithm* of Knuth and Bendix can be used. It requires the computation of all possible *critical pairs* (P,Q). They are defined in the following way: Given two rewrite rules $p_1(c_1) \rightarrow q_1$ and $p_2(c_2) \rightarrow q_2$, $P = \sigma_1(p_1[M/\sigma_2(q_2)])$, $Q = \sigma_1(q_1)$ for some subterm M of p_1 such that M and p_2 are unifiable by the substitutions σ_1 and σ_2. If for all critical pairs (P,Q) $\bar{P} = \bar{Q}$, the system is confluent (it is assumed to be noetherian).

If one specifies some kind of data as abstract data type, one may replace the equation signs in the equations by arrows, thus getting a rewrite rule system. Supposed the system is noetherian and confluent, one has implicitely defined normal forms for the terms. These normal forms can be used as representants of classes of terms and they have in general simpler forms than the other terms. For this reason, rewrite rule systems are adopted for abstract data types.

THE SCHEMA METANET

We conceive a semantic network as a graph with typed nodes and edges. Operations on networks are insertion and deletion of nodes and edges. We need further some recognizer and selector functions. Most of these operations are related to the types of nodes and edges. That means, in a specification of semantic networks as abstract data type we have to define the same operations several times, for each type separately, by means of equational axioms. To avoid such a stupid repetition of similar axioms we introduce type variables ranging over the sets of types of nodes and edges respectively. Doing this, we get axiom schemas instead of axioms and the specification defines a network schema which is called *METANET*. Here is the specification of the schema METANET with some of the equations (the total number of equations is 35, it can be found in [4 , 5]):

METANET = SET +

sorts: $Nt = \{NT_1,\ldots,NT_n\}$, $Et = \{ET_1,\ldots,ET_m\}$

operation symbols: $\forall\ i \in \{1,\ldots,n\}$, $\forall\ e \in \{1,\ldots,m\}$

EMPTYNET:		→ metanet
ADDNODE.i:	metanet NT_i	→ metanet
INSERTEDGE.e:	metanet ET_e	→ metanet
DELETENODE.i:	metanet NT_i	→ metanet
DELETEEDGE.e:	metanet ET_e	→ metanet
ISEMPTY:	metanet	→ boole
ISNODE:	metanet NT	→ boole
ISEDGE.e:	metanet ET_e	→ boole
NODES:	metanet	→ SET(NT)
EDGES.e:	metanet	→ SET(ET_e)
NEIGHBOURNODES:	metanet NT	→ SET(NT)

Remember that METANET is a Σ(Var)-termalgebra, thus "metanet" represents the whole term set $T_{\Sigma(\mathrm{Var})}$ and $NT = NT_1 \cup \ldots \cup NT_n$. Here are four of the axioms:

DELETENODE.i(INSERTEDGE.e(m,[n1_i,n2_j]),n1_i) &
    {ISNODE(m,n1_i) ∧ ISNODE(m,n2_j)} → $F_{metanet}$

ISNODE(ADDNODE.i(m,n_i),n_i) → TRUE

DELETEEDGE.e(ADDNODE.i(m,n1_i),[n2_j,n3_k])
    → ADDNODE.i(DELETEEDGE.e(m,[n2_j,n3_k]),n1_i)

DELETEEDGE.e(INSERTEDGE.e(m,[n1_i,n2_j]),[n1_i,n2_j]) &
    {ISNODE(m,n1_i) ∧ ISNODE(m,n2_j)} → m

The first axiom says that it is impossible to delete a node n1_i of type i which is connected to another node n2_j by an edge [n1_i, n2_j] (of type e), i.e. this leads to a failure element. According to the second axiom the test if a node n_i exists yields TRUE, if this node has already been added. The third axiom allows the interchanging of a deletion and an adding operation, if both concern unrelated objects. The fourth axiom describes the effect of two complementary operations: they leave the METANET, represented by the variable m, unchanged.
The schema METANET is trivially confluent because the conditions in the axioms exclude the existence of critical pairs. The proof of netheriaty is straightforward by definition of a weighting function and can be found in [5]. The normal forms of the system have a so called "minimal generating form", i.e. they consist only of insertion and adding operations, the deletion operations are all omitted. This can be proved by induction on the structure of the METANET terms.

From the schema METANET a specification of some kind of semantic network as abstract data type can be derived by instantiation, i.e. by substitution of the type variables in the axiom schemas by type constants. If one wants to specify a semantic network with e.g. the node types "concept" and "instance" and the edge types "subset_of" and "element_of", instantiation would yield four axioms from the first axiom schema above and two axioms from the fourth axiom schema. In this way specifications of various kinds of semantic networks can be automatically derived from the schema METANET.

On the basis of the METANET operations defined by the axioms algorithms on networks, e.g. for path passing, can be easily developed in a representation independent manner. To be precise, such algorithms are algorithm schemas containing type variables, and concrete algorithms can be derived from them by instantiation.

CONCLUSION

We have described the specification of a generalized kind of semantic network, the schema METANET, as an abstract data type. This specification is based on well defined mathematical concepts. The METANET can be used as a tool for the test and development of knowledge representation formalisms such as semantic networks and frames. A program that yields instantiations is already implemented. We plan to implement a program for the derivation of normal forms and some auxiliary programs that allow the use of METANET as a tool within the research project ASSIP (associative information processing) at the University of Kaiserslautern.

REFERENCES

[1] Barr, A. and E.A. Feigenbaum (ed): The Handbook of Artificial Intelligence. Stanford, 1981.

[2] Brachman, R.J.: What's in a concept: Structural foundations for Semantic Networks. Int. J. Man-Machine Studies 9 (1977) 127-152.

[3] Dershowitz, N. and Z. Manna: Proving Termination with Multiset Orderings. Comm. of the ACM 16 (1973) 465-476.

[4] Dilger, W. and W. Womann: Semantic Networks as Abstract Data Types. Proc. of the 8th Int. Conference on Artificial Intelligence Karlsruhe (1983) 321-324.

[5] Dilger, W. and W. Womann: The METANET. A Means for the Specification of Semantic Networks as Abstract Data Types. Int. J. Man-Machine Studies (1984).

[6] Goguen, J.A., J.W. Thatcher and E.G. Wagner: An initial algebra approach to the specification, correctness, and implementation of abstract data types. in Yeh R.T. (ed.): Current Trends in Programming Methodology, Volume IV, Data Structuring, 1976.

[7] Hendrix, G.G.: Encoding knowledge in Partitioned Networks. in Findler N. (ed.): Associative Networks. New York (1979).

[8] Huet, G.: Confluent Reductions: Abstract Properties and Applications to Term Rewriting Systems. Journal of the ACM 27 (1980) 797-821.

[9] Knuth, E. and P.B. Bendix: Simple word problems in universal algebras. in Leech J. (ed.): Computational Problems in Universal Algebras. Oxford (1969).

[10] Manna, Z., S. Ness and J. Vuillemin: Inductive Methods for Proving Properties of Programs. Comm. of the ACM 16 (1973) 491-504.

[11] Findler, N.V. (ed.): Associative networks representation and use of knowledge by computers. Academic Press, New York (1979).

ONE MORE PROPERTY OF ARRAY LANGUAGES

Marek Ejsmont [1)]

Abstract. We exhibit an array language which is accepted by a nondeterministic finite automaton A /without pebbles/ and which is log-space complete for the class of array languages accepted by Turing machines in logarithmic space. It follows, that if there exists any deterministic automaton with a finite number of pebbles which accepts the same language as 0-pebble automaton A then NL = L.

1. INTRODUCTION

In this paper we consider array languages and two kinds of array acceptors: pebble automaton and Turing array machine /TAM/. It is shown /see [Ej 84b]/ that TAM, which is a generalization of the k-tape Turing machine for string languages, is as powerful as the Turing array acceptor defined by Miligram and Rosenfeld in [MR 71]. By means of TAMs we can define complexity classes of array languages, for example, let NL^2 /L^2/ be the class of array languages accepted by nondeterministic /deterministic/ Turing array machines in logarithmic space. Note that all languages from L /NL/ belong to L^2 /NL^2/. We can generalize the definition of the log-space reducibility relation and define the log-space reducibility relation between array languages in such a way that if $L \leq M$ then L is reducible to M in the sense of the new definition. The following results are proved in [Ej 84b]:

1. There exists an array language which is complete for NL^2
2. Each language which is complete for NL is also complete for NL^2
3. $NL^2 = L^2$ iff NL = L
4. There exist array languages over 1-letter alphabet which are NL^2-complete.

Having proved 1-3 statements, it easy to get the 4-th one, interesting because of the unknown answer to the question whether there exists a language over 1-letter alphabet which is complete for NL.
Let us denote by $DPA^2(k)$ /$NPA^2(k)$/ the class of array languages accepted by deterministic /nondeterministic/ finite automata with k

---

1) Faculty of Applied Physics and Mathematics
Technical University of Gdańsk
Gdansk 80-952, Poland

pebbles. We will denote by DPA(k) and NPA(k) the counterparts of these classes for string languages. It is shown /see [BH 67]/ that for string languages the following classes are equal: NPA(1), DPA(1) and regular languages. This is not the case in 2-dimensional space. It turned out that the classes $DPA^2(0)$ and $NPA^2(0)$ are imcomparable with the class of isotonic regular array languages /see [Ro 76]/. Cook and Wang [CW 78] constructed special finite automata which accept precisely regular array languages. Blum and Hewitt [BH 67] showed that $NPA^2(0) \not\supseteq DPA^2(0)$ and $DPA^2(2) \not\supseteq DPA^2(1)$. On the other hand, in the string case we do not know whether DPA(2) = NPA(2) holds. Since graph accessibility problem, which is complete for NL, is accepted by some nondeterministic 2-pebble automaton we know that $NPA(2) \subset \bigcup_k DPA(k)$ implies NL = L.

In this paper we are going to introduce an array language over 1-letter alphabet, called projection accessibility problem /PAP/. We show that PAP is complete for NL^2 and it is accepted by a nondeterministic finite automaton /without pebbles/. As a corrolary we get that the positive answer to the question whether there exists such $k \geq 1$ that $NPA^2(0) \subset DPA^2(k)$ would prove L = NL and $L^2 = NL^2$.

2. PRELIMINARIES

Let Σ be a finite set and $\# \notin \Sigma$ be a distinguished symbol. The mapping E from Z^2 /where Z is the set of integers/ into $\Sigma \cup \{\#\}$ such that a preimage Pre of Σ is finite and path connected - we call an array. We shall denote the number of points under E not being # by $|E|$. The image of $(i,j) \in Z^2$ under E will be called the value of (i,j). Let us denote by $\Sigma^{\square}$ the equivalence classes of the translation relation of the set of all arrays. A k-tape Turing array machine /TAM/ consists of a 2-dimensional input tape, a finite state control, k -dimensional work tapes, a 4-way read only input head and k 2-way read/write work heads. Formally, we define TAM to be 6-tuple $M = (Q, \Sigma, \Gamma, \delta, g_s, g_a)$, where Q is the set of states, Σ is the finite input alphabet, $\# \notin \Sigma$, Γ is the finite, work tape alphabet, $g_s, g_a \in Q$ are the starting and accepting states respectively. δ is the transition function: δ: $Q \times \Sigma \times P'(\Delta) \times \Gamma^k \to P(Q \times \Delta \times \Gamma^k \times \{l,r,n\}^k)$, where $\Delta = \{l,r,u,d\}$ is the set of directions/left, right, up, down/, $P'(\Delta)$ denotes all nonempty subsets of Δ and n means "nomove". Let for each $P \in Z^2$ Pd denote the nearest point to P in the direction $d \in \Delta$. At each P of the input array E not being #, M recognizes by its input head the value of that point and the set valP, where $valP = \{d \in \Delta : E(Pd) \neq \#\}$. When the input head of M visits the point P of E, M is allowed to move its input head in the direction which belongs to valP. We assume that TAMs start at the lower left hand point of Pre /i.e. not being # /. The remaining details of the accepting computation on the input E of M and the notion of deterministic and nondeterministic TAM are defined as usual. Let us denote by NL^2 /L^2/ the class of array languages which are recognized by nondeterministic /deterministic/ TAMs with $\log|E|$ space, where E is the input array.

We define another device which is able to reduce one array language to another. A L^2-transducer is a deterministic input /output TAM with a 4-way read only input head, a 1-way write only output head and /for input array E, $|E| = n$/ log n long a 1-dimensional work tape. The output tape is a quadrant of 2-dimensional checkerboard space bounded from the bottom and left. The output head at the very beginning occupies the leftmost point of the lowest row. We assume that the output head can only shift to the right i.e. it writes down the letters from the output alphabet row by row and when it finishes writing in some row, the output head shifts immediately into the leftmost point of the row above. The function f, $f: \Sigma^{\square} \longrightarrow \Sigma^{\square}$ is said to be L^2-computable if there exists a L^2-transducer such that when it starts computation with an array E on its input tape, it halts with the array f E having been written on its output tape. Let $L, M \subset \Sigma^{\square}$ be any array languages and $\mathcal{C}$ be any class of array languages over Σ. We say that

1. L is reducible to M /written $L \leq_2 M$/ iff there exists function f, $f: \Sigma^{\square} \longrightarrow \Sigma^{\square}$ such that: f is L^2-computable and $E \in L$ iff $f(E) \in M$ for all $E \in \Sigma^{\square}$.
2. L is $\mathcal{C}$-hard iff $M \leq_2 L$ for all $M \in \mathcal{C}$.
3. L is $\mathcal{C}$-complete iff $L \in \mathcal{C}$ and L is $\mathcal{C}$-hard.

The following theorem says that the relation "$\leq_2$" has the same properties as the relation "$\leq$" in one dimensional case.

Theorem 1. Let $L, M, N \subset \Sigma^{\square}$ be any array languages over $\Sigma^{\square}$. Then
1. if $L \leq_2 M$ and $M \leq_2 N$ then $L \leq_2 M$
2. if $L \leq_2 M$ and $M \in L^2$ or $M \in NL^2$ then L belong to the same class
3. if $L \leq_2 M$ and L is NL^2-hard then M is NL^2-hard.

The proof is essentionally the same as in [Jo 75]. □

We define a finite n-pebble automaton as a system $U_n = \{Q, \Sigma, K, \delta, g_s, g_a\}$, where Q is the finite set of states, Σ is the finite input alphabet and $\# \notin \Sigma$, K is the finite set of pebbles and card(K) = n, $g_s, g_a \in Q$ are the starting and accepting states respectively. δ is the transition function $\delta: Q \times P'(\Delta) \times \Sigma \times 3^K \longrightarrow P(Q \times \Delta \times 3^K)$, which satisfies the conditions: if $(g', d, \beta) \in \delta(g, D, \sigma, \alpha)$ then $d \in D$ and $\alpha^{-1}(\{0,1\}) = \beta^{-1}(\{0,1\})$. Let $\alpha \in 3^K$ be a pebble situation and $A \in K$ be one of the pebbles, and if $\alpha(A)$ is equal to 0,1,2 that means the automaton is carrying A, the pebble A is lying at the point which the automaton is just visiting, and the pebble A is lying somewhere else respectively. A pebble automaton starts at the leftmost point not being # of the lowest row of the input array in the starting state g_s with all its pebbles. After t steps the automaton stays at the point P_t in the state g_t scanning $\sigma_t \in \Sigma$. In t+1 step the automaton recognizes the set D_t of accessible directions and the pebble situation $\alpha_t \in 3^K$. If $(g,d,\beta) \in \delta(g_t,D_t,\sigma_t,\alpha_t)$, then it means that the automaton can move in the direction $d \in \Delta$, enter the state g and change the pebble situation α_t into β. The automaton A accepts the input array E when there exists a computation of A on E such that A enters the accepting state g_a after a finite number of steps. We say that n-pebble automaton is a deterministic one if δ maps each element of $Q \times P'(\Delta) \times \Sigma \times 3^K$ into the set containing at most one element; otherwise, it is nondeterministic.

3. PROJECTION ACCESSIBILITY PROBLEM

Let us define a projection as a labyrinth /i.e. an array over 1-letter alphabet/. A projection consists of the so-called frame which is a boundary of some rectangle and of "levels" and paths between the levels. Each level is simply a horizontal line which connects the vertical sides of the frame, but is not a horizontal side of the frame. The distance between the nearest levels and between the horizontal side of the frame and the nearest level are equal to 3. For the simplicity of the description let us assume that the co-ordinates of the lower left hand point of the frame are (0,0) and the length of the vertical side of the frame is equal to 3l, where $l = 1,2,\ldots$ Let us code all levels from the lowest to the highest by the numbers $1,2,\ldots,l-1$ respectively. The path which connects the i-th level with the j-th one, $i \neq j$, is a vertical line which starts on the i-th level and ends at the point of which the vertical co-ordinate is equal to $3j + \frac{j-i}{|j-i|}$ /the line extends from the i-th level to the j-th one and has one point more/. We say that the level i is directly connected with the level j when there is a path which connects the i-th level with the j-th one. The level j is connected with the level l when there exist levels $j=i_1,i_2,\ldots,i_n=l$ for some n and i_k,i_{k+1} are directly connected for all $k=1,2,\ldots,n-1$. Projection accessibility problem denotes all projections such that the lowest level is connected with the upmost one. First we prove the following theorem.

Theorem 2. PAP is accepted by some nondeterministic finite automaton.

Proof. First the automaton checks whether the given array is a projection. At the very beginning the automaton checks the following conditions:

1. the horizontal line L, the leftmost point of which is being visited by the automaton, is the lower side of the frame.
2. an input array consists of rectangles the horizontal length of which is equal to 3, the lower side of the lowest rectangle is the line L, the upper side of each rectangle is the lower side of the next rectangle, the upper side of the upmost rectangle is the upper side of the frame.
3. the horizontal sides of these rectangles create the horizontal sides of the frame.

It is not difficult to prove that there exists a deterministic automaton A which is able to check conditions 1-3. When conditions 1-3 are valid, then we know that the input array satisfies conditions according to the frame and levels. Let us observe that the conditions 1 and 2 imply that no vertical line has a common point with the frame. Next, the automaton A checks conditions according to the paths. At each point P of each level, which does not belong to the frame and such that $valP \not\supseteq \{l,r\}$, A checks the following conditions:

A. at the point P a path starts /card(valP) = 3/.

B. at the point Pd or Pu a path ends /card(valPd) = 1 or card(valPu) = 1 /.

C. card(valP) = 4 and the points Pd, Pdd, Pu, Puu belong to the array.

When A /B/ is valid, then the automaton A goes to the last /to the starting/ point of the path, checks whether that path satisfies the appropriate conditions and comes back to the point P. When C is valid, then A will check the conditions of that path when it visits another level. When $valP \not\supseteq \{l,r\}$ and none of A,B,C /for the lowest and the upmost level: neither A nor B/ is valid, the automaton rejects the array. Having decided that the array is a projection, the automaton checks whether the array belongs to PAP. Starting from the first level A chooses /nondeterministically/ one of the paths which starts on this level, goes to the before last point of this path and reaches a new level. On each level the automaton checks whether it is the upmost one and if it is not, it chooses one of the paths which starts on this level and reaches a new level. When the lowest level is connected with the upmost one, then the automaton finds a way to the upmost level using the above algorithm and accepts the projection.□

In order to prove that PAP is NL^2-complete we would like to recall the graph accessibility problem /GAP/. Let $G = (V,E)$ be a finite directed graph, where $V = \{1,2,\ldots,k\}$ for some $k \geq 1$. By the encoding code (G) of G we denote the list $[bin(1),bin(n_1^1),\ldots,bin(n_{t(1)}^1)]$ $[bin(2),\ldots,bin(n_{t(2)}^2)]$ ... $[bin(k),bin(n_1^k),\ldots,bin(n_{t(k)}^k)]$, where bin(j) denotes the binary representation of the integer j /with no leading zeroes/ and for $1 \leq i \leq k$, $1 \leq l \leq t(i)$ n^i occurs on the list iff $(i, n_1^i) \in E$. GAP denotes the set of all encoding of graphs $G = (V, E)$, which possess a path from the vertex 1 to k.

Using the properties of the transformation relation between array languages we are able to prove

Theorem 3. PAP is NL^2-complete.

Proof. PAP belongs to NL^2 because it is accepted by a 0-pebble automaton. In [Ej 84b] it is shown that GAP is NL^2-complete. We have only to prove that GAP $\leq_2$ PAP. We describe the construction of L^2-transducer M which transforms the set of all encodings of graphs to the set of projections which have the following properties:

- the horizontal length of the frame is equal to k^2+1 /where k is the number of the vertexes of the input graph/
- the output projection has k levels.

If the input array is not a code of any graph, M writes on its output only the letter "a". Let us assume that on the input tape of M there is the encoding code(G) of a graph $G = (V, E)$. We may assume that the co-ordinates of the edges of the frame will be $(0,0)$, $(3(k+1),0)$, $(3(k+1),k^2+1)$, $(0,k^2+1)$. The projection which M will draw on the output tape will have a path from the i-th level to the n_1^i-th one iff $(i, n_1^i) \in E$. The horizontal co-ordinate of that path will be $(i-1)k+1$. Let M write the letter "a" at the point P to mark that P belongs to the output projection. We describe how M writes the letter "a" drawing the $(3m-1)$-th row /i.e. the row below to the m-th level/. First M writes the letter "a" at the point $(0, 3m-1)$ because this point belongs to the frame of the projection. Now suppose that $m \neq j$ and M's output head occupies the point $((j-1)\cdot k+1, 3m-1)$. M considers first the n_1^j-th node and checks whether one of the following inequalities holds: $n_1^j \leq m < j$ or $j < m \leq n_1^j$. If it is the case, then M writes down the letter "a" at the $((j-1)\cdot k+1, 3m-1)$ point and shifts the output head to the right. Then it considers the n_2^j-th node etc. Having considered the $n_{t(j)}^j$-th node, M shifts its output head to the point $(j\cdot k+1, 3m-1)$ and if $j < k$ then M considers the n_1^{j+1}-th node etc. In the case when $m = j$, the output head writes down the letter "a" at the points $((j-1)\cdot k+p, 3m-1)$ iff $j > n_p^j$, where $1 \leq p \leq t(m)$. /Similarly the machine draws the $3m+1$-th row./ Drawing the $(3m)$-th row /i.e. the m-th level/ M writes the letter "a" at each point from $(3m, 0)$ to $(3m, k^2+1)$. Let us observe that M uses not more than logarithmic space and it follows from the construction that the graph G has a path from the node 1 to k iff the first level of the output projection is connected with the last one. This completes the proof of the Theorem 3. □

Using the result from [Ej 84b] that $NL^2 = L^2$ iff $NL = L$ we get

Theorem 4. There exists $k \geq 1$ such $NPA^2(0) \subset DPA^2(k)$ iff $NL = L$ /$NL^2 = L^2$/.

REFERENCES

[BH 67] Blum, M. and C. Hewitt: Automata on 2-dimensional tape. - In: Proc. 8 th IEEE Symp. Switching Theory, 1967, 155-160.

[CW 78] Cook, C. R. and P. S. P. Wang: A Chomsky hierarchy of isotonic array grammars and languages. - In: Comp. Graphics Image Processing 8, 1978, 144-152.

[Ej 84a] Ejsmont, M.: Problems in labyrinth decidable by pebble automata. Elektron. Informationsverarb. u. Kybernetik 12 (1984), 623-632.

[Ej 84b] Ejsmont, M.: Array languages acceptable in logarithmic space. submitted to Information and Control, 1984.

[Jo 75] Jones, N. D.: Space bounded reducibility among combinatorial problems. J. Comput. System Sci. 11 (1975), 62-85.

[MR 71] Miligram, D. L. and A. Rosenfeld: Array automata and array grammars. - In: Proc. IFIP Congres 71, Ljubljana, Yugosl., Aug. 23 - 28, 1971. - Amsterdam: North-Holland Pub. Comp., 1972, 166-173.

[Ro 76] Rosenfeld, A.: Some notes on finite-state picture languages. Inform. Control 29 (1976), 177-184.

THEORETICAL ASPECTS OF Σ-PROGRAMMING

Goncharov S.S., Sviridenko D.I.

1. Introduction

Logical-mathematical ideas have lately gained great recognition and popularity in programming. It is sufficient to mention such directions as logical and functional programming, relational data bases, synthesis of programs, abstract data types, languages of specifications and design of programs. The analysis of these and related approaches allows one to make a conclusion that they have certain conceptual similarity. For instance, the concept of logical programming may be satisfactorily realized in functional environment. At the same time, functional programming may be considered as a special (equational) case of logical programming. The same might be said about the relational approach as well. One can easily trace the connection of the abstract data types (ADT) concept with the relational approach. In terms of abstract data types there is well set-up and solved the problem of extracting programs from the proofs (synthesis of programs). Such a conceptual unity makes one think that certain synthesis of logical-mathematical concepts of computer information processing is possible which, in its turn, will make it possible to uniformly interpret a lot of programming problems. The present article belongs to such investigations on developing common logical apparatus of programming treating all these concepts from the same viewpoint.

Described in the article are theoretical aspects of a new concept of programming, called Σ-programming. The foundation of this concept is made up of ideas and methods of mathematical logic and, in particular, of the fact that computable functions admit "simple" formula description. As the foundation of such descriptions in Σ-programming there were chosen the so-called Σ-formulae of the language of the first-order predicate calculus.

2. Methodology of Σ-programming

One of the basic notions of Σ-programming is that of "a task". A task in Σ-programming is represented by its specification. Among specifications of tasks there is a separate class of the so-called Σ-specifications which may be "executed". It is supposed that the "execution" of specifications is realized by some device - Σ-computer. Such Σ-specifications are Σ-programs. Thus, in the concept of Σ-programming one points out a language in which specifications of tasks are written, in particular, Σ-specifications, and Σ-computer is some abstract device "executing" specifications. The present paper deals, in the main, with the methodology and theory of Σ-language, specifications and Σ-programs.

The process of Σ-programming starts with writing a rather abstract (with respect to the level of Σ-computer) specification of the task which is to be solved and finishes with the creation of a rather concrete (i.e. perceptible by Σ-computer) Σ-program. Since the initial specification may essentially differ in its form from Σ-specification, then there arises the problem of constructing (by the specification of the problem) the corresponding Σ-program (program design). In mathematical and programming practice of solving problems the dynamic aspects are interwoven with the static ones. Therefore, the language in which the problems are formulated and their solutions are written as Σ-programs must allow one to completely and conveniently represent specific peculiarities of problem domains under investigation, their dynamic and static aspects. To do this, a language contains a developed <u>system of imperatives</u> (the initial operations and means of combining new ones) and <u>system of declaratives.</u> The latter are represented by formulae of the special language of logic of the first-order predicates. From the fact that Σ-specifications should be "executed" descriptions there follows the requirement of the existence of their "natural" imperative interpretation. This circumstance explains the fact that, as Σ-specification, formulae of special kind have been chosen - the so-called <u>Σ-formulae</u>. "Execution" of Σ-formulae implies the verification of their <u>truthfulness</u> in a model. Such verification may be realized in various ways, syntactic ones (deducibility) among them. The main thing here is the efficiency of the methods used (i.e. the efficiency of "computations"). If the users of Σ-language are only interested in the possibility of task specification in the form of Σ-specification, then the choice of the strategy of execution is performed by Σ-translator. Thus, we speak about universal "built-in" verification strategies of Σ-formula to be true. But if the user is interested in the efficiency of Σ-specification, then Σ-language should allow one to describe the "computation" strategy, assuming such a description to be one of components of Σ-programs. Thus, in the general case Σ-program is expressed by a construction consisting of 2 components: the former shows <u>what</u> Σ-program must do (the logical component), the latter determines <u>how</u> this"<u>what</u>" should be done. Here both components have particularly declarative form - the form of Σ-formulae.Such a viewpoint upon Σ-programs gives essentially mathematical character to the process of Σ-designing.

Another way of improving efficiency of Σ-programs is their <u>transformation</u>. It is natural to expect such transformations to be realized within the framework and by means of Σ-language. Moreover, we demand that within the framework of Σ-language the possibility of logical foundation of correctness of Σ-program transformations could be realized. Here we touched upon the fact we would like to consider in more detail. That is <u>the problem of self-applicability</u>. In the present case this problem is of interest to us not only in the sense it is understood in the mathematical computation theory (for instance, when the sensibility of functional expressions of the form $f(f)$ is studied), but in the sense that the investigation of a language, the description of constructions over it could be realized within the framework and by means of this very language. Besides, unlike, say, Peano arithmetic where the hierarchy of descriptions of constructive objects and of constructions themselves can be imbedded into the initial formalism by means of suitable enumerations which are arithmetic constructions themselves, we mean the explicit description and presentation of all the necessary constructions. For instance, for a user, the requirements of simplicity,convenience and clearness are essential. Such "self-applicable" languages (for instance, a natural language) which possess, on the one hand, the above advantages, are rather difficult to be studied semantically. Therefore, demanding "explicit self-applicability" of a Σ -language one should expect non-trivial arrangement of this language and its theory, and non-traditional architectural solutions in creating a Σ -computer.

Creating a programming language one should, first of all, have a good idea of its semantics, and, in particular, solve in advance the problem of semantic representation of the notion "constructive object". By a constructive object we mean the finite object equipped with "the inner system of coordinates" (together with the indication of some initial element - "beginning of coordinates") which allows one to uniquely sinle out in an object any of its components. Finite words, graphs, trees, automata, etc. may serve as examples of constructive objects. For us, the most adequate semantic representation of the notion "constructive object" is the finite list: on the one hand, finite lists have certain codifying universality - all the above examples of constructive objects admit their natural representation in the form of lists, on the other hand, the structure of data "list" admits satisfactory algorithmic realization.

A constructive object may be considered as an element of some "real world" formally assigned, say, in the form of a multi-base model (maybe, with some "superstructure" above this model). Since we deal with the constructivity of representations, it is most natural to concieve such a model intensionally: either as some procedure generating the elements of a model (and those of the "superstructure"), or as a constructive (positive or strongly constructive) model. It is natural to call such models (even if they are of rather abstract character) as data structures or just data, and their elements are said to be data elements. Besides, a constructive object may be considered as an object of a "world" represented as a system of knowledges about this world, for instance, as a formal theory. Such a theory, among all data, points out those which are its models. In certain sense the theory is some single (indivisible) description of the entire class of its models, i.e. as a type of a class of data structures. Just for this reason we will below consider formal theories as the most adequate formalization of the notion "abstract data type". At the same time, the theory itself acts as some abstract structure of data which is realized in our language.

When solving some problem, we will have, besides the use of knowledge about some models representing the "world" to which the problem belongs, create some additional, auxiliary constructions above the model, handle them and discuss them. Since we are interested in a constructive, algorithmic solution, it is natural that such auxiliary constructions should necessarily be constructive objects and have, as it has already been mentioned, explicit character. So, we need a model for which one could simply and conveniently realize all the necessary constructions of constructive objects to solve problems. It is therefore that , speaking of a model above as of a formal representation of problem domain, we have mentioned some "superstructure" above it. Such a superstructure may be expressed by list structures above multi-base models. A model and its superstructure are just the formal construction in which both the interesting for us subject domain and all the means of handling the necessary constructions are contained. Dealing with such a "two-tier" model we use syntactically described constructions in terms of a Σ-language. Therefore, it is natural to require that for "reasonable" descriptions in our model there exist the corresponding constructions (realizations of descriptions). In this case the structurality of a list superstructure is naturally reflected in a language.

List superstructure, as the one of all finite lists above the initial multi-base model, turns out to be arranged rather uniformly. Therefor it may be regarded as a model (data structure) of some formal theory. Thus, in the framework of Σ-language we will deal with formal theories where one part is the theory of subject domain, the other being the formal theory of lists above the given domain. Investigation of such formal theories will be made in the framework of the so-called theory of list extensions GES. A meaningful mathematical theory of list extensions is our further tool in constructing both the theory of Σ-language and the theory of Σ-computer. Within the framework of this theory one could study logical-mathematical models of designing systems of Σ-programs as well. Thus, the theory GES may be considered as the theoretical foundation of programming. The present paper concerns mainly with this theory.

As we will see below, there are very efficient means in the GES theory to represent and study a wide class of effective constructions used in programming. The totality of these constructions turns out to be closed with respect to various recursive definitions. The main body of a Σ-language is a set of initial imperatives (which may be considered to be the simplest operations of a language) and a set of initial predicates. In terms of this basis one may construct rather complicated Σ-programs. However, in a Σ-language there is the possibility of natural extension of basis notions. The necessity of such an extension is due to many reasons. The main of them is the convenience of using Σ-language.

The basic mechanism of the conservative extension of the signature of a Σ-language is the construction of initial objects for systems of quasi-identities, Σ-definability and representability. It also seems rather perspective (but it requires additional argumentation) for conservative extension of the basis of a Σ-language to use a mechanism similar to that of "extracting programs from constructive proofs". Note that this mechanism is used in Σ-programming when designing Σ-programs. Such mechanisms of constructive extension play the main role in the problem of orientation of a Σ-language. The solution for this problem is the generation of abstract data types which formally represent the notion of a subject domain under consideration. And again, due to the "self-applicability" property of a Σ-language, the above mechanisms and constructions are used and improved in the framework of a language under consideration.

3. The theory of list extension GES

Let σ_0 be a multi-sorted signature with a set of sorts I. Denote by σ the signature $\sigma_0 \cup \{\underline{head}, \underline{tail}, \underline{cons}, \underline{conc}, \underline{nil}, \in, \sqsubseteq, S'\}$ with a set of sorts $I \cup \{S\}$, and by σ^* - the signature $\sigma \cup \{Q_1^{m_1}, \ldots, Q_n^{m_n}, \ldots; F_1^{n_1}, \ldots, F_\ell^{n_\ell}, \ldots\}$ with a set of sorts $I \cup \{S\}$, where Q_i and F_j are predicate and functional variables not contained in σ. The terms and formulae of the signatures σ_0, σ and σ^* are defined as usual. It should only be noted that the following item is added to the definition of the notion of the formula: if Ψ is a formula, t is a term of a sort S, and x is a variable, then the expressions $(\forall x \in t)\Psi$, $(\exists x \in t)\Psi$, $(\forall x \sqsubseteq t)\Psi$ and $(\exists x \sqsubseteq t)\Psi$ are also formulae; in these recordings the quantors are called <u>restricted.</u>

The notion of a Δ_0-formula, Σ- and Π-formulae are introduced similar to [1]. Note that for Σ-formulae of the signature σ^* it is necessary that predicate and functional variables are contained in such formulae <u>positively</u>.

Consider a model $\mathfrak{M}$ of signature σ. Objects of the sort S are called <u>lists</u> below. We say that a list α is an ordered pair of elements α_1 and α_2 and denote it by $\langle \alpha_1, \alpha_2 \rangle$ if the following Δ_0-property is valid:

$$\underline{ORDPAIR}(\alpha) \leftrightharpoons (\exists \alpha_1 \in \alpha)(\exists \alpha_2 \in \alpha)(\alpha = \underline{cons}(\underline{cons}(\underline{nil}, \alpha_1), \alpha_2))$$

Thus, the recording $\langle \alpha_1, \alpha_2 \rangle$ is in fact the shortening for $\underline{cons}(\underline{cons}(\underline{nil}, \alpha_1), \alpha_2)$.

Consider also the Δ_0-property $LF(\alpha, \beta)$ ("a list α is a list function of the list β"):

$$\underline{LF}(\alpha,\beta) \leftrightharpoons (\forall \gamma \in \alpha)(\underline{ORDPAIR}(\gamma) \& (\forall \alpha_1 \in \gamma)(\forall \alpha_2 \in \gamma)((\langle \alpha_1, \alpha_2\rangle = \gamma \rightarrow \alpha_1 \sqsubseteq \beta)) \& (\forall \delta \sqsubseteq \beta)(\exists \gamma \in \alpha)(\underline{cons}(\underline{nil},\delta) = \underline{tail}(\gamma) \& (\forall \alpha^1 \sqsubseteq \alpha)(\forall \alpha^2 \sqsubsetneq \alpha)(\exists \delta' \in \underline{tail}(\underline{head}(\alpha^1))(\exists \delta'' \in \underline{tail}(\underline{head}(\alpha^2))(\delta'' \sqsubsetneq \delta')).$$

A list α which is a list function of the list β may be interpreted as a tabular function whose arguments are the first segments of the list β.

Call α a <u>hereditary list function</u> β (the corresponding predicate denote as $HLF(\alpha,\beta)$ if α is a list function β, and for any $\gamma \in \alpha$ there holds:

1. If $\underline{head}(\underline{tail}(\gamma)) = \underline{nil}$, then $\underline{head}(\gamma) = \underline{nil}$;
2. If $\gamma = \langle \alpha_1, \alpha_2\rangle$ and $\alpha_1 = \underline{cons}(\alpha_1', a)$, then $\alpha_2 = \underline{cons}(\alpha_2', b)$ and $\langle \alpha_1', \alpha_2'\rangle \in \alpha$.

Note that the pair $\langle \alpha_1', \alpha_2'\rangle$ in the list α should be located just before the pair $\langle \alpha_1, \alpha_2\rangle$. The hereditary list function α of the list β may be considered as a "properly arranged" tabular function inheriting its previous values.

The formal theory GES of list superstructures above the model $\mathfrak{M}$, as its axioms, has the universal closures of the following formulae:

<u>Axiom of empty list:</u> $\neg(\exists \delta)(\delta \in \underline{nil})$.

<u>Uniqueness axiom:</u> $[\underline{cons}(\alpha,\delta) = \underline{cons}(\alpha',\delta') \rightarrow \alpha = \alpha' \& \delta = \delta']$, where α, α' are the variables of the type $\langle\{s\}\rangle$ (i.e. of the type <u>list</u>) and δ, δ' - of the type $\langle I \cup \{s\}\rangle$.

Below, where one uniquely sees from the context what type of variables is considered, we omit the description of these variables.

<u>Axioms of list operations:</u> $\underline{tail}(\underline{cons}(\alpha,\delta)) = \alpha$;
$\underline{head}(\underline{cons}(\alpha,\delta)) = \delta$;

$(\neg(\alpha = \underline{nil}) \rightarrow \underline{cons}(\underline{tail}(\alpha), \underline{head}(\alpha)) = \alpha)$;
$\underline{tail}(\underline{nil}) = \underline{head}(\underline{nil}) = \underline{nil}$;
$\underline{cons}(\underline{conc}(\alpha,\beta),\gamma) = \underline{conc}(\alpha,(\underline{conc}(\beta,\gamma))$;
$\underline{cons}(\underline{conc}(\alpha,\beta),\delta) = \underline{conc}(\alpha, \underline{cons}(\beta,\delta))$;
$\underline{conc}(\underline{nil},\alpha) = \underline{conc}(\alpha,\underline{nil}) = \alpha$.

<u>Axioms of list predicates:</u>

$\alpha \in \beta \leftrightarrow \exists \gamma_0, \gamma_1 (\beta = \underline{conc}(\underline{cons}(\gamma_0, \alpha), \gamma_1))$;

$\alpha \sqsubseteq \beta \leftrightarrow \exists \gamma_0 (\beta = \underline{conc}(\alpha, \gamma_0))$.

Induction axioms: $([\Phi]^{x}_{nil} \,\&\, (\forall\alpha)(\forall\delta)([\Phi]^{x}_{\alpha} \rightarrow [\Phi]^{x}_{\underline{cons}(\alpha,\delta)}) \rightarrow$
$\rightarrow \forall\alpha\,\Phi$,

where Φ is an arbitrary formula and the recording $[\Phi]^{x}_{t}$ means the substitution, instead of all free occurences of the variable x into Φ, of the term t so that there is no collision of variables.

Extensionality axiom: $\alpha = \beta \leftrightarrow (\forall\gamma \sqsubseteq \alpha)(\gamma \sqsubseteq \beta \,\&\, [\neg(\gamma = \beta) \rightarrow$
$\rightarrow (\exists\delta \in \alpha)(\underline{cons}(\gamma,\delta) \sqsubseteq \alpha \,\&\, \underline{cons}(\gamma,\delta) \sqsubseteq \beta)])$

Axiom of Δ_0-separation: if $\Phi(\alpha)$ is a Δ_0-formula with free variable α, then there takes place

$$(\forall\beta)(\exists\alpha)(\underline{HLF}(\alpha,\beta) \,\&\, (\forall\beta' \sqsubseteq \beta)(\forall\delta \in \beta)(\underline{cons}(\beta',\delta) \sqsubseteq \beta \rightarrow$$
$$\rightarrow (\forall\gamma_1 \in \alpha)(\forall\gamma_2 \in \alpha)(\underline{head}(\underline{tail}(\gamma_1)) = \beta' \,\&\, \underline{head}(\underline{tail}(\gamma_2)) =$$
$$\underline{cons}(\beta',\delta) \rightarrow (\Phi(\delta) \rightarrow \underline{cons}(\underline{head}(\gamma_1),\delta) = \underline{head}(\gamma_2)) \,\&\, (\neg\Phi(\delta)$$
$$\rightarrow \underline{head}(\gamma_1) = \underline{head}(\gamma_2)))) \,\&\, (\forall\gamma \in \alpha)(\underline{head}(\underline{tail}(\gamma)) = \underline{nil} \rightarrow$$
$$\rightarrow \underline{head}(\gamma) = \underline{nil}))$$

The present axiom states that for each list there is a tabular function selecting from it only the elements on which the property Φ holds.

Axiom of Δ_0-collection: if $\Phi(\alpha,\beta)$ is a Δ_0-formula, then the following holds:

$$(\forall\beta)((\forall\alpha \in \beta)(\exists\delta)\Phi(\alpha,\delta) \rightarrow (\exists\alpha)(HLF(\alpha,\beta) \,\&\, (\forall\gamma \in \alpha)$$
$$((head(tail(\gamma)) = nil \rightarrow (head(\gamma) = nil)) \,\&\, (\neg(head(tail(\gamma))$$
$$= nil) \rightarrow \Phi(head(head(tail(\gamma))), head(head(\gamma)))))).$$

This axiom implies the possibility, in every particular case (i.e. for each list β), to realize "functional correspondence" defined by the formula Φ, having restricted ourselves by some list α only, not by the whole universe.

This completes the list of axioms describing the list superstructure above the model $\mathfrak{M}$. We would like to draw the readers' attention to the following fact. The form of the axioms is rather cumbersome, but if you analyse them carefully you will see the reason for this inconvenience - the axioms <u>are constructive</u> in their nature since they not only state the existence of the necessary objects, but they also tell us how they are to be constructed. Such constructivity is the result of <u>determinedness</u> of list constructions unlike, say, theoretical-multiple constructions [1,3].

Consider some properties of the GES theory illustrating its adequacy to the goals mentioned in Section 2.

Let Φ be some formula and v be a variable absent from its recording. We write $\Phi_{\in}^{(v)}$, denoting by this result the replacement of all contained in Φ unbounded quantors by the bounded ones:

$$\exists\alpha \quad \text{for} \quad \exists\alpha\in v, \text{ and}$$

$$\forall\alpha \quad \text{for} \quad \forall\alpha\in v,$$

and we write $\Phi_{\subseteq}^{(v)}$ realizing the replacements of the form:

$$\exists\alpha \quad \text{for} \quad \exists\alpha\subseteq v,$$

$$\forall\alpha \quad \text{for} \quad \forall\alpha\subseteq v.$$

But if there were changes in Φ of all unbounded quantors for the bounded ones without indication of the kind of change ($\in$ or $\subseteq$), then we denote the result of the change by $\Phi^{(v)}$. Note that $\Phi_{\in}^{(v)}$, $\Phi_{\subseteq}^{(v)}$ and $\Phi^{(v)}$ are Δ_0-formulae. But if Φ is already a Δ_0-formula, then

$$\Phi = \Phi_{\in}^{(v)} = \Phi_{\subseteq}^{(v)} = \Phi^{(v)}.$$

<u>Theorem 3.1</u> (the principle of Σ-reflexion). For any Σ-formula of the signature σ there holds:

a) $GES \vdash \Phi \leftrightarrow (\exists v)\Phi_{\in}^{(v)}$;

b) $GES \vdash \Phi \leftrightarrow (\exists v)\Phi_{\subseteq}^{(v)}$;

c) $GES \vdash \Phi \leftrightarrow (\exists v)\Phi^{(v)}$.

Below the formula of the form $(\exists\alpha)\Phi(\alpha)$, where Φ is a Δ_0-formula, is called <u>Σ_1-formula.</u> Thus, Theorem 3.1 implies that every Σ-formula is equivalent in GES to Σ_1-formula.

Above we have pointed out a class of Σ-formulae. On the other hand, one may point out a class of Π-formulae - the smallest class containing Δ_0-formulae and closed with respect to disjunction, conjunction, bounded quantification and unbounded generality quantor. It is obvious that the negation of Σ-formula is logically equivalent to Π-formula and vice versa. The formula, which is logically equivalent to Σ-formula and at the same time to Π-formula, is called <u>Δ-formula</u>. It turns out that in the GES theory the axiom of Δ_0-collection is generalized to Σ-collection, and the axiom of Δ_0-separation to Δ-separation.

<u>Definition 3.2.</u> Let $\Phi(\bar{x},y)$ be an Σ-formula of the signature σ, for which there holds

$$GES \vdash (\forall\bar{x})(\exists! y)\Phi(\bar{x},y), \text{ where } \bar{x} = \langle x_1, \ldots, x_n\rangle$$

and F is an n-dimensional functional symbol not belonging to the signature σ. Put

$$(F) \quad F(\bar{x}) = y \leftrightarrow \Phi(\bar{x}, y)$$

and assume that F is <u>Σ -definable</u> in GES. Similarly one may introduce the notion of Σ -definable predicate.

<u>Theorem 3.3.</u> For any formula $\Phi_1(\bar{z}; F)$ of the signature $\sigma \cup \{F\}$ there exists the formula Φ_2 of the signature σ such that

$$GES + (F) \vdash \Phi_1(\bar{z}, F) \leftrightarrow \Phi_2(\bar{z}).$$

If Φ_1 is a Σ -formula, then Φ_2 is also a Σ -formula. If Φ_1 is a Δ_0 -formula, then there exist such Σ - and Π -formulae Φ_2 and Φ_3 respectively (of the signature σ) that

$$GES + (F) \vdash \Phi_1 \leftrightarrow \Phi_2,$$
$$GES + (F) \vdash \Phi_1 \leftrightarrow \Phi_3$$

and GES + (F) is a conservative extension of GES.

<u>Remark</u>. Analogous theorem can be proved for predicates as well. These results and, in particular, the last item, are very important for Σ -programming in connection with remarks made in Section 2 with respect to relatively definable constructions in a Σ -language which extend it conservatively.

The construction TC(α), which is the transitive closure of the list α plays a very important role in the GES theory and in Σ -programming. Its definition is cumbersome and therefore we do not give it here. We only say that in its sense it is similar to the notion of the transitive closure of a set but which was considered together with the process of its construction.

TC(α), as a Σ -definable function is of importance in the theory of Σ -recursion making it possible to construct by any Σ -definable functions a new Σ -definable function. The possibility and correctness of such a construction is established by Theorem 3.4 which may be considered to be the analogy of Gandy theorem in the theory of admissible sets [1,2]. Before passing over to formulation let us define some constructions.

Let $\mathfrak{M}^{\sigma_0}$ be a model of signature σ_0 . A multi-base model $\mathfrak{A}(\mathfrak{M})$ of signature σ , obtained from $\mathfrak{M}$ by joining to it objects of a new sort S , we call a <u>list extension of the model</u> $\mathfrak{M}$ if $\mathfrak{A}(\mathfrak{M}) \models GES$. If $\mathfrak{A}(\mathfrak{M})$ is the list extension of $\mathfrak{M}$, then the totality of all objects of the sort S we denote by $S(\mathfrak{M})$ and call them <u>lists</u> over $\mathfrak{M}$, the set $S(\mathfrak{M})$ itself we call the <u>list superstructure</u> above $\mathfrak{M}$. Below we often denote the list extension $\mathfrak{A}(\mathfrak{M})$ by the pair $\langle \mathfrak{M}, S(\mathfrak{M}) \rangle$. The model $\langle \mathfrak{M}, S^{fin}(\mathfrak{M}) \rangle$ where $S^{fin}(\mathfrak{M})$ is a set of all finite lists above $\mathfrak{M}$ may be an example of list extension.

Let $\Phi(\bar{x},\bar{y};Q)$ where $\bar{x}$ and $\bar{y}$ are sets of free variables, Φ is the formula of the signature σ^* having positive occurences of only one predicate variable $Q \notin \sigma$, and $Q(\mathfrak{M})$ is the list extension of the model $\mathfrak{M}$. Define the operator

$$\Gamma_{\Phi,\bar{y}}(\tilde{Q}) \rightleftharpoons \{\bar{a} \mid Q(\mathfrak{M}) \models \Phi(\bar{a},\bar{y};\hat{Q})\}$$

Due to positivity of occurences of a veriable Q in Φ the operator $\Gamma_{\Phi,\bar{y}}$ is monotone, and it has the least fixed point.

<u>Theorem 3.4.</u> For any Σ-formula $\Phi(\bar{x},\bar{y};Q)$ of the signature σ^* having positive occurence of a predicate variable Q there exists a Σ-formula $\Psi(\bar{x},\bar{y})$ determining the least fixed point of the operator $\Gamma_{\Phi,\bar{y}}$ for any fixed value of parameters.

The theory of Σ-recursion may be developed in various directions. For instance, similar to paper [3] by Yu.L.Ershov, one can extend a first-order logic over the lists, having defined the dynamic logic over list extensions which possesses the same good properties as the dynamic logic above the admissible sets. The infinite variant of Σ-formulae turns out to be useful. The problem of the abstract data type and the representability problem of one data type in another are solved in GES just as naturally as in [3].

4. Conclusion

We conclude theppresent paper by considering an example of a Σ-program solving the sorting problem. The basic notions concerning Σ-programs may be found in [4].

Let σ_0 be a signature of elementary arithmetic. Suppose that one must write a Σ-program which, by every list of numbers construct an ordered list of its elements. If one does not care about the efficiency of executing a Σ-program, then it might be recorded as follows:

$$
\begin{aligned}
&S(\underline{SORT}(\alpha,\beta),\ x \le y):\\
&\quad \underline{def}\ \underline{SORT}(\alpha,\beta): [S^1(\alpha) \to (\forall x \in \alpha)(\neg S^1(x)\ \&\ (\forall y \in \beta)\\
&\qquad\qquad (\neg(\underline{tail}(y) = \underline{nil}) \to \underline{head}(\underline{tail}(y)) \le \underline{head}(x)))\\
&\qquad\qquad \&(\forall x \in \beta)(x \in \alpha)\ \&\ (\forall x \in \alpha)(x \in \beta)];\\
&\quad \underline{def}\ x \le y: (\neg S^1(x)\ \&\ \neg S^1(y)\ \&\ (\exists z)(\neg S^1(z)\ \&\ y = x + z));\\
&\qquad\qquad\qquad \underline{end}
\end{aligned}
$$

The execution of such a program means sorting out elements of the model in order to verify the truthfulness of a Σ-program S on the model. The given program may be considered as an executed Σ-specification. But if we care about the efficiency of execution, then in the Σ-program one may show more or less explicitly the algorithm (strategy) of searching the necessary elements (sorting out algorithm):

$$
\begin{array}{l}
S1(\underline{SORT}(\alpha,\beta),\ x \le y):\\
\quad \underline{def}\ \underline{SORT}(\alpha,\beta): [S^1(\alpha) \rightarrow (\exists \gamma)(\underline{LF}(\alpha,\gamma) \,\&\, \beta = \gamma(\alpha) \,\&\\
\qquad\qquad \underline{if}\ \alpha = \underline{nil}\ \underline{then}\ \gamma(\alpha) = \underline{nil}\ \underline{else}\ [(\forall x \sqsubseteq \alpha)\\
\qquad\qquad (\forall a \in \alpha)((\underline{cons}(x,a) \sqsubseteq \alpha \rightarrow (\exists \alpha_2)(\exists \alpha_1 \sqsubseteq x)(\\
\qquad\qquad \gamma(\underline{cons}(x,a)) = \langle\langle \alpha_1, a\rangle, \alpha_2\rangle \,\&\, \underline{conc}(\alpha_1,\alpha_2) = \gamma(x)\\
\qquad\quad \&\, (\forall y \in \alpha)(a \le y) \,\&\, \underline{head}(\alpha_1) \le a))]];\\
\quad \underline{def}\ x \le y : (\neg S^1(x) \,\&\, \neg S^1(y) \,\&\, (\exists z \in \langle 0,1,\ldots,y\rangle)(y = x + z);\\
\qquad\qquad\qquad \underline{end}
\end{array}
$$

Here LF is considered to be a built-in predicate. If we are not satisfied with the efficiency of the program S1,one may search for more efficient variants.

Note that Σ -programs are multipurpose since it is possible to address any of its Σ -definitions (the construction beginning with def). In Σ -programs recursive definitions are possible, one may use the call of Σ -definitions from other Σ -programs, etc. To illustrate these constructions, we write down the Σ -program of sorting out a list of numbers as follows:

$$
\begin{array}{l}
S2(\underline{SORT}(\alpha,\beta),\ \underline{PERM}(\gamma,\delta),\ \underline{ORDLIST}(\mu)):\\
\quad \underline{def}\ \underline{SORT}(\alpha,\beta): \underline{PERM}(\alpha,\beta) \,\&\, \underline{ORDLIST}(\beta);\\
\quad \underline{def}\ \underline{PERM}(\gamma,\delta): ((\forall x \in \gamma)(x \in \delta) \,\&\, (\forall x \in \delta)(x \in \gamma));\\
\quad \underline{def}\ \underline{ORDLIST}(\mu): (S^1(\mu) \rightarrow (\forall x \in \mu)[\neg S^1(x) \,\&\, (\neg(\underline{tail}(\mu)\\
\qquad\qquad = \underline{nil}) \rightarrow (\forall \beta \sqsubseteq \mu)(\underline{ORDLIST}(\beta) \,\&\\
\qquad\qquad [\underline{head}(\beta), \underline{head}(\mu) =: x,y]\ S1.\le))];\\
\qquad\qquad\qquad \underline{end}
\end{array}
$$

Note that the given program may give a list, as a sorted-out one, in which the repetitions of occurences of elements are removed.

The results of Section 3 guarantee the correctness of execution of the given Σ -program.

References

1 Barwise J. Admissible sets and structures, B., Springer-Verlag, 1975.

2 Ershov Yu.L. The principle of Σ-enumeration, Doklady AN SSSR, 1983, v.270, No 5, p. 786-788.

3 Ershov Yu.L. The dynamic logic over admissible sets, Doklady AN SSSR, 1983, v.273, No 5, p. 1045-1048.

4 Goncharov S.S., Sviridenko D.I. Σ -programming. In: Vychislitel'nye sistemy, vyp.107, Novosibirsk, 1985.

DECIDABILITY IN PRATT'S PROCESS LOGICS

Z. Habasiński [1)]

0. INTRODUCTION

We redefine here (cf. [Hab 84]) the class DPL of the Dynamic Process Logics which form a generalization of the logics from [Pra 79, Har 79]. DPL is a class of logics designated for reasoning about events during regular programs computations. For this purpose they have path formulae (interpreted over sequences of states) which describe properties of paths. The "proper" statements of the logic are interpreted over states (state formulae). A definition of a logic L from the class DPL consists in giving an interpretation to operators which create (when applied to state formulae) the elementary path formulae. If the operators meet a regularity condition then L is decidable in time $O(\exp cn^3)$. For example some logics strictly stronger than PL from [Har 79] are still decidable in that time. DPL^+ is an extension of DPL allowing Boolean combinations of the elementary path formulae. Any DPL^+-logic meeting the same regularity condition is decidable in time $O(\exp(n^3 \exp ck))$ where k is a number appreciable less than the length n of the given formula. Any DPL^+-logic with zero-ary regular operators remain decidable in contrast to the non-local PL from [HKP 82] which is known to be undecidable. At the end we list some open problems.

1. DEFINITION OF DPL^+ AND DPL

Assume we have given three countable, pairwise disjoint sets of actions: $A_0, A_1, \ldots$ propositions: $P_0, P_1, \ldots$ and operators: $O_0, O_1, \ldots$ Programs are defined exactly as in the Propositional Dynamic Logic [FL 79] with tests over state formulae, see below.

State- and path formulae are built accordingly to the following rules:

F1. any proposition is a state formula

F2. if a is a program and p is a path formula then $\langle a \rangle p$ is a state formula (called a "diament" formula)

1) Computer Centre, Technical University
Pl. Skłodowskiej-Curie 5 60-965 Poznań, Poland
and Mathematical Institute of PAS, Poznań

F3. state formulae are closed under the Boolean connectives

F4. if O is an operator of arity m and $p_1,\dots,p_m$ are state formulae then $O(p_1,\dots,p_m)$ is an (elementary) path formula

F5. path formulae are closed under the Boolean connectives

The set of DPL^+ (DPL) -formulae consists of all the state formulae defined by F1 - F5 (F1 - F4 resp.).

Let S be a nonempty set. By $\underline{S}$ we denote the set of all (finite or not) nonempty sequences of elements from S. A structure for DPL^+ is any triple $(S, \models, Tr)$ where S is a nonempty set of states, $\models$ is a relation such that $\models \subseteq S \times \{\text{state formulae}\} \cup \underline{S} \times \{\text{path formulae}\}$, $Tr: \{\text{programs}\} \longrightarrow \text{Powerset}(\underline{S})$. A structure is a model iff it fulfils the following semantic conditions:

S1. $Tr(a;b) = \{(s_0,\dots,s_i,\dots) \mid (s_0,\dots,s_i) \in Tr(a)$ and $(s_i,\dots,s_j,\dots) \in Tr(b)$ for some $i \geq 0\}$

S2. $Tr(a \cup b) = Tr(a) \cup Tr(b)$

S3. $Tr(a^*) = \{(s) \mid s \in S\} \cup \bigcup_n Tr(a^n),\ n \geq 1$

S4. $Tr(p?) = \{(s,s) \mid s \models p\}$

S5. $s \models \langle a \rangle \underline{p}$ iff there is $\underline{s} \in Tr(a)$ such that $\underline{s} \models \underline{p}$ and the first element of $\underline{s}$ is s

S6. describe the standard behaviour of $\models$ on the Boolean connectives

Example

In order to fix a logic in the DPL^+-framework we have to define the operators. Let $\underline{s} = (s_0,\dots,s_i,\dots)$ be a path in a structure. We write simply p until q instead of until(p,q) etc.

$\underline{s} \models p$ until q	iff	$\exists i : s_i \models q$ and $\forall j \leq i \quad s_j \models p$
$\underline{s} \models p$ while q	iff	$\forall i : (\forall j \leq i \quad s_j \models q) \Longrightarrow s_i \models p$
$\underline{s} \models$ next p	iff	there exists s_1 on $\underline{s}$ and $s_1 \models p$
$\underline{s} \models p$ since q	iff	$\exists i : s_i \models q$ and $\forall j > i \quad s_j \models p$
$\underline{s} \models p$ imp q	iff	$\forall i : s_i \models p \Longrightarrow \exists j > i \quad s_j \models q$
$\underline{s} \models$ even p	iff	$\forall i : s_{2i} \models p$

Using this operators some other constructs may be defined:

some p is simply true until p, all p corresponds to p while true and last p to false since p. Thus Pratt's "during" is expressible in DPL^+ as [a]some p and in DPL as $\neg\langle a \rangle$all$\neg p$. Harel's ψ-formula is expressible in DPL^+ as [a](p imp q) or as $\neg\langle a \rangle(\neg q$ since $p)$ in DPL, and is not definable in PL from [Har 79].

2. DECIDABILITY CRITERION

In this chapter we restrict the semantics of programs to sets of finite path only. Let $D \subseteq \text{Subformulae}(p) \cup \{\neg q \mid q \in \text{Subformulae}(p)\}$

be a <u>description</u> <u>of</u> p iff the following holds for any $q \in$ Subformulae(p) : $q \in D$ iff $\neg q \notin D$. The set of all descriptions for p is denoted by Des(p). An automaton $\mathfrak{A}$ accepting finite strings on the alphabet Des(p) <u>defines</u> the path formula <u>p</u> iff for any path $(s_0,\dots,s_k)$ in any model we have:

$(s_0,\dots,s_k) \models \underline{p}$ iff $\mathfrak{A}$ accepts $D_0 \dots D_k$ where $D_i = \{q \mid s_i \models q$ and q is a subformula of $p\}$.

Let O be an operator of arity m. O is <u>regular</u> iff there is a constant c such that for any state formulae $q_1,\dots,q_m$ there is an usual finite-state automaton $\mathfrak{A}$ on the alphabet $Des(O(q_1,\dots,q_m))$ such that:

$\mathfrak{A}$ defines $O(q_1,\dots,q_m)$, the number of states in $\mathfrak{A}$ is less than c and $\mathfrak{A}$ can be constructed in time proportional to the cardinality of its alphabet.

Note that each operator quoted in the example is regular as well as is Pratt's "preserve"-operator. Therefore the logic above is an actual extension of PL from [Har 79] and it is decidable by our criterion.

An elementary path subformula of p is called <u>maximal</u> iff it is not in the scope of any operator.

<u>Theorem</u>

Let us fix certain finite set of regular operators and restrict the semantics of programs to sets of finite paths. For any state formula p_0 of the DPL$^+$-logic the satisfiability problem is decidable in time proportional to $\exp(n^3 \exp ck)$ where: n is the length of p_0, $k = \max\{k_1,\dots,k_N\}$, k_i is the number of occurrences of the maximal subformulae in p_i, $(i = 1,\dots,N)$ and $p_1,\dots,p_N$ are all the diament subformulae of p_0.

<u>Corollary</u>

The same problem for DPL-logics with regular operators is decidable in time $O(\exp cn^3)$.

The proof of the criterion may be found in [Hab 84], cf. also [Str 81].

3. OTHER PROPERTIES

The complexity bound from the DPL$^+$-criterion remains unchanged if we restrict the semantics of actions to paths of length one as in [SPH 81] or - more generally - shorter than a fixed number. However, in general DPL-logics <u>cannot</u> be simulated using binary programs in the way that to an action A (interpreted as a set of finite paths) corresponds a program B^* (all traces of B are of length one). A simple counterexample is a model in which $Tr(A) =_{df} \{(s_0,s_2,s_3),(s_1,s_2,s_4)\}$. The simulation suggested above would lead to a trace $(s_0,s_2,s_4) \in Tr(B^*)$

not in Tr(A). In other words in our semantics the set of traces need not to be generable by a binary relation.

Following [Wol 82] one can prove that the set of paths $EVEN(P_0) = \{(s_0,\ldots,s_i,\ldots) \mid s_{2i} \models P_0\}$ (P_0 is a fixed proposition) cannot be defined in PL from [HKP 82]. In contrast any DPL-logic with regular operators remains decidable when augmented by the regular operator even, cf. the example.

The arity of the operators in the logics presented does not make any difficulties in the decision procedure. The zero-ary operators become non-local atomic formulae in parlance of [ChHMP 81]. As far as they are regular the resulting logic remains decidable in contrast to the non-local PL from [HKP 82] which is known to be undecidable.

4. OPEN PROBLEMS

(1) Axiomatization of DPL and DPL^+ (cf. [Wol 82])

(2) Expressibility. Suppose we have two DPL- (DPL^+-) logics with operators $O_0,\ldots,O_k$ and $O_0,\ldots,O_k,O_{k+1}$ resp. Under what conditions on O's is the first logic less expressive than the second one?

(3) Definability of the operators. In the example we have defined the operators using a kind of a first order language. However, adding the equality results in a language in which context free properties of traces may be defined. Therefore we ask about a convenient first order language in which exactly all the regular operators are definable.

REFERENCES

ChHMP 81 Chandra, A., J. Halpern, A. Meyer and R. Parikh: "Equations between regular terms and an application to Process Logic", STOC'81, 384-390.

FL 79 Fischer, M. J. and R. E. Ladner: "Propositional Dynamic Logic of regular programs", JCSS 18(2), 194-211.

Hab 84 Habasiński, Z.: "Process Logic: two decidability results", LNCS 176, 282-290.

Har 79 Harel, D.: "Two results on Process Logic", Inf. Processing Letters, 8(4), 195-198.

HKP 82 Harel, D., D. Kozen and R. Parikh: "Process Logic: expressiveness, decidability, completeness", JCSS 25, 144-170.

Pra 79 Pratt, V. R.: "Process Logic: preliminary report", POPL'79, 93-100.

SPH 81 Sherman, R., A. Pnueli and D. Harel: "Is the interesting part of Process Logic uninteresting?", Rep. of Weizmann Inst. of Sci. Rehovot.

Str 81 Street, R. S.: "Propositional Dynamic Logic of Looping and Converse", STOC'81, 375-381.

Wol 82 Wolper, P. L.: "Synthesis of the Communicating Processes from Temporal Logic specifications", Rep. of Dep. Comp. Sci., Stanford.

A PROGRAM SYNTHESIS ALGORITHM EXEMPLIFIED

Steffen Lange[1)]

ABSTRACT. We present a algorithm for synthesizing programs from input/output examples of their behavior. This method is a prototype of a feasible inductive inference algorithm. It is able to synthesize programs from a considerably small number of examples, which, in fact, provide only incomplete information, in general. The main computational work performed during the synthesis process consists in deducations of term equations and inequalities. The investigated synthesis algorithm is well-structured and assumes some basic knowledge formalized as a heterogeneous signature with some first order axioms. We introduce this synthesis algorithm in detail by means of a particular program for a sorting algorithm.

INTRODUCTION

Throughout the present draft we will suppress of technical details as much as possible. Instead, we will investigate a particular problem in detail for illuminating the underlying ideas.

The synthesis algorithm to be introduce is an inductive inference algorithm. Inductive inference is a mathematical theory of learning objects of some underlying well-defined class in processing incomplete information like input/output examples or sample computations. For more information we refer to the survey /1/.

The aim of the present paper is to introduce a quite general program synthesis algorithm by a case study. The method we have in mind is a generalization of Summers' approach (cf./3/). It assumes any finite, hetereogeneous and finitary signature with a set of operators divided into so-called selectors and constructors. For more information about technical details in this regard we direct the reader to the paper of Jantke in this volumne.

Our program synthesis algorithm is able to synthesize any loop program build over this assumed signature from any potentially complete list of input/output examples in the limit. We supplement that a program is said to be a loop program, if every recursive call assumes an application of a selector function before executing the call. Additionally, it is forbidden to take off the effect of the selector application within the execution of the call.

---

1) Steffen Lange, Humboldt University Berlin, Department of Mathematics DDR-1086 Berlin, P.O.Box 1297

THE BASIC EXAMPLE

Throughout the present paper we focus on an application of the general synthesis algorithm by means of a detailed case study assuming an appropriate signature for describing sorting algorithms. As the underlying set of elements of lists we take the Latin alphabet of lower case letters. These letters will be underlined. By = we denote the usual lexicographical ordering.
For our basic case study Mid, In and Fi are selectors. In and Fi computing in dependence on any file f the longest possible initial resp. final segment of f such that In(f) and the inverted version of Fi(f), respectively, is ordered.
o, Merge and Inv are constructors, o denotes the concatenation of lists and Merge denotes the merging of two ordered lists. Inv is the unary operator inverting any list.
We assume also the standard functions Ord and Empty. These are names which denote Boolean-valued functions checking wether a given list is ordered or checking a list of emptyness, resp. Note that E denotes the empty list.
For the sake of shortness, we present only two of the axioms describing the underlying knowledge.

Ord(o(x,y) = TRUE $\Longrightarrow$ o(x,y) = Merge(x,y) (1)
f = o(In(x),o(Mid(x),Fi(x))) (2)

Our main concern is the synthesis of programs from input/output examples. Examples of that kind are pairs of lists of constants. We consider a recursively defined sorting algorithm which is defined by an iterated application of some subprogram called NEXT:

SORT(f) := IF Ord(f) = TRUE THEN f ELSE SORT(NEXT(f)

IF ... THEN ... ELSE is an assumed language construct as usual.
f denotes a variable for lists.
As target algorithm we choose the sorting algorithm explained in chapter 5.2.4. of the standard reference /2/. Its subprogram named NEXT can be explained by means of the following input/output examples, where X_1 and X_2 are given lists and Y_1 and Y_2 are the corresponding results after applying NEXT.

X_1 = x.m n v.s t.a q.c.d b.u.w k.z y

Y_2 = x y z.s t u.c.q d b a.w v n m k

The dots do not belong to the lists under consideration. They are inserted to indicate segments of the files which play an important role during the algorithmic process to be learned.

$X_2 = \underline{y}\ \underline{z}.\underline{u}.\underline{k}\ \underline{m}.\underline{e}\ \underline{d}.\underline{c}.\underline{a}.\underline{b}.\underline{f}.\underline{g}.\underline{n}\ \underline{l}.\underline{w}.\underline{x}$

$Y_2 = \underline{x}\ \underline{y}\ \underline{z}.\underline{k}\ \underline{l}\ \underline{m}\ \underline{n}.\underline{d}\ \underline{f}.\underline{a}.\underline{c}\ \underline{b}.\underline{g}\ \underline{e}.\underline{w}\ \underline{u}$

Our goal is to synthesize a program which is a correct description of NEXT from input/output examples like the pairs (X_1,Y_1) and (X_2,Y_2). In working up any list of examples $(X_1,Y_1) \ldots (X_n,Y_n)$ our inductive inference algorithm generates a program being consistent with the information processed (cf./1/). This algorithm will be exemplified in the sequel by the two given examples.

GLOBAL STRUCTURE OF THE SYNTHESIS ALGORITHM

An algorithm of the type proposed which synthesizes programs from input/output examples consists of three successive parts A, B and C. Although all parts play an important role in the synthesis process, and each part incorporates some original ideas, we especially focus on a detailed investigation of Part B by means of the examples introduces before.
Part A takes a list of input/output examples $(X_1,Y_1),\ldots,(X_n,Y_n)$ as its input and expresses every output Y_i in terms of the corresponding input X_i. This is quite similar to the approach proposed by Summers (cf./3/). Within the general framework underlying our approach, there is no uniquely determind solution of expressing Y_i in terms of X_i. We will describe, for our basic example, how to overcome this difficulty. In general, let us denote by S(T) the set of all terms build from terms of a set T by applications of selectors. Similary, C(T) defines the set of terms resulting from applications of constructors to terms of T for some set T of given terms. Expressing some Y_i in terms of the corresponding X_1 means finding a term $T_i \in C(S\{X_i\})$ such that $T_i = Y_i$ is valid with respect to the given axioms. Part A is based on some lexicographical ordering of the underlying signature and tries to the lexicographical first term T_i satisfying $T_i = Y_i$. These terms generated by Part A are fed on to Part B. Part B takes these input terms $T_1,\ldots,T_n$ and generates one output term T as described in detail in the following chapter. The final component Part C takes T as input and generates a program P as output. The work performed by Part C is quite similar to the work for synthesizing finite deterministic automata from examples of their behavior, which

is introduced by Trachtenbrot and Barzdin in chapter IV.5. in their book /4/. Our algorithm generalizes this approach with respect to two particular points. First, in the case of deterministics automata, each node of a given tree represents a state, i.e. it denotes an application of a state transition function. In the general case, every node represents an application of some constructors. But two nodes labelled by different constructors may denote the same subprogram call, if there is a transformation of at least one of the corresponding nodes yielding a subterm being equivalent with respect to the underlying knowledge, such that the outermost operator become identical to each other. Therefore, Part C tries to substitute subterms of T by semantically equivalent terms, for being able to guess the equivalence of subprogram calls denoted by different nodes of T. We will come back to this point.

Figures 1 illustrates the global structure of our program synthesis algorithm, which results from the general method being proposed by fixing a signature, indicating selectors and constructors, introducing a lexicographical ordering, formalizing dependencies by means of first order axioms, and fixing the parameters of Part B explained below.

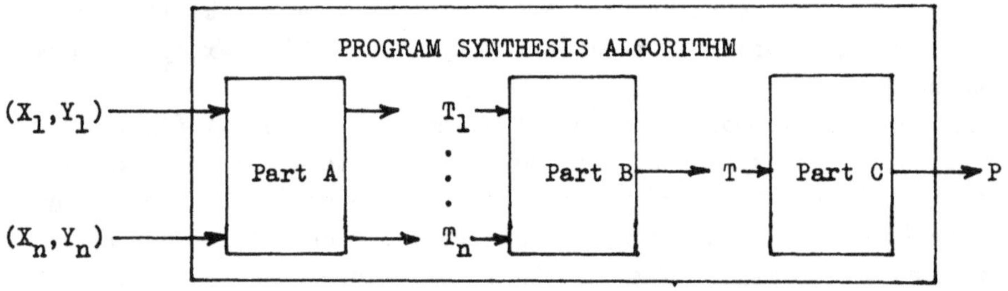

Figure 1

PROCESSING THE BASIC EXAMPLE

The present chapter is devoted to an explanation of Part A and B on the basis of the examples above. We intend to illuminate some key ideas and their mathematical background.

We assume that the basic knowledge about constructors and selectors is specified by some set E of first order axioms. Let us investigate the pairs (X_1,Y_1) and (X_2,Y_2). Part A computes the lexicographically first term t such that $t \in C(S\{Y_1\}))$ and $E \models t = Y_1$. Let us describe Part A of the algorithm in detail for the pair (X_1,Y_1).

The following term t' is the lexicographicall first term with

$$t' = \underline{o}(\underline{In}(Y_1),\underline{o}(\underline{Mid}(Y_1),\underline{Fi}(Y_1))) = Y_1$$

It is easy to see that an application of the selectors $\underline{In}$, $\underline{Fi}$ or $\underline{Mid}$ to $\underline{In}(Y_1)$ resp. $\underline{Fi}(Y_1)$ describes the empty list or the same list, respectively. Consequently, the algorithm proceedes in processing the subterm $\underline{Mid}(Y_1)$ only. It substitutes for $\underline{Mid}(Y_1)$ the lexicographically first term t'' with

$$t'' = \underline{o}(\underline{In}(\underline{Mid}(Y_1)),\underline{o}(\underline{Mid}(\underline{Mid}(Y_1),\underline{Fi}(\underline{Mid}(Y_1)))) = \underline{Mid}(Y_1)$$

This work is performed as long as possible. It is done, if the application of any selector to all subterms yields the empty list or the same list, i.e. the termination condition is satisfied. For Y_1 we obtain:

$$t = \underline{o}(\underline{In}(Y_1),\underline{o}(t'',\underline{Fi}(Y_1))) = Y_1$$

Now the algorithm tries to express the constituents of t in terms of X_1, i.e. it computes the lexicographically first terms which are equal to $\underline{In}(Y_1)$, $\underline{In}(\underline{Mid}(Y_1))$, ... , or $\underline{Fi}(Y_1)$.
Figures 2 shows the complete description of Y_1 resp. Y_2 in terms of the corresponding input X_1 and X_2, respectively. For visibility, we describe T_1 and T_2 as trees reflecting only the application of constructors. The circles on the leafs abbreviate subterms belonging to $S(\{X_1\})$ resp. $S(\{X_2\})$. If the outermost operator is $\underline{In}$, $\underline{Fi}$, or $\underline{Mid}$, the corresponding circle is ⊘, ⦸, or ⊗.

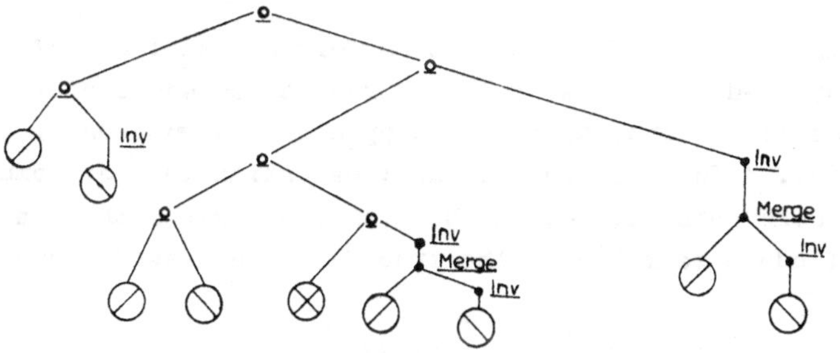

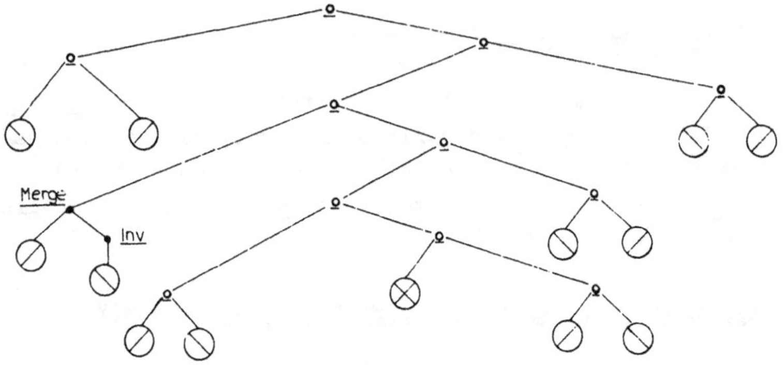

Figure 2

These two trees T_1 and T_2 are fed on to part B. We are especially in the left hand part of each tree interested. From the figure above we deduce

Y_1 = NEXT(X_1) = o(o(In(X_1),Inv(Fi(X_1))), ...)
Y_2 = NEXT(X_2) = o(o(Fi(X_2),In(X_2)), ...)

The corresponding subterms seem to be quite different in structure. But the goal of the work performed is to detect subprograms F and F' such that the program for computing Next may be decomposed into F and F' by

NEXT(x) := o(F(x),F'(x))

To reach this goal Part B tries to transform at least one of the subterms indicated above. Naturally, a search procedure of this kind requires some time bound, as it may happen that a successful result does not exist. A function for calculating estimations of computation time is one more parameter of the program synthesis method developed.

Part B finds a term R with the free variable x as follows.

R(x) abbreviates Merge(Inv(Fi(x)),In(x))

The following equalities are valid as logical consequences of the properties of the standard functions assumed.

$R(x\ \ X_1) = \underline{o}(\underline{In}(X_1),\underline{Inv}(\underline{Fi}(X_1))) = \underline{x}\ \underline{y}\ \underline{z}$

$R(x\ \ X_2) = \underline{o}(\underline{Fi}(X_2),\underline{In}(X_2)) \qquad = \underline{x}\ \underline{y}\ \underline{z}$

Note that equations like $R(x) = \underline{o}(\underline{Fi}(x),\underline{In}(x))$, e.g., are not true. That means that the synthesis algorithm did not prove that R is the correct term for describing the subprogram F. It only proved that taking R does not yield any contradiction provable from the basic knowledge and the examples (X_1,Y_1) and (X_2,Y_2). More abstractly, if BK denotes our basic knowledge, it holds that

$$BK \quad NEXT(X_1) = Y_1 : NEXT(X_2) = Y_2 \qquad R(x) \neq F(x)$$

R is the lexicographically first term such that the corresponding inequality is not provable from the information provided. Transformations being similarly to the one above yield the term (or tree, equivalently) T constructed by Part B in processing (X_1,Y_1) and (X_2,Y_2). It is shown by figure 3. Part B works iteratively, i.e. if Part B generates T from $T_1,\ldots,T_n$ (in fact from $(X_1,Y_1),\ldots,(X_n,Y_n)$), an additional input/output example (X_m,Y_m) is processed by taking T_m produced by Part A and matching T and T_m assdescribed before. (Note that $m = n+1$)

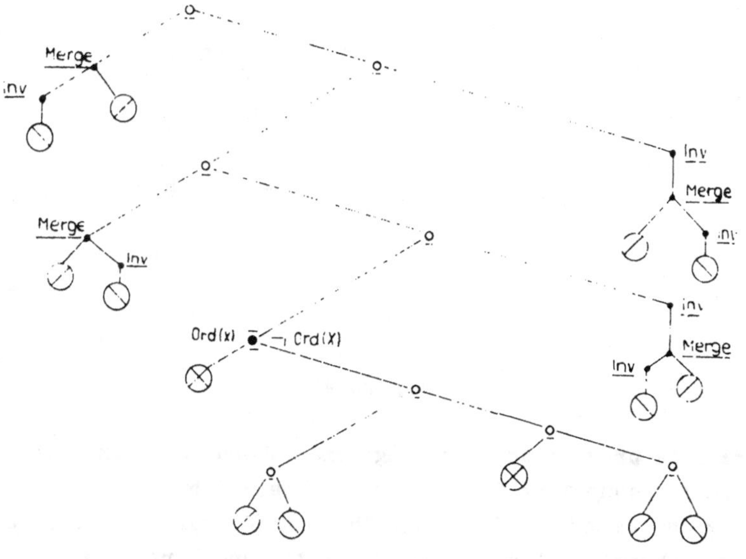

Figure 3

The resulting term T shown by figure 3 contains a special subterm with the outermost operator C. Considering T as a tree, the edges outgrowing from the node labelled by C are labelled by some conditions, i.e. by Boolean-valued terms. This indicates calls of the corresponding subterms. A term matching as above may yield such a node labelled by C, if and only if (1) one of the two subterms matched consists only of selectors whereas the other contains at least one constructor and (2) it turns out to be impossible to match both terms as described above within the given time limit. We suppress further details, for shortness.

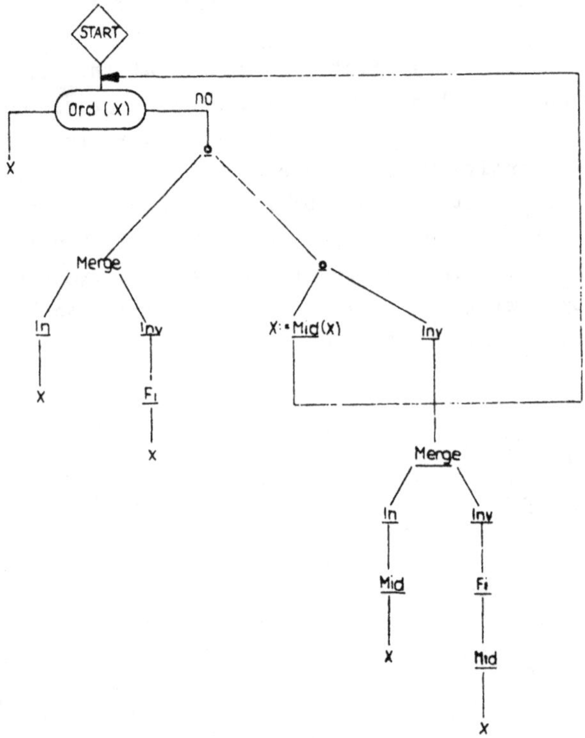

Figure 4

Figure 5 is presenting a drawing which shows in an informed way the program for computing NEXT being synthesized by Part C in processing the term T of figure 4. The method applied is a straightforward generalization of Trachtenbrot's and Barzdin's method. We direct the reades to /4/ in this regard.

CONCLUSIONS

The aim of the present paper is to explain a quite general inductive inference method which yields, by fixing certain parameters, a family of similar inductive inference algorithms for different problem domains. An exemplification of this method is the focus of our paper. For the sake of shortness and readability, we have suppressed almost all formalisms and technical details.

REFERENCES

/1/ Angluin, D. and Smith, C.H.: Inductive inference-theory and method. Computing Surveys, Vol. 15, No.3, Sept. 1983, 237-269

/2/ Knuth, D.E.: The art of computer programming, Vol.3, sorting and searching, Adison-Wesley, 1973

/3/ Summers, P.D.: A methodology for LISP program construction from examples, J.A.C.M.,24, 1978, 161-175

/4/ Trachtenbrot, B.A. and Barzdin, J.M.: Finite Automata-Synthesis and behaviour (russ.), Moskau 1970

THE ALGORITHMIC SPECIFICATION METHOD OF ABSTRACT DATA TYPES: AN OVERVIEW

Jacques Loeckx
Fachrichtung 10.2 Informatik
Universität des Saarlandes
D - 6600 Saarbrücken

1. INTRODUCTION

The practical relevance of abstract data types is twofold. First, their use may support the design of modular programs by stepwise refinement. Second, mechanical correctness proofs of these programs may become feasible in practice.

Classically, a data type is considered to be a multisorted algebra. This algebra consists of carrier sets - one for each sort - and of operations on these sets. Essentially, there exist two different specification methods. An *operational* specification [Sh 81, Li 81, NY 83] is embedded in an imperative programming language; the carrier sets are built up with the help of the data structures of this programming language and the operations are defined with the help of program pieces. An *algebraic* specification [GTW 78, GHM 78, BW 82, Re 80, EM 85, etc.] essentially consists of a set of equalities. The algebra thus defined is a special model of this set of equalities, generally the initial model.

A shortcoming of the operational specification method is its lack of abstraction. In fact, an operational specification constitutes an implementation (of a specification) rather than a specification. The main drawback of the algebraic specification method is related to its generality and, in particular, to its non-constructive nature. This leads to the difficult problems of consistency and completeness.

The specification method to be presented here has been called *algorithmic* to stress its constructive nature. In this method each (new) carrier set is defined by a (constructively defined) formal language; each (new) operation is defined by a recursive program. By its constructive nature the algorithmic specification method essentially avoids the problems of the algebraic specification method. On the other hand it differs from the operational specification method by being more "abstract". Being fundamentally different by their very definition the algebraic and algorithmic specification methods are nevertheless related. For instance, in many "simple" cases algorithmic specifications may be transformed into algebraic ones by mere rewriting. Other constructive specification methods may be found in [Ca 80, Kl 84].

In the frame of this paper it is not possible to present a complete description of the algorithmic specification method and of its applications. The interested reader is referred to [Lo 84, Lo 81 a, Lo 81 b, Lo 80, Le 85]. Instead, Section 2 explains the main ideas of the method. Section 3 shortly discusses the logic in which properties of the data types may be expressed and proved. Section 4 provides a glimpse of a specification language based on the algorithmic specification method and of its implementation.

2. THE SPECIFICATION METHOD

2.1 The introduction of new sorts

In order to introduce a new sort it is sufficient to define its carrier set and its operationa.

The carrier set is defined as a term language, i.e. as a particular formal language. In the case of Figure 1 the carrier set is the term language generated by the operation symbols characterized by the word *constructor*. The elements of this carrier set are words such as ε, App(ε,o), App(App(ε,4),2), etc.

The definition of the operations is different for the constructors and the other operation symbols. The interpretation of the constructors is the Herbrand interpretation. For instance, the value of the operation App for the arguments ε and o is the word App(ε,o). The other operation symbolsare defined as recursive programs (in the sense of [Ma 74, LS 84]). For instance, Insert appends an integer to a sequence provided the integer does not yet occur in this sequence; Delete deletes the rightmost occurrence of an integer; Memberof tests whether a (given) integer occurs in a sequence.

2.2 The operations *subset* and *quotient*

The method of Section 2.1 does not allow to specify "elaborate" sorts such as the sort consisting of (finite) sets (of integers). In fact, let us try to modify the specification of Figure 1, being understood that a term such as App(App(ε,o),1) now stands for the set {o,1}. Clearly, a term with "duplicates" such as

App(App(ε,o),o)

```
sort seq
signature
     constructor ε : → seq
     constructor App : seq × int → seq
     Insert : seq × int → seq
     Delete : seq × int → seq
     Memberof : seq × int → bool
     Subset : seq × seq → bool
operations
     Insert(s,i) ← if Memberof(s,i) then s else App(s,i) fi
     Delete(s,i) ← case s of
          ε : s
          App(s',i') : if i=i' then s' else App(Delete(s',i),i') fi
                                                            esac
     Memberof(s,i) ← case s of
          ε : false
          App(s',i') : if i=i' then true else Memberof(s',i) fi
                                                            esac
     Subset(s1,s2) ← case s1 of
          ε : true
          App(s1',i) : if Memberof(s2,i) then Subset(s1',s2)
                                          else false fi esac
```

FIGURE 1: A specification of the sort *seq*, which consists of finite sequences of integers

may not occur in the carrier set. Moreover, terms such as

$$\mathrm{App}(\mathrm{App}(\varepsilon,o),1)$$

and

$$\mathrm{App}(\mathrm{App}(\varepsilon,1),o)$$

have to stand for the same set. The first of these difficulties is solved by introducing an operation which defines a subset of the carrier set; an example of such an operation is the operation Nodup of Figure 2. The second difficulty is solved by introducing an equivalence relation such as Eq of Figure 2; the carrier set then consists of a set of equivalence classes.

It is well-known that such a *subset operation* or *quotient operation* yieldsan algebra only if the *closure condition* and the *congruence condition* respectively are fulfilled (see e.g. [GM 83]). Informally, the closure condition expresses that arguments from the subset lead to a value from the subset; the congruence condition expresses that equi-

signature

    Nodup : *seq* → *bool*

    Eq : *seq* × *seq* → *bool*

operations

    Nodup(s) ⇐ case s of
        ε : true
        App(s',i) : if Memberof(s',i) then false
                                   else Nodup(s') fi esac

    $Eq(s_1,s_2)$ ⇐ if $Subset(s_1,s_2)$ then $Subset(s_2,s_1)$
                                   else false fi

FIGURE 2: The specification of Figure 1 together with Nodup as subset operation and Eq as quotient operation defines the sort consisting of finite sets of integers. The operation App is not put at the disposal of the user of the specification, as it does not fulfil the closure condition.

valent arguments lead to equivalent values. These conditions have to be fulfilled by all operations put at the disposal of the user of the specification; they have to be proved once and for all by the designer of the specification.

3. THE LOGIC OF STRICT ALGEBRAS

The *logic of strict algebras* [Lo 84] allows to express and prove properties of the data types introduced by algorithmic specifications. The logic is similar to LCF (see [Mi 72 , LS 84]) and takes account of the fact that the operations constitute partial computable functions. An example of a formula referring to Figure 1 is:

$\forall s \in seq,\ i \in int.\ \mathrm{Memberof}(s,i) = \underline{\mathrm{false}} \supset \mathrm{Delete}(s,i) = s$

An important proof rule is structural induction on the carrier set [Lo 80, Lo 84]. For "non-trivial" properties it may be necessary to use fixpoint induction [Lo 81 b].

4. THE SPECIFICATION LANGUAGE OBSCURE

4.1 The language

The specification language OBSCURE [Le 85] is similar to CLEAR [Sa 84] but is based on the algorithmic specification method instead of the algebraic one. Essentially OBSCURE allows to construct an algebra from a given one.

OBSCURE contains among others three constructs which correspond to the extension described in Section 2.1, to the subset operation and to the quotient operation respectively. Moreover OBSCURE allows the specification and use of parameterized data types. Finally, it provides the possibility to define implementations of abstract data types.

4.2 The implementation

An implementation of OBSCURE is under construction at the university of Saarbrücken. It consists of a programming and a verification part.

The programming part supports the top-down development of programs by stepwise refinement. In particular, it generates the closure and congruence conditions which are to be proved.

The verification part allows interactive correctness proofs and bears similarities with the AFFIRM system [Mu 80, Th 79, Lo 80]. Essentially, the computer performs the formula manipulation and takes care of the administration; the user is responsible for the choice of the proof strategy. The readability of the intermediate results produced by the computer is given particular attention to.

REFERENCES

[BW 82] Broy, M., Wirsing, M., Partial abstract types, *Acta Inform.* 18 (1982), 47 - 64

[Ca 80] Cartwright, R., A constructive alternative to abstract data type definitions, Proc. 1980 LISP Conf., Stanford Univ. (1980), 46 - 55

[EM 85] Ehrig, H., Mahr, B., Fundamentals of Algebraic Specification, Springer-Verlag, 1985

[GHM 78] Guttag, J.V., Horowitz, E., Musser, D.R., Abstract data types and software validation. *Comm. ACM* 21 (Dec. 1978), 1048 - 1069

[GM 83] Goguen, J.A., Meseguer, J., *Initiality, Induction and Computability*, SRI-CSL Techn. Rep. 140, Stanford Research Institute, December 1983

[GTW 78] Goguen, J.A., Thatcher, J.W., Wagner, E.G., An initial algebra approach to the specification, correctness and implementation of abstract data types. *Current Trends in Programming Methodology IV* (Yeh, R., Ed.), Prentice-Hall, 1978, 80 - 149

[Kl 84] Klaeren, H.A., A constructive method for abstract algebraic software specification, *Theor. Comp. Sc.* 30, 139 - 204 (1984)

[Le 85] Lermen, C.W., OBSCURE, a specification language for algorithmic specifications, Intern. Rep., FR 10.2, Univ. Saarbrücken (in preparation)

[Li 81] Liskov, B., et al, *CLU Reference Manual*, LNCS 114, 1981

[Lo 80] Loeckx, J., Proving properties of algorithmic specifications of abstract data types in AFFIRM. AFFIRM-Memo-29-JL, USC-ISI, Marina del Rey, 1980

[Lo 81 a] Loeckx, J., Algorithmic specifications of abstract data types, Proc. ICALP 81, LNCS 115 (1981), 129 - 147

[Lo 81 b] Loeckx, J., Using abstract data types for the definition of programming languages and the verification of their compilers, Int. Rep. A 81/13, FB 10, Univ. Saarbrücken (1981)

[Lo 84] Loeckx, J., Algorithmic specifications: A constructive specification method for abstract data types, to appear in *TOPLAS*

[LS 84] Loeckx, J., Sieber, K., *The Foundations of Program Verification*, J. Wiley/Teubner-Verlag, New York/Stuttgart (1984)

[Ma 74] Manna, Z., *Mathematical Theory of Computation*, McGraw-Hill (1974)

[Mi 72] Milner, R., Implementation and application of Scott's logic for computable functions. Proc. ACM Conf. on Proving Assertions about Programs, SIGPLAN Notices 7 (Jan. 1972), 1 - 6

[Mu 80] Musser, D.R., Abstract data type specification in the AFFIRM System. *IEEE Trans. on Softw. Eng.* SE-6 (1980), 24 - 32

[NY 83] Nakajima, R., Yuasa, T., *The IOTA Programming System*, LNCS 160, 1983

[Re 80] Reichel, H., Initially-restricting algebraic theories, Proc. 9th FCS, LNCS 88, 460 - 473 (1980)

[Sa 84] Sannella, D., A set-theoretic semantics for CLEAR, *Acta Inform.* 21, 5, 443 - 472 (1984)

[Sh 81] Shaw, M. (ed.), *ALPHARD, Form and Content*, Springer-Verlag, 1981

[Th 79] Thompson, D.H. (Ed.), AFFIRM Reference Manual. Internal Report, USC-ISI, Marina del Rey (1979)

ORIENTATION PROBLEMS ON SEQUENCES BY RECURSIVE FUNCTIONS

Péter Komjáth[1/]
Szabó Zsolt [2/]

Physicists often say that our universe is homogeneous and isotropic, i.e. neither distinguished place nor distinguished direction exists. This means that the space is filled with matter essentially uniformly. We are not interested of the physical aspects of this observation but in a mathematical model. We define homogeneity and isotropy of integer sequences in a recursion theoretic way. We show that there exist extremally irregular sequences which are homogeneous and isotropic contradicting the popular notion on these concepts.

Throughout this paper N and Z denote the set of non-negative integers and integers respectively. Let Z^* be the set of all finite sequences of Z. We fix a 1-1 recursive encoding $\langle \dots \rangle$ of Z^* onto Z. Let φ be a fixed Gödel numbering of $Z \to Z$ type partial recursive functions. We denote by P an R the classes of partial recursive and total recursive functions respectively, and Ω shall denote the class of functions from Z to Z. We think Ω as the set of all possible one-dimensional, discrete universes, and a member - a given world - will be denoted by α, β, γ. A universe α possesses a distinguished place if it can be localised by an algorithm in any point of α. That is to say if a spaceship, if lost, can find her way home /with a good navigator/. Obviously, if a universe has one distinguished point then each point is such, so this is a property of the universe /and not of the point/. We are interested in this class of universes.

For convenience's sake throughhout the paper we denote by $\alpha[n]$ the segment $\langle \alpha(-n), \dots, \alpha(0), \dots, \alpha(n) \rangle$ of $\alpha \in \Omega$ and by α^k the translated copy of α by k steps, i.e. $\alpha^k(i) = \alpha(i+k)$.

1./ Department of Computer Sci. Institute of Mathematics, Eötvös Univ.H-1445.Budapest,P.O.B. 323.

2./ Enterprise for Computing Applications, H-15o2.Budapest, P.O.B. 146.

Definitions 1. There is a distinguished place of the sequence $\alpha \in \Omega$ iff there exists a $f \in P$ such that for all $k \in Z$ it holds that

a/ For all $n \in N$ $f(\langle \alpha^k[n] \rangle)$ is defined.

b/ $\lim_{n \to \infty} f(\langle \alpha^k[n] \rangle)$ exists.

c/ $\lim_{n} f(\langle \alpha^k[n] \rangle) = k$.

Remark 1. This definition is similar to the definition of inductive inference (see [1]).

Definition 1. suggests that "navigator f" has a map with an origin and has to find out in which point k he actually is. In every step he learns two more points of the neighbourhood and guesses where he is. Therefore, he gives an infinite sequence of guesses and though he will never be convinced he knows where he is, his guesses converge to the right answer and this is practically enough.

Let $\mathcal{A}$ denote the set of sequenses $\alpha \in \Omega$ for which there is a distinguished place and let $\mathcal{A}^f$ denote the set of sequences $\alpha \in \Omega$ for which the $f \in P$ determines a distinguished place. Denote by Per the set of periodic functions in Ω (i.e. $\mathrm{Per} := \{\alpha \in \Omega \mid \exists n \in Z \ \forall i \in Z \ \ \alpha(i) = \alpha(i+n)\}$).

It is easy to see that:

Proposition 1. $\mathcal{A} \cap \mathrm{Per} = \emptyset$

We say that the sequence $\alpha \in \Omega$ is homogeneous if there is no distinguished place and it is not periodic either. Denote by $\mathcal{H}$ the set of homogeneous sequences, i.e. $\mathcal{H} := \Omega - (\mathcal{A} \cup \mathrm{Per})$.

Theorem 1. $R - \mathrm{Per} \subseteq \mathcal{A}$

Sketch of proof: Let $g \in R - \mathrm{Per}$ be given. We know that $g^k = g^m$ implies $k=m$. Define the recursive predicate h the folloing way:

$h(\langle x_{-n}, \dots, x_0, \dots, x_n \rangle, j) = \text{"true"} \quad \forall i(-n \leq i \leq n \ \& \ x_i = g(i+j))$

It is easily seen that the f is able to determine a distinguished place for the given sequence g, where f is defined for arbitrary $\beta \in \Omega$:

$f(\langle \beta[0] \rangle) = 0$;

$$f(\langle\beta[n+1]\rangle)=\begin{cases}+f(\langle\beta[n]\rangle) & \text{if } h(\langle\beta[n+1]\rangle, f(\langle\beta[n]\rangle)) = \text{'true'}\\ -f(\langle\beta[n]\rangle) & \text{if } h(\langle\beta[n+1]\rangle, f(\langle\beta[n]\rangle)) = \text{'false'} \text{ and } f(\langle\beta[n]\rangle)>0\\ 1-f(\langle\beta[n]\rangle) & \text{otherwise;}\end{cases}$$

□

Define a partial order $\subseteq$ on Z^* as follows:
$u \subseteq v$ iff there is a $x,y \in Z^*$ that $v=xuy$.
Denote by W_n the set of those $\alpha\in\Omega$ sequences for which there exists a segment $u\in Z^*$ of α occuring at most n times.

$$W_n=\{\alpha\in\Omega \mid \exists u\in Z^* \ \exists k\in N\,(u\subseteq\alpha[k] \ \&\ (\forall x_1,\dots,x_n\in Z^* \ \forall m\in N: (ux_1ux_2\dots ux_n \not\subseteq \alpha[m])))\}.$$

Let $\overline{W}$ denote the set of sequences $\alpha\in\Omega$ for which every segment of α occurs in α at infinitely many places, i.e. $\overline{W}=\Omega-(\bigcup_{n=1}^{\infty}W_n)$.

The reader can readily verify that:

Proposition 2. $W_n \subseteq \mathcal{A}$ for all $n\in N$.

Proposition 3. If $\alpha\in\mathcal{K}$ then $\alpha\in\overline{W}$.

Our next theorem says that no cleverest navigator exists:
Theorem 2. There is no $f\in P$ such that $\mathcal{A}^f=\mathcal{A}$.

Sketch of proof: Assume, indirectly, that there exists an $f\in P$ with $\mathcal{A}^f=\mathcal{A}$. By Theorem 1 R-Per $\subseteq\mathcal{A}^f$ and obviously $f\in R$. Choose $\gamma\in$ R-Per with the property that $\forall u\in Z^*\ \exists n\in N$ with $u\subseteq\gamma[n]$. Clearly, $\gamma\in\overline{W}$. If $\gamma\in\mathcal{A}^f$, then it is easy to find algorithm, which defines for every pair $(i,n)\in Z\times N$ another one $(j,m)\in Z\times N$ with $m>n$, $\gamma^i[n]=\gamma^j[n]$ and $f(\langle\gamma^i[m]\rangle)\neq f(\langle\gamma^j[m]\rangle)$. Using this one can also construct a sequence $\beta\in$ R-Per without $\lim_{k\to\infty} f(\langle\beta[k]\rangle)$ so $\beta\notin\mathcal{A}^f$, a contradiction.

The next theorem is an improvement of Theorem 2.

Theorem 3. There are f_1, $f_2\in P$ such that there is no $f_3\in P$ for which $\mathcal{A}^{f_1}\cup\mathcal{A}^{f_2}\subseteq\mathcal{A}^{f_3}$.

Sketch of proof: Let σ be a recursive and bijective encoding of Z^2 onto Z, and let σ_1 and σ_2 be such that if $\sigma(x,y)=z$ then $\sigma_1(z)=x$ and $\sigma_2(z)=y$ .Denote by $\gamma\in$ R-Per a such function for which there exists $n\in N$ for all $u\in Z^*$ that $u\subseteq\gamma[n]$.

Define the following two sets of sequences:

$$A_1=\{\alpha\in(\Omega-\mathrm{Per}) \mid [\forall i,j\in Z: \sigma_1(\alpha(i))=\sigma_1(\alpha(j))] \text{ and } [\exists m\in Z(\forall n\in Z: \varphi(\sigma_1(\alpha(n)),n)=\sigma_2(\alpha^m(n)))]\};$$

$$A_2=\{\alpha\in\Omega \mid \forall i\in Z: \sigma_2(\alpha(i))=\gamma(i)\}.$$

It is easy to show such functions $f_1,f_2\in P$ for which $A_1\subseteq\mathcal{A}^{f_1}$

and $A_2 \subseteq \mathcal{A}^{f_2}$. Now assume that there exists an $f_3 \in P$ with $A_1 \cup A_2 \subseteq \mathcal{A}^{f_3}$. For $i \in Z$ let $\beta_i \in \Omega$ be a sequence such that for every $j \in Z$ $\sigma_1(\beta_i(j)) = i$ and it is constructed similarly to the β of Theorem 2. Then $\beta_i \notin \mathcal{A}^{f_3}$ for $i \in Z$. It is easy to see that there exist a total recusive $g: Z^2 \to Z$ with $g(i,j) = \sigma_2(\beta_i(j))$ for all $i, j \in Z$. By the recursion theorem there is a $k \in Z$ such that $g(k,n) = \varphi(k,n)$ for $n \in Z$ and so $\beta_k \in A_1$. This contradicts $\beta_k \in \mathcal{A}^{f_3}$.

□

Remark 2. The proof of Theorem 3 is similar to the proof of the theorem which says inductive identifiable classes are not closed under union (see [2]).

Theorem 4. $\mathcal{H} \neq \emptyset$

We cannot simply prove this result from cardinality considerations; though the cardinality of Ω is continuum and P is countable, as there exists an $f \in P$ with $V \subseteq \mathcal{A}^f$ where $V = \{\alpha \in \Omega \mid \alpha(i) = 0 \Leftrightarrow i = 0\}$ and the cardinality of V is also continuum.
It is necessary to make arrangements for proving the theorem.

Let us introduce the metric ρ on Ω as follows:

$$\rho(\alpha,\beta) = \begin{cases} 0 & \text{if } \alpha = \beta \\ \dfrac{1}{k+1} & \text{if } k \in N \text{ is such that } k = \min\{i \in N \mid \alpha[i] \neq \beta[i]\} \end{cases}$$

It is easy to see that Ω is complete space via ρ.

Let us introduce the following notation:

$G(x_{-n}, \dots, x_0, \dots, x_n) = \{\alpha \in \Omega \mid \alpha[n] = (x_{-n}, \dots, x_0, \dots, x_n)\}$.

So $G(\alpha[n])$ is a neighbouhood of with radius $\frac{1}{n+2}$. In the proof we are going to use the Baire category theorem, i.e. that a complete, metric, separable space, if uncontable, is not the union of countably many nowhere dense sets.

Proof of Theorem 4. By definition, $\mathcal{H} = \Omega - (\mathcal{A} \cup \mathrm{Per})$. By the Baire category theorem it is enough to show that $\mathcal{A} \cup \mathrm{Per}$ is the union of countably many nowhere dense sets. As Per is countable, there is no problem with it.
Now define

$C_k^f(x_{-n}, \dots, x_0, \dots, x_n) = \{\alpha \in \Omega \mid \alpha[n] = (x_{-n}, \dots, x_n)$ and for every $i \in N$ $f(\langle \alpha[k] \rangle) = f(\langle \alpha[k+i] \rangle)\} \cap \overline{W}$.

Clearly,

$$\mathcal{A} = \bigcup_{\substack{f\in P\\ k,n\in N\\ (x_{-n},\dots,x_n)\in Z^{2n+1}}} \left(\mathcal{A}^f \cap C_k^f(x_{-n},\dots,x_0,\dots,x_n)\right) \cup \bigcup_{m=1}^{\infty} W_m .$$

It is easy to see that W_m is nowhere dense.

It suffices to show that $\mathcal{A}^f \cap C_k^f(x_{-n},\dots,x_0,\dots,x_n)$ is nowhere dense, as well. To this, it is enough to find an open set in every neighourhood $G(y_{-m},\dots,y_0,\dots,y_m)$ with $m > n$, $m > k$, and $\langle y_{-n},\dots,y_n\rangle = \langle x_{-n},\dots,x_0,\dots,x_n\rangle$ which is disjoint from $\mathcal{A}^f \cap C_k^f(x_{-n},\dots,x_n)$. If $\alpha \in G(y_{-m},\dots,y_0,\dots,y_m) \cap (\mathcal{A}^f \cap C_k^f(x_{-n},\dots,x_0,\dots,x_n))$, then $\alpha \in \bar{W}$ by the definitions of C_k^f, so there exists a $d > m$ with $\alpha^d[m] = \alpha[m]$. Therefore, $\lim_{i\to\infty} f(\langle\alpha^d[i]\rangle) = f(\langle\alpha[k]\rangle) + d$, i.e. there exists a $c > m$ (so $c > k$) with $f(\langle\alpha^d[c]\rangle) = f(\langle\alpha[k]\rangle) + d$. As $f(\langle\alpha^d[k]\rangle) = f(\langle\alpha[k]\rangle)$, $G(\alpha^d[c]) \cap C_k^f(x_{-n},\dots,x_n) \neq \emptyset$ will hold. $G(\alpha^d[c])$ will be the open set we where seeking for.

□

Next, we are going to define the notion of distinguished direction. A universe has a distinguished direction if a good navegator can tell α from its reverse, independently of his actual location.

For convenience's sake denote by α_q^k the sequence defined from $\alpha\in\Omega$ by the following way:

$$\alpha_q^k(i) = \alpha(k+qi) \quad \text{for} \quad i\in Z \quad \text{where} \quad k\in Z \quad \text{and} \quad q=\pm 1.$$

Definition 2. There is a distinguished direction of the sequence $\alpha\in\Omega$ iff there exists a $f\in P$ such that for all $k\in Z$ and for all $q\in\{+1,-1\}$ it holds that

a/ For all $n\in N$ $f(\langle\alpha_q^k[n]\rangle)$ is defined.

b/ $\lim_{n\to\infty} f(\langle\alpha_q^k[n]\rangle)$ exists.

c/ $\lim_{n\to\infty} f(\langle\alpha_q^k[n]\rangle) = q$.

In the Definition above q shows whether "navigator" is in a reverse position or not. We cannot omit clause "for all $k\in Z$ ", otherwise only symmetrical universes would not have distinguished direction.

Let $\mathcal{T}$ denote the set of sequence $\alpha\in\Omega$ for which there is a distinuished direction.

Denote by $\mathcal{S}$ the set of symmetrical functions in Ω i.e.

$$\mathcal{S} := \{\alpha\in\Omega \mid \exists k\in Z : \forall i\in Z \ \alpha(k-i) = \alpha(k+i) \text{ or } \forall i\in Z \ \alpha(k-i) = \alpha(k+i+1)\}.$$

We say that the sequence $\alpha \in \Omega$ is <u>isotropic</u> if there is no distinguished direction and it is not symmetrical either. Denote by $\mathcal{J}$ the set of isotropic sequences, i.e. $\mathcal{J} = \Omega - (\mathcal{T} \cup \mathcal{S})$.

Similarly to Theorem 4 one can show

<u>Theorem 5.</u> $\mathcal{J} \neq \emptyset$.

To formulate a result saying there exists a homogeneous, isotropic, and "highly irregular" universe in Ω, we define for every $k,n \in N$ a set $\mathcal{K}_{k,n} \subseteq \Omega$ of sequences, as follows:

$$\mathcal{K}_{k,n} = \{\alpha \in \Omega \mid \forall m > n \ \left| \frac{1}{2m+1} \sum_{i=-m}^{m} \alpha(i) - \frac{1}{2n+1} \sum_{i=-n}^{n} \alpha(i) \right| \leq k \}.$$

Put $\mathcal{K} = \bigcup_{k,n \in N} \mathcal{K}_{k,n}$ Therefore,

$$\overline{\mathcal{K}} = \{\alpha \in \Omega \mid \overline{\lim_{n \to \infty}} \frac{1}{2n+1} \sum_{i=-n}^{n} \alpha(i) - \underline{\lim}_{n \to \infty} \frac{1}{2n+1} \sum_{i=-n}^{n} \alpha(i) = \infty \}.$$

We can regard $\overline{\mathcal{K}}$ as the set of very irregular and non-uniform universes.

It is easy to show that $\mathcal{K}_{k,n}$ is nowhere dense for $k,n \in N$. From this, our concluding theorem, which says that there exist homogeneous, isotropic and highly irregular sequences in Ω follows:

<u>Theorem 6.</u> $\mathcal{H} \cap \mathcal{J} \cap \overline{\mathcal{K}} \neq \emptyset$.

We hope that the generalisations of the results in this paper may have some /mathematical/ interest. It would be desirable to find other classes similar to $\mathcal{H}$ and $\mathcal{J}$.

REFERENCES

[1] GOLD,E.M.:Limiting recursion,J.of Symbolic Logic <u>30</u> 1965.pp.28-48

[2] BLUM,L.BLUM,M.:Inductive inference: a recursion theoretic approach. Memorandum No. EHL-M 386.University of California,Berkeley,1973.

The solution of discrete problems by means of ternary representations

Posthoff, Ch., Reiß, J.

1. Introduction and function

On principle, there are possibilities for solving binary problems by manual algebraic transformations of binary terms or manual analyses of karnaugh diagrams or similar methods. They are not usable for practically relevant problems because of the high consumption of time and the risk of errors. Using computers is the only alternative.

At present, we can see two lines of developing methods for solving binary problems:

1. A concrete, sharply limited problem is given, and a particular solving method will be created by utilizing all properties of the problem. Such specific solutions do not sufficiently cover the complete field of binary problems; they are rarely flexible and cannot be generalized.
2. A large class of discrete problems is modelled by binary equations. Their solutions will be composed by available universal basic algorithms.

It must be paid attention to both lines; to the first one because of the high possible operation speed, and to the second one because of the good universality or good economy of the produced software, respectively. Based on a great number of studies we have accomplished research work with regard to the second line.

We have to consider that the boolean operations for logical variables or binary vectors, respectively, are included in the most programming languages, complying the requirement for universality, but they do not meet the criteria for efficiency. This is caused by the low complexity of binary data which are directly operated. Our research works show that fundamental binary objects can be found at the level of binary functions, binary equations and solution sets of binary equations.

Based on a careful analysis and selection of data structures, it was necessary to develop algorithms and programs complying the following intentions:

- solving binary equations and systems of binary equations;
- executing operations with solution sets of binary equations;
- executing operations of the boolean differential calculus;

Prof.Dr.sc.techn.Christian Posthoff, Dr.rer.nat.; Dr.-Ing.Joachim Reiß; Techn. Hochschule Karl-Marx-Stadt, Sektion Informatik 901 Karl-Marx-Stadt, Straße der Nationen 62.

- executing basic operations for processing graphs;
- dialogue possibilities;
- linguistic description of problems;
- problem-oriented input and output operations.

2. Data structures

The selection of suitable data structure exercises an important influence on the efficiency of the processing algorithmus. There are any usual requirements for data structures as, for instance, low storage requirements and universal applicability. These requirements are completed by the following aspects for binary problems:

- consideration of both functional and structural aspects (optimization, minimization, decomposition);
- changing the number of relevant variables during the operation.

a) Binary vector lists

A binary vector list is a set of l binary vectors with length k, $k \geq 1$, $0 \leq l \leq 2^k$, which are solutions of a binary equation of k variables (especially of the equations $f(x_1,\ldots,x_k)=0$ or $f(x_1,\ldots,x_n)=1$ for any function $f(x_1,\ldots,x_n)$).

Advantages are:

- the direct use of availability vectors $\underline{x}$ within the data structure;
- the fixed correspondance between the elements of all binary vectors and the binary variables x_i, for $i=1,\ldots,k$;
- the direct notation of canonical normal forms of binary functions.

The required storage for such a list not containing any binary vector several times is equal to $l \cdot k$ with $0 \leq l \cdot k \leq 2^k \cdot k$.

b) Ternary vector lists

A ternary vector list reduces the required storage capacity compared with a binary vector list by concentrating several binary vectors of binary vector list to one data element called ternary vector.

- If two binary vectors with the same length differ only at position i, then they can be combined to one ternary vector containing the element "-" (stroke) at position i.
- If two ternary vectors with the same length differ only at position i and the combination "0,1" appears at this position, then the two ternary vectors can be concentrated to one ternary vector containing the stroke element at the position i.

It can be easily shown that the required average storage capacity is less than the required storage capacity for binary vector lists, generally much more less. The most unfavourable case for this representation are linear boolean functions.
The ternary vector lists produced in this way are not uniquely determined but depend on the order of the binary vectors and the comprehensions. The reverse procedure dissolving any stroke in two vectors with "0" and "1" in this position, respectively, leads to an uniquely determined list of binary vectors (by deleting vectors occurring several times).

3. Interpretation of ternary vector lists

A set of binary vectors described by a ternary vector list can be interpretated directly as a solution set of a binary equation. Since a set of binary vectors is represented by a ternary vector list, it is necessary to provide the known set operations (union, intersection, difference, symmetric difference, complement of symmetric difference, complementation) for solving binary problems by means of ternary vector lists. The operation "ternary vector list number 3 is equal to the intersection of ternary vector list 1 and ternary vector list 2" is performed in such a way that the ternary vector list 3 describes all binary vectors which are represented both of the ternary vector list 1 and the ternary vector list 2 (set operations in the meaning of corresponding sets of binary vectors).
In this representation, ternary vector list 3 does not contain all ternary vectors contained both in the ternary vector list 1 and the ternary vector list 2. This is only the matter of the chosen sementic, the other meaning being useful too.
The representation of binary functions in normal forms is the next essential interpretation of ternary vector lists.

disjunctive form: $$f(\underline{x}) = \bigvee_{i=1}^{n_1} K_i$$

conjunctive form: $$f(\underline{x}) = \bigwedge_{i=1}^{n_2} D_i$$

exclusive-or form: $$f(\underline{x}) = \sum_{i=1}^{n_3} K_i$$

equivalence form: $$f(\underline{x}) = \mathop{E}_{i=1}^{n_4} D_i$$

One of three cases is possible in a conjunction (disjunction) for each variable x_j, $j=1,\dots,k$:

a) x_j appears non-negated, coded by 1;

b) x_j appears negated, coded by 0;

c) x_j does not appear, coded by -.

Please, look at a sample for this:

1. disjunctive form:

$f(\underline{x}) = \bar{x}_1 x_2 \vee \bar{x}_2 x_3$ $\qquad M(D_f) = \begin{array}{ccc} x_1 & x_2 & x_3 \end{array} \begin{bmatrix} 0 & 1 & - \\ - & 0 & 1 \end{bmatrix}$

2. conjunctive form:

$f(\underline{x}) = (x_2 \vee x_3) \wedge (\bar{x}_1 \vee \bar{x}_2)$ $\qquad M(K_f) = \begin{array}{ccc} x_1 & x_2 & x_3 \end{array} \begin{bmatrix} - & 1 & 1 \\ 0 & 0 & - \end{bmatrix}$

3. exclusive-or form:

$f(\underline{x}) = \bar{x}_2 x_3 \not\sim \bar{x}_1 x_2$ $\qquad M(A_f) = \begin{array}{ccc} x_1 & x_2 & x_3 \end{array} \begin{bmatrix} - & 0 & 1 \\ 0 & 1 & - \end{bmatrix}$

4. equivalence form:

$f(\underline{x}) = (\bar{x}_1 \vee \bar{x}_2) \sim (x_2 \vee x_3)$ $\qquad M(E_f) = \begin{array}{ccc} x_1 & x_2 & x_3 \end{array} \begin{bmatrix} 0 & 0 & - \\ - & 1 & 1 \end{bmatrix}$

If this assignment of ternary vectors is made for each appearing conjunction (disjunction), and if these vectors are written one beneath the other, then a ternary vector list is created definitely related to the specific normal form (the type of the normal form must be stored).

The operations union, intersection, negation, exclusive-or and equivalence are defined for binary functions.

Let $f(x_1,\dots,x_k)$ and $g(x_1,\dots,x_k)$ binary functions and $L_o(f)$, $L_1(f)$, $L_o(g)$, $L_1(g)$ the sets of solutions of the equations $f(\underline{x})=0$, $f(\underline{x})=1$, $g(\underline{x})=0$, $g(\underline{x})=1$, respectively.

Because of the isomorphy between the boolean lattices $[P(M), \cap, \cup, -, \emptyset, E]$ and $[B^k, \wedge, \vee, \bar{}, \underline{0}, \underline{1}]$ or boolean rings $[P(M), \cap, \Delta, \emptyset]$, $[P(M), \cup, \bar{\Delta}, E]$ and $[B^k, \wedge, \not\sim, \underline{0}]$ or $[B^k, \vee, \sim, \underline{1}]$, respectively, a defined correspondence consists between operations in binary equations and set operations for solution sets (M being any set with k elements, P(M) the power set of M, B^k the set of all binary vectors with k components).

<u>binary equation</u>	<u>solution set</u>
$f \wedge g = 0$	$L_o(f) \cup L_o(g)$
$f \wedge g = 1$	$L_1(f) \cap L_1(g)$

$f \vee g = 0$	$L_0(f) \cap L_0(g)$	
$f \vee g = 1$	$L_1(f) \cup L_1(g)$	
$f \not\sim g = 0$	$L_0(f) \overline{\Delta} L_0(g)$	
$f \not\sim g = 1$	$L_1(f) \Delta L_1(g)$	
$f \sim g = 0$	$L_0(f) \Delta L_0(g)$	
$f \sim g = 1$	$L_1(f) \overline{\Delta} L_1(g)$	
$\bar{f} = 0$	$\overline{L_0(f)}$	$= L_1(f)$
$\bar{f} = 1$	$\overline{L_1(f)}$	$= L_0(f)$
$f \rightarrow g = 1$	$\overline{L_1(f)} \cup L_1(g)$	
$f \rightarrow g = 0$	$\overline{L_0(f)} \cap L_0(g)$	

A lot of different problem-oriented interpretations can be related to the universal interpretation of a ternary vector list as a binary function or equation.

A ternary vector list can be interpretated directly as a graph. Therefore the variable vector is decomposed in at least two parts $\underline{x}$ and $\underline{x}'$ (or d$\underline{x}$, respectively) with length k.

For each edge from $\underline{x}$ to $\underline{x}'$, a function $f(\underline{x},\underline{x}')$ will get the value 1. Any ternary vector including s stroke elements describes a set of 2^s graph edges by start and end nodes (start node and direction). Set operations for ternary vector lists are transferable to set operations with graph edges etc .

4. Orthogonal ternary vector lists

Two vectors $\underline{x}$ and $\underline{y}$ are called orthogonal to each other iff $\underline{x} \cdot \underline{y} = \underline{n}$, $\cdot$ being the ring multiplication and $\underline{n}$ the zero element of the ring. For the both boolean rings that means:

$$\underline{x} \wedge \underline{y} = \underline{0}, \quad \underline{x} \vee \underline{y} = 1.$$

Between the boolean lattice $[B^k, \wedge, \vee, \bar{\ }, \underline{0}, \underline{1}]$ and the boolean ring $[B^k, \wedge, \not\sim, \underline{0}]$, the following holds:

$$\underline{a} \vee \underline{b} = \underline{a} \not\sim \underline{b} \not\sim (\underline{a} \wedge \underline{b}).$$

For orthogonal elements $\underline{a}$ and $\underline{b}$, this relation is changed to

$$\underline{a} \vee \underline{b} = \underline{a} \not\sim \underline{b}$$

because of $\underline{a} \wedge \underline{b} = 0$ and $\underline{x} \not\sim \underline{0} = \underline{x}$.

In the same way:

$$\underline{a} \wedge \underline{b} = \underline{a} \sim \underline{b} \ .$$

If K_i or D_i are conjunctions or disjunctions of a binary function $f(\underline{x})$ in disjunctive or exclusive-or form (conjunctive or equivalence form) and if $K_i \wedge K_j = 0$ ($D_i \vee D_j = 1$) for all $i \neq j$, then

$$\bigvee_{i=1}^{l} K_i = \sum_{i=1}^{l} K_i, \quad \text{or} \quad \bigwedge_{i=1}^{l} D_i = \mathop{E}_{i=1}^{l} D_i, \text{ respectively.}$$

If applied to ternary vectors, the following holds for orthogonality:

Two ternary vectors are called orthogonal to each other if the combination "0,1" appears at least once in case of componentwise comparison.
A ternary vector list is called orthogonalized if all pairs of ternary vectors are orthogonal to each other.
Orthogonal ternary vector lists have any advantages for solving binary problems compared to non-orthogonal ternary vector lists.
An orthogonal ternary vector list can represent optionally a disjunctive and exclusive-or form or a conjunctive and equivalence form, respectively.
Therefore, it is not necessary to provide converting algorithms.
If necessary, each processing activity can be completed by a non-orthogonal minimization.

5. Operations with ternary vector lists

Set algorithms are realized in a program system called BOOLE solving the following problems:
- union of ternary vector lists ($\cup$),
- intersection of two orthogonal ternary vector lists ($\cap$),
- difference of ternary vector lists ($\setminus$),
- symmetric difference of ternary vector lists (Δ),
- complement of symmetric difference of ternary vector lists ($\overline{\Delta}$),
- complementation of a ternary vector list ($^{-}$),
- minimization of a ternary vector list.

They are based on basic algorithms solving the following problems:
a) orthogonalizing ternary vectors,
b) reducing the number of ternary vectors by minimization.

6. Solution of binary equations and systems of equations given in an arbitrary form

The binary equation, $f(\underline{x}) = g(\underline{x})$, can be transformed to a homogenous equation form by applying the exclusive-or or the equivalence operation:

$$f(\underline{x}) \nsim g(\underline{x}) = 0, \qquad f(\underline{x}) \sim g(\underline{x}) = 1.$$

A homogenous binary equation is called to be in arbitrary form if the term $h(x)$ in the equation $h(\underline{x}) = 0$ or $h(\underline{x}) = 1$, respectively, is not a normal form. Binary equations in arbitrary form will be solved by decomposition of the binary function $h(\underline{x})$. The function $h(\underline{x})$ is decomposed in possible parts $h_i(\underline{x})$, $i=1,\dots,n$, representing each one a normal form. In borderline case, a binary variable or a constant is used as a normal form.
At first the functions $h_i(\underline{x})$ are solved providing the solution sets

$L_1(h_i)$. (The solution sets $L_1(h_i)$ are uniquely used in BOOLE because of standardization).

The solution set of the arbitrary equation composed of $h_i(\underline{x})$ is determined by applying the described set algorithms to the solution sets $L_1(h_i)$ corresponding to the given table. The operation priorities in binary equations of arbitrary form are considered by using the Polish Notation.

7. Language definition of the program system BOOLE (Subset)

A command language is provided by the program system BOOLE for solving binary problems. The main functions are:

Set operations – This commands will be used for the given set operations with ternary vector lists: BBT – minimization, NEG – complementation of a ternary vector list, NDM – negation for realizing the transformations between disjunctive and conjunctive as well as exclusive-or and equivalent forms, respectively, V – union, D – intersection, A – exclusive-or (symmetric difference), E – equivalence (complement of symmetric difference).

Input operations – The input operation of a binary equation activates the solution of the equation. The input operation of a ternary vector list corresponding to the type statement provides the changing of a ternary vector list to a disjunctive form equal to 1.

$$\left\{\begin{matrix} EBS \\ ELK \\ EMP \end{matrix}\right\} \left\{\begin{matrix} M(type) \\ G \end{matrix}\right\} [L] \; [P] \; [S.BN]$$

storage with an inventory
name in a library

print

list

The operand is a ternary vector list corresponding to the type statement or a binary equation in arbitrary form

Input from display unit, card reader or megnatic disk

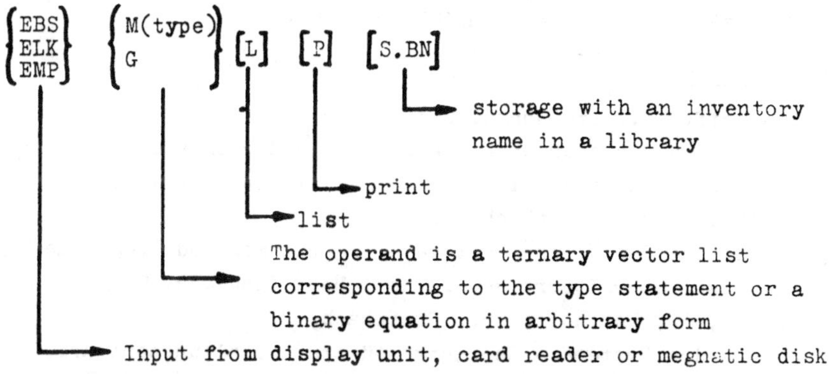

Output operations – They are used for transfering solutions to the desired devices.

Variable correspondance – The correspondance between columns of a ternary vector list and the variables can be changed. It is a basic command for the composition and decomposition of ternary vector lists.

Editor commands – An efficient EDITOR-system is provided. It is possible to apply some operations to the inventories. This is very precious for the dialogue mode.

Processing command sequences - The command language of the realized program system permits the extension of the language by commands representing command sequences.

8. Summary

We have represented the foundations of a program system permitting the handling of logic problems up to 64 variables. The realized program system can be used under control of the operating system OS/MVT and OS/MVS. A combination of dialogue and closed shop computing is possible. The program is written in PASCAL and ASSEMBLER.

Some fields of application for the realized algorithms vicarious for other thinkable utilizations:

- Synthesis of switching networks;
- Decomposition of switching networks;
- Analysis, checking, diagnosis and simulation of switching networks;
- Software solutions for binary controls;
- ROM and RAM network synthesis;
- Microprogramming;
- Solving graph problems;
- Tasks of discrete optimization;
- Logics;
- Discrete problems (finite mathematics).

9. Literature

- Posthoff, Ch., Steinbach, B.:
  Binäre Gleichungen - Algorithmen und Programme,
  Wiss. Schriftenreihe, TH Karl-Marx-Stadt, 1/1979
- Posthoff, Ch., Steinbach, B.:
  Binäre dynamische Systeme - Algorithmen und Programme,
  Wiss. Schriftenreihe, TH Karl-Marx-Stadt, 9/1979
- Fehmel, J., Posthoff, Ch., Steinbach, B.:
  Binäre Systeme - Rechnergestützter Schaltungsentwurf,
  Wiss. Schriftenreihe, TH Karl-Marx-Stadt, 7/1982
- Reiß, J.:
  Ein Beitrag zur rechentechnischen Lösung analytisch formulierter, binärer Problemstellungen hoher Variablenzahl im Dialog,
  Dissertation, IHS Mittweida, 1984
- Steinbach, B.:
  Theorie, Algorithmen und Programme für den rechnergestützten logischen Entwurf digitaler Systeme, Diss., TH Karl-Marx-Stadt, 1984

FORMALIZING ANALOGICAL REASONING

Dieter Pötschke [1)]

1. Introduction

Analogical reasoning or problem solving by analogy was studied by different authors in logic [1],[2] and artificial intelligence, e.g. [3] - [7]. Mathematical well-founded approaches, which can lead to programs which can check analogies between structures or transformations of structures can be found in [6] and [7].

Analogical transformation of programs for robots are studied in [8], [9]. Checking the analogy between chemical reaction equations is studied in [6] and plays an important role in our project RDX (=reaction design expertsystem), which can simulate organic synthesis and is now under development.

From a more general point of view a mathematical theory of analogical reasoning has

(i) to explain how to reason analogically in the simplest cases

(ii) to give a formal basis on which computational algorithms can be constructed to solve formalized problems by analogical reasoning.

2. The model

The analogy problem

G1 : G2 = H1 : H2

can be formalized in two steps:

(i) Give mathematical representations of the objects G1,G2,H1,H2, e.g. as relational algebras or labelled digraphs, see [6].

(ii) If we consider the model

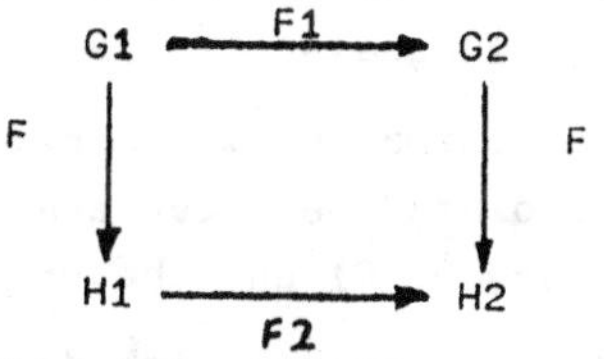

then F,F1,F2,G can be formalized as graphhomomorphisms, homomorphisms with defect or as graphtransformations, compare [6].

---

1) Dept. Art. Int., Central Inst. of Cyb. and Inform. Proc. Academy of Sc. GDR, GDR-1080 Berlin, Kurstr. 33.

There are strong connections with the theory of graph grammars, the categorial theory of pullback diagrams and the theory of inductive learning in the sense of K.-P. Jantke on which we handle in another paper.

3. The algorithm

The analogy algorithm A-2 works in the following steps:

(i) Describe G1,G2,H1,H2 as labelled digraphs.

(ii) Determine a maximal common partial graph of G1 and G2.

(iii) Compute the difference G1\G2.

(iv) Generate a minimal set of graph transformations $F1 = \{F_1, \ldots, F_k\}$ with

$$F_1(\ldots F_k(G1)\ldots) = G2.$$

(v) Check whether

$$F1(F^{-1}(H1)) = F^{-1}(H2).$$

4. A PROLOG-program for the algorithm A-2

In principle the program is independent from the kind of representationof the graphs, but the representation in PASCAL is more effective than in Standard PROLOG.

We define the following basic functions for edges and vertices:

```
edge(G,N,X/A-Y/B) :- ([P=..[x,G,N,X/A,Y/B],P=..(x,G,N,Y,B,X/A])),
                     call(P),
   where  G  - name of the graph
          N  - label of the edge X-Y
          X,Y- labels of the vertices
          A,B- numbers of the vertices A,B ∈{1,...,M}

verlist (G,[X/A,X1/A1,...,XM/AM]).
```

The function analog(-,-,-,-,-) checks the analogy of F1 and F2. Therefore it is structured in three subgoals:

delteil(G1,G2,F1): builds the maximal common partial graphs of G1 and G2; identical edges and isolated vertices are retracted; F1 is the mapping between the vertices of G1 and the vertices of G2.

embedding (G1,H1,F): looks for a mapping which determines an embedding from G1 into H1.

isom(G2,H2,F): checks the existence of an isomorphism between G2 and H2 with help of the detected embedding F, if there exists one.

The following program is written in DEC-10-PROLOG and runs on a SM 52 computer.

program:

```
   analog(G1,G2,H1,H2,F) :- delteil(G1,G2,F1),delteil(H1,H2,F2),!,
                             embedding(G1,H1,F), isom(G2,H2,F).
```

As an example we give delteil in detail.

```
delteil(GX,GY,FF):- vertlist(GX,L1),vertlist(GY,L2),
                    knozu (L1,L2,L3,F1),
                    pass1 (G1,G2,F1),
                    pass2 (G1,G2,L3,L4),
                    assertz(y(G1,L4)),assertz(y(G2,L4)).
  knozu([ ],[ ],[ ],[ ]).
  knozu([X/A | L4 ,L5, [ X/A | L3],[X/A*X/A | F ] ) :- moveon(X/A,L5,L6),
                                                        knozu (L4,L6,L3,F).
  knozu([X/A|L4],L5,[X/A,Y/A|L3],[X/A*Y/A|F]):- moveon(Y/A,L5,L6),
                                                knozu(L4,L6,L3,F).
  moveon(Z,[Z/Z1],Z1):-!.
  moveon(Z,[Z1 |Z2],[Z1|Z3]):- moveon(Z,Z2,Z3).
  pass1 (G1,G2,[_/A*_/A|FF]):- edge(G1,N,_/A-_/C1),
                               edge(G2,N,_/A-_/C1),
                               retractall(x(G1,N,_/A,_/C1)).
                               retractall(x(G2,N,_/A,_/C1)),
                               pass(G1,G2,FF).
  pass1(G1,G2,[_/A*_A/FF]):- pass1(G1,G2,FF).
  pass2(G1,G2,[X/A | L3],[X/A| L4]):-(edge(G1,N,X/A-_/_),
                                      edge(G2,N,X/A-_/_)),
                                      pass2(G1,G2,L3,L4).
  pass2(G1,G2,[X/A|L3],L4):- pass2(G1,G2,L3,L4).
  pass2(G1,G2,[ ],[ ]).
```

This program was written by U.Zöphel from the Technical University Dresden under the author's guidance.

Literature:

[1] J.LINDENBAUM-HOSIASSON:
Induction et Analogie. In: Mind, vol.L, October 1941.

[2] Ch.G.MORGAN:
Modality, analogy, and ideal experiments according to C.S.Peirce. Synthese 41(1979),65-83.

[3] P.H.WINSTON:
Artificial Intelligence.Addison-Wesley Publishing Comp.,Reading, Mass.1977.

[4] B.V.FUNT:
Analogical modes of reasoning and process model_ing. Computer 16(1983)10,99-1o4.

[5] J.W.ULRICH,R.MOLL:
Program synthesis by analogy. Symp.Art. Int. and Programming Languages, Rochester, N.Y., Aug.1977, 22-28.

[6] D.PÜTSCHKE:
Toward a mathematical theory of analogical reasoning. Proc. 1982 European Conf. on Artificial Intelligence, 12-14 July, Orsay, France, 48-53.

[7] M.HARAGUCHI:
Towards a mathematical theory of analogy.
Bull.Inf.Cyb. 21(1985), 3/4,29-56.

[8] S.TANGWONGSAN,K.S.FU:
An application of learning a robot planning. Int. J. of Computer and Information Sciences. 8(1979), 3o3- 333.

[9] D. PÖTSCHKE:
Generation of analogical programs for robots. Res. Rep. ZKI/1983, 64-1o2.

Some Results in the Theory of Effective Program Synthesis: Learning by Defective Information

Gisela Schäfer [1)]

INTRODUCTION

Since the early paper of Gold [4] a lot of research has been done in the theory of Inductive Inference (see [1], [5]). This has been motivated by questions that arise in Artificial Intelligence and in Cognition. In order to illuminate the theoretical background of these fields, a lot of modifications of the original Gold model have been studied. While usually the input information of an inferential process is modelled by an exact and complete enumeration of the graph of a (partial) recursive function, we are concerned with a modification of the information presentation here:
we allow as input graph enumerations which include mistakes at finitely many arguments x, i.e. tuples (x,y) where y is not the right image for the enumerated function. The aim of an inferential process on such a 'noisy' input e is to compute in the limit a program for one of the functions e enumerates in such a defective way. This modification of the Gold paradigm is motivated by real learning processes (e.g. observation of experiments, language learning) where there are often several functional values for one input argument, i.e. the input graph enumerations define multivalued functions.
Our aim is to study the effect of input mistakes on the power of different types of inferential strategies.

PRELIMINARIES AND DEFINITIONS

N denotes the set of natural numbers, P is the set of all partial recursive functions. Let $(\phi_i)_{i=0}$ be an acceptable numbering of P (see [6]). For $\phi \in P$, graph(ϕ) is the set of all tuples $(x,\phi(x))$ for $x \in$ domain(ϕ). A graph enumeration e of $\phi \in P$ is a total recursive function from **N** to $\mathbf{N}^2 \cup \{*\}$ such that graph(ϕ) $\subseteq$ range(e) and $e(i)=(x,y) \implies \phi(x)=y$ for all $i \in \mathbf{N}$. We write e[n] to denote the initial segment e(0) e(1) ... e(n) of e. In the following let always $n,m \in \mathbf{N}$ and $a,b \in \mathbf{N} \cup \{*\}$. For $\phi,\phi' \in P$ we write $\phi \subseteq^n \phi'$ ($\phi \subseteq^* \phi'$) iff for all but at most n (finitely many) arguments x

$$\phi(x)\downarrow \implies \phi'(x)\downarrow \wedge\ \phi(x)=\phi'(x).$$

An inference machine M (in the sense of Gold [4]) works in a limiting recursive manner as follows:
M reads successively larger initial segments of some graph enumeration of a partial recursive function ϕ; if the computation of M does not diverge on some initial segment M outputs an infinite sequence M(e[0]), M(e[1]), ... of hypothesized programs for ϕ. M is said to <u>EX^a-identify ϕ</u> (see [3]), iff on any graph enumeration e of ϕ and for all n: $M(e[n])\downarrow$ and (1) and (2) hold.

1) Lehr- und Forschungsgebiet Theoretische Informatik, RWTH Aachen, Büchel 29-31, 5100 Aachen, BRD

(1) $\lim_n M(e[n]) =: i$ exists.

(2) $\phi \subseteq^a \phi_i$.

We write $M(e)\downarrow$ to indicate that $\lim_n M(e[n])$ exists, we also write $M(e)=i$.

Let $EX^a := \{U \subseteq P | (\exists M)\ M\ EX^a\text{-identifies any } \phi \in U\}$. $EX^0 \subset EX^1 \subset \ldots \subset EX^*$ is shown in [3].

In order to include 'noisy' information in our learning model, we define 'anomalous' graph enumerations and distinguish them by the number of arguments where anomalies occur and by the degree of multivaluedness at such arguments:
We call a total function $e: N \to N^2 \cup \{*\}$ n-single-valued, iff

$$AN(e) := \{x \in N | (\exists y_1, y_2 \in N)\ y_1 \neq y_2 \wedge (x,y_1) \in range(e) \wedge (x,y_2) \in range(e)\}$$

has cardinality less than n. e is called *-single-valued, iff the cardinality of An(e) is finite. e is called a,*-single-valued, iff e is a-single-valued and for all $x \in An(e)$ the cardinality of $\{y | (x,y) \in range(e)\}$ is finite.
There are at least two reasonable ways to define an anomalous graph enumeration of a function $\phi \in P$; first we are concerned with the following:

Definition 1

Let $\phi \in P$. A total function $e: N \to N^2 \cup \{*\}$ is an a(,*)-anomalous graph enumeration of ϕ, iff (1) and (2) hold.

(1) e is a(,*)-single-valued.

(2) $graph(\phi) \subseteq range(e)$ and $(\forall (x,y) \in range(e))\ \ x \in domain(\phi)$.

That means, that e enumerates some 'noisy' elements **besides** the original graph of ϕ, and noise can only appear at arguments of domain(ϕ). We write $e \in SV^{a(,*)}(\phi)$.

Definition 2

An inference machine M is said to ^{a}EX-identify (^{a,*}EX-identify) a function $\phi \in P$, iff M on any a-anomalous (a,*-anomalous) graph enumeration e of ϕ outputs an infinite sequence of hypothesises M(e[0]), M(e[1]), ... with (1) and (2).

(1) $\lim_n M(e[n]) =: i$ exists.

(2) $(\exists \phi' \in P)\ \ e \in SV^a(\phi')\ \ \ (\text{rsp. } \ e \in SV^{a,*}(\phi')) \wedge\ \ \phi' \subseteq \phi_i$,
that means ϕ_i is an extension of one of the (with respect to graph inclusion) maximal functions enumerated by e.

Let $^{a(,*)}EX := \{U \subseteq P | (\exists M)\ M\ ^{a(,*)}EX\text{-identifies any } \phi \in U\}$.
Our aim is to study the effect of input mistakes on the power of different types of inference machines. For that purpose we extend the definition of some well known properties of inference machines to our new model:

Definition 3

An inference machine M is called

(i) <u>reliable on a-single-valued input</u>, iff

$$M(e)\downarrow \implies (\exists \phi \in P)\ e \in SV^a(\phi) \wedge \phi \subseteq \phi_{M(e)}$$

for any a-single-valued e;

(ii) <u>weak on a-single-valued input</u>, iff $M(e)\downarrow$ for any a-single-valued e;

(iii) <u>normal on a-single-valued input</u>, iff M is neither reliable nor weak on a-single-valued input;

(iv) <u>finite on a-single-valued input</u>, iff whenever on some a-single-valued e two successive hypothesises i_n and i_{n+1} of M are equal, then $M(e)=i_n$;

(v) <u>consistent on a-single-valued input</u>, iff whenever M outputs some hypothesis i after having seen e[n] of some a-single-valued e, then

$$(\forall x)\ [(\exists y)\ (x,y) \in \{e(0), \dots , e(n)\} \implies \phi_i(x)\downarrow \wedge (x,\phi_i(x)) \in \{e(0), \dots , e(n)\}\ ].$$

(vi) <u>iterative on a-single-valued input</u>, iff there is a partial recursive function F: $(\mathbf{N}^2 \cup \{*\}) \times \mathbf{N} \to \mathbf{N}$ such that for all a-single-valued e and for all $n \geq 1$:

$$M(e[n]) = F(e(n), M(e[n-1])).$$

The properties 'reliable on a,*-single-valued input', 'weak on a,*-single-valued input' etc. are defined analoguously. For I ∈ {REL,WEAK,NORM,CONS,FIN,IT} let ${}^aI$ (${}^{a,*}I$) denote the class of all sets of partial recursive functions which are ${}^{a(,*)}EX$-identified by some machine M having the property corresponding to I, that means M is reliable, weak, ..., iterative on a(,*)-single-valued input.

RESULTS

Since for any $\phi \in P$ and a<b we have $SV^{a,*}(\phi) \subseteq SV^{b,*}(\phi) \subseteq SV^b(\phi) \subseteq SV^*(\phi)$, the following scheme holds for any I:

$$\begin{array}{ccccccccc} {}^{*,*}I & \subseteq \dots \subseteq & {}^{n+1,*}I & \subseteq & {}^{n,*}I & \subseteq \dots & \subseteq & & \\ \cup\!\!| & & \cup\!\!| & & \cup\!\!| & & & {}^0I & . \\ {}^{*}I & \subseteq \dots \subseteq & {}^{n+1}I & \subseteq & {}^{n}I & \subseteq \dots & \subseteq & & \end{array}$$

These relations can be specified depending on the choice of I, indicating that the inferential power of different types of machines is affected in different ways by the presence of input anomalies, depending on the number of arguments where faulty images occur, and depending on the degree of ambiguity of the input enumeration; only the power of reliable machines remains unaffected:

<u>Theorem 1</u>

(i) ${}^aREL = {}^{a,*}REL = {}^0REL$ for any a.

(ii) ${}^*WEAK \subset \dots \subset {}^{n+1}WEAK \subset {}^nWEAK \subset \dots \subset {}^0WEAK = {}^{a,*}WEAK$ for any a.

(iii) $$\begin{array}{ccccccccl} {}^{*,*}I & \subset \dots \subset & {}^{n+1,*}I & \subset & {}^{n,*}I & \subset \dots & & & \\ \cup & \# & \cup & \# & \cup & & \supset & {}^{0}I & \text{for } I \in \{EX, NORM\}, \\ {}^{*}I & \subset \dots \subset & {}^{n+1}I & \subset & {}^{n}I & \subset \dots & & & \end{array}$$

where for two sets A,B '$A \# B$' means $A \not\subseteq B \wedge B \not\subseteq A$.

(iv) ${}^{*,*}I \subset \dots \subset {}^{n+1,*}I \subset {}^{n,*}I \subset \dots \subset {}^{0}I$ and ${}^{a,*}I = {}^{a}I$ for any a and $I \in \{FIN, CONS\}$.

(v) $$\begin{array}{cccccccl} {}^{*,*}IT & \subset \dots \subset & {}^{n+1,*}IT & \subset & {}^{n,*}IT & \subset \dots & & \\ \cup\!\! \mid & & \cup\!\! \mid & & \cup\!\! \mid & & \supset & {}^{0}IT \;, \\ {}^{*}IT & \subset \dots \subset & {}^{n+1}IT & \subset & {}^{n}IT & \subset \dots & & \end{array}$$

it is open by now, whether ${}^{a}IT \neq {}^{a,*}IT$ or not.

Sketch of proof:

For any I a claim '$I_1 = I_2$', where $I_1 \subseteq I_2$ is already known, is proved by simulation: assuming $U \in I_2$ via some machine M_2 we construct an inference machine M_1 which identifies any $\phi \in U$ on the sort of graph enumerations according to I_1, M_1 uses M_2 as 'subprogram'. For example, (i) is proved by verifying $REL \subseteq {}^{*}REL$:
if M_2 is a reliable machine ${}^{0}EX$-identifying some $U \subseteq P$, a reliable machine M_1 ${}^{*}EX$-identifying U may be constructed. On any anomalous graph enumeration e M_1 searches for some maximal exact graph enumeration e' included in e with $M_2(e')\downarrow$ and outputs in the limit a program for $\phi_{M(e')}$. We omit details here.

When verifying proper inclusionships, although for any type of inference machines the proof of a corresponding claim $I_1 \subset I_2$ is different in detail, we only need two sorts of inferable sets as 'witnesses' for all these claims:
one is the family of sets

$$S^n := \{\phi \in P \mid (\forall x \leq n)\ \phi(x) = \phi(0) \ \wedge \ \phi \subseteq \phi_{\phi(0)}\},$$

the other is the family of sets $T^n \cup L_0$, where

$$T^n := \{\phi \in P \mid (\forall x \in N)\ (\phi(x)=1 \Longrightarrow \phi \subseteq \phi_x) \ \wedge \ (\exists x_0, \dots, \exists x_n)\ [(\forall i,j \leq n)\ i \neq j \Longrightarrow x_i \neq x_j \ \wedge \ \phi(x_i) = 1]\},$$

and

$$L_0 := \{\phi \in P \mid (\overset{\infty}{\forall} x)\ \phi(x) = 0 \wedge 1 \notin range(\phi)\}.$$

For these sets we can prove the following lemmata:

(i) $S^n \in {}^{n}FIN \cap {}^{n}IT \cap {}^{n}SW \cap {}^{*,*}NO$.

(ii) $S^n \notin {}^{n+1}EX \cup {}^{n+1,*}IT$.

(iii) $T^n \cup L_0 \in {}^{n}CONS \cap {}^{n}NO$.

(iv) $T^n \cup L_0 \notin {}^{n+1,*}EX$.

The theorem follows as a combination of these results. Positive inclusionships claimed in the lemmata are always proved by constructing the desired inference machine, see [7] for details. We concentrate on the negative subclaims here.

$S^n \notin {}^{n+1}EX$:

To see $S^0 \notin {}^{1}EX$ (the case $n \geq 1$ is analoguous), assume $S^0 \in {}^{1}EX$ via some inference machine M. Let $a_0\, a_1\, a_2 \dots \in (N^2 \cup \{*\})^{\mathbf{N}}$ be any exact graph enumeration of some $\phi \in S^0$, then M identifies $\phi \in S^0$ on the graph enumeration

$$e(\phi) := (0,0)\ a_0\ (0,1)\ a_1\ (0,2)\ a_2 \ldots (0,n)\ a_n \ldots$$

as well, where anomalies occur only at the argument 0 and all natural numbers occur as a value there. Since for any $\phi \in P$ there is a function $\phi' \in S^0$ with $\phi(x) = \phi'(x+1)$ for any $x \in \mathbf{N}$, M can be used to construct some M' which EX^0-identifies any $\phi \in \mathbf{P}$: on some graph enumeration of $\phi \in \mathbf{P}$, M' simulates M on an enumeration $e(\phi')$ of the corresponding function ϕ' and reconstructs ϕ from the hypothesis of M. Since the problem of EX^0-identifying any $\phi \in P$ is unsolvable (see [3] or [4]), this leads to a contradiction.

$S^n \not\in {}^{n+1,*}IT$:

the assumption $S^0 \in {}^{1,*}IT$ via some M is let to a contradiction by use of the double recursion theorem of Smullyan (see [6]), the case $\underline{n \geq 1}$ is analoguous. We define two functions ϕ_n, ϕ_m simultanously by the following algorithm:

```
start:      φm(0) = m;
            φn(0) = n;
            goto 1.1;

stage 1.x:  (φn and φm are already defined for arguments ≤ x-1)
            let σx := (0,n)(0,m)(1,φn(1))...(x-1,φn(x-1));
            if M(σx^(x,0)) ≠ M(σx):
               φn(x) = φm(x) := 0;
               goto 1.x+1;
            else if M(σx^(x,1)) ≠ M(σx):
                  φn(x) = φm(x) := 1;
                  goto 1.x+1;
                else φn(x) := 0;
                     φm(x) := 1;
                     goto 2.x+1;

stage 2.x:  φn(x) = φm(x) := 0;
            goto 2.x+1;
```

M cannot diverge on some $\sigma_x\hat{}(x,0)$ or $\sigma_x\hat{}(x,1)$: w.l.o.g. suppose $M(\sigma_x\hat{}(x,0))\uparrow$, then M diverges on some 1,*-single-valued graph enumeration of the function

$$\phi_k(z) := \begin{cases} k & \text{for } z = 0, \\ \phi_n(z) & \text{for } 1 \leq z \leq x-1, \\ 0 & \text{for } z \geq x; \end{cases}$$

since $\phi_k \in S^0$ this is a contradiction. Thus, ϕ_n and ϕ_m become total.
If the above algorithm never reaches some stage 2.x, then M changes the hypothesis infinetely often on a 1,*-single-valued graph enumeration of ϕ_n, thus M does not identify $\phi_n \in S^0$, a contradiction. If M reaches some stage 2.x, then since M is iterative it will reach the same final hypothesis on 1,*-single-valued graph enumerations of ϕ_n and ϕ_m although $\phi_n(x-1) \neq \phi_m(x-1)$, again a contradiction, since M should EX^0-identify both functions on those enumerations.

$T^n \cup L_0 \not\in {}^{n+1,*}EX$ is finally proved using the recursion theorem by transferring a well known idea of Blum and Blum [2] to our new input conventions. We omit details. #

Combining input anomalies with output anomalies as they are implicit in the definition of EX^a-identification leads to the concept of <u>$^aEX^b$-identification</u> (rsp. <u>$^{a,*}EX^b$-identification</u>) in a straight forward way.

<u>Theorem 2</u>

$$\begin{array}{ccccccccc}
EX & \subset & \dots & \subset & EX^m & \subset & EX^{m+1} \subset & \dots \subset & EX^* \\
\cup & & & & \cup & & \cup & & \cup \\
{}^nEX & \subset & \dots & \subset & {}^nEX^m & \subset & {}^nEX^{m+1} \subset & \dots \subset & {}^nEX^* \\
\cup & & & & \cup & & \cup & & \cup \\
{}^{n+1}EX & \subset & \dots & \subset & {}^{n+1}EX^m & \subset & {}^{n+1}EX^{m+1} \subset & \dots \subset & {}^{n+1}EX^* \\
\cup & & & & \cup & & \cup & & \cup \\
{}^*EX & \subset & \dots & \subset & {}^*EX^m & \subset & {}^*EX^{m+1} \subset & \dots \subset & {}^*EX^*
\end{array}$$

The same scheme holds for $^{a,*}EX^b$-identification.

The horizontal inclusions are proved the same way Case and Smith proved their EX^a-hierarchy (see [3]), the vertical inclusions are proved the same way as the analoguous claim of theorem 1, (iii).
Furthermore, we can prove that in general the tolerance of output anomalies cannot help to deal with input anomalies, as well as output anomalies cannot be reduced by offering a 'more precise' input enumeration: part (i) of the following theorem says that both sorts of anomalies cannot be traded against each other.

<u>Theorem 3</u>

(i) $^{n(,*)}EX^m \;\#\; ^{b(,*)}EX^a$ for b>n and a>m.

(ii) $^aEX^n \subset {}^aEX^b \cap {}^mEX^n$ for a>m and b>n.

The analogy to (ii) is an open question for $^{a,*}EX^b$-identification.

<u>Sketch of proof:</u>

(i) Because of theorem 2 we only have to prove

(1) $^nEX^m \setminus {}^{n+1}EX^* \neq \emptyset$ and

(2) $^*EX^{m+1} \setminus {}^nEX^m \neq \emptyset$.

A witness for (1) is the set $S^{n,m} := \{\phi \in P \mid (\forall x \leq n)\ \phi(x) = \phi(0) \wedge \phi \subseteq^m \phi_{\phi(0)}\}$: by techniques sketched above it can be verified that $S^{n,m} \in {}^{n+1}EX^*$ implies the existence of a machine M which EX^*-identifies any $\phi \in P$, a contradiction to a result in [3]. (2) can be proved by verifying $T^{0,m+1} := \{\phi \in P \mid (\exists x)\ \phi(x)=1 \wedge (\forall x)\ (\phi(x)=1 \implies \phi \subseteq^{m+1} \phi_x)\} \in {}^*EX^{m+1} \setminus EX^m$, where $T^{0,m+1} \notin EX^m$ is proved via the recursion theorem by transferring an idea of Case and Smith [3].

(ii) The set $S^{n/m+1} := \{\phi \in P \mid (\forall x \leq n)\ \phi(x) = \phi(0) \wedge \phi \subseteq^m \phi_{\phi(0)} \wedge \phi \subseteq^{m+1} \phi_{\phi(n+1)}\}$ is in $({}^{n+1}EX^{m+1} \cap {}^nEX^m) \setminus {}^{n+1}EX^m$, because the assumption $S^{n/m+1} \in {}^{n+1}EX^m$ implies the existence of a machine M which EX^m-identifies any $\phi \in P$, a contradiction to a result in [3]. #

MODIFICATIONS

Besides other possibilities (which will lead to similar results) another way to define an anomalous graph enumeration of a function $\phi \in P$ is the following:

Definition 1'

Let $\phi \in \mathbf{P}$. A total function e: $\mathbf{N} \to \mathbf{N}^2 \cup \{*\}$ is an a(,*)-anomalous graph enumeration of ϕ, iff e is a(,*)-single-valued and (1)' and (2)' hold:

(1)' $(\forall x \in \text{domain}(\phi))\ (\exists y \in \mathbf{N})\ \ (x,y) \in \text{range}(e)$.

(2)' For all but at most a (rsp. finitely many if a=*) $x \in \mathbf{N}$ the following holds: $(\forall y \in \mathbf{N})\ (x,y) \in \text{range}(e) \implies \phi(x)=y$.

That means that e enumerates various functions which are equal to ϕ and have the same domain as ϕ up to at most a (rsp. finitely many) arguments. We write $e \in \widetilde{SV}^{a(,*)}(\phi)$. $^{a(,*)}\widetilde{EX}$-identification is defined as $^{a(,*)}EX$-identification with $\widetilde{SV}^{a(,*)}(\phi)$ instead of $SV^{a(,*)}(\phi)$. We define $^{a}\widetilde{I}$ and $^{a,*}\widetilde{I}$ for $I \in \{REL, WEAK, \ldots\}$ in a similar way as above. The situation is less complicated now:
We get $^{*}\widetilde{REL} = {}^{0}\widetilde{REL}$ and $^{*}\widetilde{I} \subset \ldots \subset {}^{n+1}\widetilde{I} \subset {}^{n}\widetilde{I} \subset \ldots \subset {}^{0}\widetilde{I}$ and $^{a}\widetilde{I} = {}^{a,*}\widetilde{I}$ for any a and $I \in \{EX, WEAK, NORM, CONS, FIN, IT\}$. This is easily proved by a simple construction verifying $^{a}\widetilde{I} = {}^{a,*}\widetilde{I}$ for any I and using the set S^n as a witness for the proper inclusionships. All further results carry over to this situation.

CONCLUSIONS

From our proofs we know that there may be certain sensitive points in the domain of a function where input mistakes may confuse a certain type of identifying machines more than mistakes at other arguments. Also the sort of faulty images offered as input may increase the confusion more or less. This should be inspected for concrete inferential processes. Similar investigations are open for other identification types (e.g. BC-identification, see [3]).

LITERATURE

[1] ANGLUIN, D. and C.H. SMITH : A Survey of Inductive Inference: Theory and Methods, Computing Surveys 15 (237-269), 1983.

[2] BLUM, E. and M. BLUM : Towards a Mathematical Theory of Inductive Inference, Inform. Control 28 (125-155), 1975.

[3] CASE, J. and C.H. SMITH : Comparison of Identification Criteria for Machine Inductive Inference, TCS 25 (193-220), 1983.

[4] GOLD, E.M. : Language Identification in the Limit, Inf. and Contr. 10, (447-474), 1967.

[5] KLETTE, R. and R. WIEHAGEN : Research in the Theory of Inductive Inference by GDR mathematicians - a Survey, Inf. Sciences 22 (149-169), 1980.

[6] ROGERS, H.Jr. : Theory of Recursive Functions and Effective Computability, McGraw-Hill, New York, 1967.

[7] SCHÄFER, G. : Über Eingabeabhängigkeit und Komplexität von Inferenzstrategien, Dissertation, RWTH Aachen 1984.

DEDUCTIVE NORMAL FORMS OF RELATIONS

B. Thalheim [1)]

The "normalization" of relations is one of the most important tools for database design. The concept of special kinds of dependencies has been proved to be useful in the design and analysis of relational databases. By using this concept, a new ("deductive") normal form of relational databases is defined. This deductive normal form is better than other known normal forms in the most cases. By using special tuple-generating dependencies as deduction rules we get the entry relation from its deductive normal form. During the query phase, the rules are used to generate all possible derivations of facts and thereby make them again explicit in the database. But from recursive deduction rules arises the termination problem when the rules are used since potentially they may lead to infinite derivation paths. However, in the case of single decomposition dependencies as deduction rules or in the case of classes of decomposition dependencies generated by a single decomposition dependency it is possible to find a termination condition which cuts potentially infinite derivation paths. Therefore in this paper a condition for classes of decomposition dependencies to be generated by single decomposition dependencies is given moreover.

1. Basic notions and problems

We assume some familiarity with the relational model. In this section we define the elements of the model used in the paper.

Attributes or column names are symbols from a given finite set $U = \{A_1, A_2, \ldots, A_n\}$ with a given fixed natural number n . We assume that with each attribute A there is associated a set, called its domain. Since in this paper are discussed only dependencies and deductive normal forms, w.l.o.g., we assume that there is one domain G .

A relational data structure (on U) is a system $\langle G , R \rangle$, where R is a finite subset of G^U called relation.

For a subset X of U , a relation R and a tuple r of R we denote by $r(X)$ the restriction of r to X .

A special Horn-formula

$$P(x_{11},\ldots,x_{1n})\&\ldots\&P(x_{m1},\ldots,x_{mn}) \longrightarrow P(x_{01},\ldots,x_{0n})$$

is called strong tuple-generating dependency (TGD) ,

1) Sektion Mathematik, Technische Universität Dresden
DDR - 8027 Dresden

if $x_{ij} = x_{kl}$ then $j = l$ $(0 \le i,k \le m,\ 1 \le j,l \le n)$ and
if for all x_{oj} there is a k, $1 \le k \le m$, with $x_{oj} = x_{kj}$,
and is called decomposition dependency (DD) if moreover for all i,j $(1 \le i < j \le m)$ and k $(1 \le k \le n)$ from $x_{ij} = x_{jk}$ follows $x_{ik} = x_{ok}$ (no hidden conditions in premise).

A tuple-generating dependency means that if some tuples, fulfilling certain conditions, exist in the relation then another tuple must also exist in the relation.

A join dependency (JD) is a cover $(X_1,\dots,X_k)$ of U. A DD

$$P(x_{11},\dots,x_{1n}) \,\&\, \dots \,\&\, P(x_{m1},\dots,x_{mn}) \longrightarrow P(x_{o1},\dots,x_{on})$$

is equivalent to the JD $(X_1,\dots,X_m)$
with $X_i = \{ A_j \mid x_{ij} = x_{oj} \}$.

Given a set of strong tuple-generating dependencies, a set G, a relation R on U and a set of interpretations $I(\Sigma) = \{ Pr^1 \,\&\, \dots \& \, Pr^k \longrightarrow Pr \}$ of Σ in G. Then we define

$$/R/_{\Sigma,0} = R ,$$

$$/R/_{\Sigma,i+1} = \{ r \in G^U \mid r^1,\dots,r^k \in /R/_{\Sigma,i} ,\ Pr^1 \& \dots Pr^k \rightarrow Pr \in I(\Sigma) \} \cup /R/_{\Sigma,i}$$

$$/R/_{\Sigma} = \bigcup_{i=o}^{\infty} /R/_{\Sigma,i} .$$

The set $/R/_{\Sigma}$ is called the Σ-closure of R.

Corollary 1. Given a finite relation R and a set of TGD , there is a natural number i such that $/R/_{\Sigma} = /R/_{\Sigma,i}$.

A relation $R \subseteq G^U$ is called Σ-closed if holds $R = /R/_{\Sigma}$.

A set of TGD Σ is true in R if holds $R = /R/_{\Sigma}$. A TGD β follows from a set Σ if all Σ-closed relations R are $\{\beta\}$-closed $(\Sigma \models \beta)$.

Given a set of TGD Σ and a Σ-closed relation R. A subset R' of R is called Σ-deductive subset if holds $/R'/_{\Sigma} = R$.

A Σ-deductive subset R' of R is called *Σ-deductive normal form of R* if there is no Σ-deductive subset R'' of R with $R'' \subsetneq R'$.

Given a relation R. Let be Σ_R the set of all TGD β with $/R/_{\{\beta\}} = R$. A Σ_R-deductive normal form of R is called *deductive normal form of R*.

Example 1. Given $G = \{0,1\}$, $n = 3$, $U = \{1,2,3\}$,
$\beta = P(x_1,x_2',x_3) \& P(x_1,x_2,x_3') \longrightarrow P(x_1,x_2,x_3)$ and
$R = \{(0,0,0),(0,0,1),(0,1,0),(0,1,1),(1,0,0)\}$.
The subsets $R' = \{(0,1,0),(0,0,1),(1,0,0)\}$ and
$R'' = \{(0,0,0),(0,1,1),(1,0,0)\}$ are $\{\beta\}$-deductive normal forms of R.

There are two main problems.

1. Given a deductive normal form R of a relation $/R/_{\Sigma}$. How many steps are needed for construction of the Σ-closure of R? For a given set Σ are there bounds for construction of Σ-closure of relations?
2. Given R and Σ. How to construct a Σ-deductive normal form of R?

For the second problem there are some algorithms. The first problem is harder. If for a given Σ the construction of Σ-closure is unlimited then the using of Σ-deductive normal forms is unprofitable.

Example 2. Given $U = \{1,2,3,4\}$, $G = \mathbb{N}'$,
$\beta_1 = P(x,y,z,u') \& P(x,y,z',u) \longrightarrow P(x,y,z,u)$,
$\beta_2 = P(x,y,z,u) \& P(x',y',z,u) \longrightarrow P(x,y',z,u)$, $\Sigma = \{\beta_1,\beta_2\}$,
$r_1 = (0,0,0,0)$ and for $i \geq 1$
$r_{2i}(\{1,2,3\}) = r_{2i-1}(\{1,2,3\})$, $r_{2i}(4) = r_{2i-1}(4) + 1$,
$r^+_{2i}(\{1,2,4\}) = r_{2i-1}(\{1,2,4\})$, $r^+_{2i}(3) = r_{2i-1}(3) + 1$,
$r_{2i+1}(\{1,3,4\}) = r_{2i}(\{1,3,4\})$, $r_{2i+1}(2) = r_{2i}(2) + 1$,
$r^+_{2i+1}(\{2,3,4\}) = r_{2i}(\{2,3,4\})$, $r^+_{2i+1}(1) = r_{2i}(1) + 1$.
Let be $R_1 = \{r_1\}$ and for $i \geq 2$ $R_i = R_{i-1} \setminus \{r_{i-1}\} \cup \{r_i, r^+_i\}$.
Then holds $(0,0,0,0) \in /R_{i+1}/_{\Sigma,i}$ and $(0,0,0,0) \notin /R_{i+1}/_{\Sigma,i-1}$,
i.e. $/R_{i+1}/_{\Sigma,i} \neq /R_{i+1}/_{\Sigma,i-1}$.

We get that for all natural numbers i exists a relation R with $/R/ \neq /R/_{\Sigma,i}$.

2. A solution of the first problem

Example 2 shows that there are sets of TGD and of DD without bounds for closure.

A set of DD Σ is called Sheffer-set if there is a DD β with $\Sigma \subseteq \{\beta' \mid \{\beta\} \models \beta'\}$, $\Sigma \models \beta$.

Theorem 1. Given a Sheffer-set Σ of DD. For any relation R holds $/R/_{\Sigma} = /R/_{\Sigma,1}$.

Theorem 1 cannot be extended to TGD.

Example 3. The TGD

$P(x,y',z,u')\&P(x',y,z,u')\&P(x,y',z',u)\&P(x',y,z',u) \longrightarrow P(x,y,z,u)$

is equivalent to the set Σ in example 2.

Proof.

For the proof of theorem 1 we use the approach of /3/ to recursive axioms.

We introduce some useful definitions. Given a TGD β with the set $Var(\beta)$ of variables and a subset V of $Var(\beta)$, a substitution $S_{\tilde{x}}^{\tilde{y}}$ of old variables $\tilde{x} = (x_1,\ldots,x_k)$ and corresponding new variables $\tilde{y} = (y_1,\ldots,y_k)$. The substitution $S_{\tilde{x}}^{\tilde{y}}$ is said to be safe for β and V if holds $\{y_1,\ldots,y_k\} \wedge Var(\beta) = \emptyset$ and $\{x_1,\ldots,x_k\} \cap V = \emptyset$.

Given two formulaes $\beta = \beta_1\&\ldots\&\beta_p$ and $\gamma = \gamma_1\&\ldots\&\gamma_q$ with atomar formulaes $\beta_1,\ldots,\beta_p,\gamma_1,\ldots,\gamma_q$.

Given $V \subseteq Var(\beta) \cup Var(\gamma)$.

A pair $\langle S_1,S_2\rangle$ of safe substitutions for β resp. γ and V is called safe unificator if holds

$\{S_1(\beta_1),\ldots,S_1(\beta_p)\} \subseteq \{S_2(\gamma_1),\ldots,S_2(\gamma_q)\}$.

Now we consider special derivations $\Delta(\Sigma,P(\tilde{x}))$ for formulaes $P(\tilde{x})$: $\beta_1,\beta_2,\ldots,\beta_i,\ldots$ with $\beta_1 = P(\tilde{x})$ and for any i,

$\beta_{i-1} = \beta_{i-1}^1\&\ldots\&\beta_{i-1}^k$, $\beta_i = \beta_i^1\&\ldots\&\beta_i^{k'}$ there exist some j,

$P(y_1)\&\ldots\&P(y_s) \longrightarrow P(y) \in \Sigma$ and a safe substitution S with

$\beta_i^m = \beta_{i-1}^m$ $(1 \le m \le j)$, $\beta_i^{j+s+1} = \beta_{i-1}^{j+1}$ $(1 \le l \le k-j+1)$, $\beta_{i-1}^{j+1} = S(P(\tilde{y}))$,

$\beta_i^{j+t} = S(P(\tilde{y}_t))$ $(1 \le t \le s)$ and $k' = k+s-1$.

Any such derivation $\Delta(\Sigma,P(\tilde{x}))$ correspond to the generation of a new element in $/R/_{\Sigma,i}$ for a interpretation I and vice versa.

Therefore our first problem is solved if a halting condition exists for derivations.

<u>Corollary 2</u> (/1,3/). Given some derivation $\Delta(\Sigma,P(\tilde{x})) = \beta_1,\ldots,\beta_i,\ldots$ If for some j, a safe unificator exists for $\langle \beta_j,\beta_{j+1}\rangle$ then the derivation $\Delta(\Sigma,P(\tilde{x}))$ is equivalent to the derivation $\beta_1,\ldots,\beta_j$.

Example 4 (Continuation of example 2)

$\Delta(\{\beta_1,\beta_2\},P(x,y,z,u)) = P(x,y,z,u)$, $P(x,y,z,u')\&P(x,y,z',u)$,

$P(x,y',z,u')\&P(x',y,z,u')\&P(x,y,z',u)$,

$P(x,y',z,u'')\&P(x,y',z'',u')\&P(x',y,z,u')\&P(x,y,z',u)$,

$P(x,y'',z,u'')\&P(x',y',z,u'')\&P(x,y',z'',u')\&P(x',y,z,u')\&P(x,y,z',u)$,

...

Obviously, for no j a safe unification exists for $\langle \beta_j,\beta_{j+1}\rangle$.

Now we can prove theorem 1.

Given a DD $\mathcal{B}$. Any derivation $\Delta(\{\mathcal{B}\},P(\tilde{x})) = \mathcal{B}_1,\ldots,\mathcal{B}_i,\ldots$ is equivalent to $\mathcal{B}_1,\mathcal{B}_2$.

Let be $\mathcal{B} = P(\tilde{x}_1)\&\ldots\&P(\tilde{x}_k) \longrightarrow P(\tilde{x}_0)$, $\mathcal{B}_1 = P(\tilde{x})$,

$\mathcal{B}_2 = \mathcal{B}_{21}\&\ldots\&\mathcal{B}_{2k}$, $\mathcal{B}_3 = \mathcal{B}_{31}\& \ldots \& \mathcal{B}_{3\ (2k-1)},\ldots$

By definition of $\mathcal{B}_i$ we get for some i,j: $\mathcal{B}_{2l} = \mathcal{B}_{3l}$ $(1\leq l\leq j)$, $\mathcal{B}_{3\ j+k+i} = \mathcal{B}_{2\ j+i}$ $(1=i=k-j)$. A safe unification exists for the pair $<\mathcal{B}_{2\ j+1}, \mathcal{B}_{3\ j+1}\&\ldots\&\mathcal{B}_{3\ j+k}>$ and therefore also for $<\mathcal{B}_2,\mathcal{B}_3>$.

Given a Sheffer-set Σ of DD with $\Sigma\subseteq\{\mathcal{B}' \mid \{\mathcal{B}\}\models \mathcal{B}'\}$. It is easy to prove that for every derivation $\Delta(\Sigma,P(\tilde{x}))$ exists an equivalent derivation $\Delta(\{\mathcal{B}\},P(\tilde{x}))$.

3. Characterization of Sheffer-sets

In /2/ a characterization of Sheffer-sets is given in the special case of binary JD. This result can be extended to bigger classes of JD.

A set of JD Σ is called $\cap$-closed if holds $(X_1,\ldots,X_{i-1},X_i\cap Y,X_{i+1},\ldots,X_k)\in\Sigma$ for any $(X_1,\ldots,X_k)$, $(X_1,X_2,\ldots,X_{i-1},Y,X_{i+1},\ldots,X_k)\in\Sigma$.

Corollary 3. Given a DD $\mathcal{B}$ and the corresponding JD D. The set $M = \{D' \mid \{D\}\models D'\}$ is $\cap$-closed.

A JD (DD) $(X_1,\ldots,X_m)$ is called full first-order hierarchical dependency (FOHD) if holds $X_i\cap X_j = X_k\cap X_l$ for any pairs with $i\neq j$, $k\neq l$.

In /4/ is proved

Theorem 2. Let Σ be a set of FOHD. The following are equivalent:

(1) Σ is equivalent to a single JD D.

(2) Σ is $\cap$-closed.

References

/1/ C.L. Chang, R.C.-T. Lee: Symbolic logic and mechanical theorem proving. Academic press, New York 1973.

/2/ N. Goodman, Y.C. Tay: A characterization of multivalued dependencies equivalent to a join dependency. Information Processing Letters 18 (1984), 261-266.

/3/ J. Minker, J.M. Nicolas: On recursive axioms in deductive databases. Information Systems 8, 1, 1-13, 1983.

/4/ B. Thalheim: Dekompositionsabhängigkeiten in Relationen. Manuscript, Dresden 1984.

HOW FAST IS PROGRAM SYNTHESIS FROM EXAMPLES

Rolf Wiehagen [1)]

Synthesis of programs of recursive functions from input/output examples is investigated. Necessary and sufficient conditions are derived that the synthesis can be done if the admissible number of examples is bounded.

Let P, P^2 denote the set of all partial recursive functions of one, two arguments, respectively. Let R, R^2 denote the corrsponding subsets of all recursive functions. Let N denote the set of natural numbers 1,2,... Every function Num $\in P^2$ is called a numbering. Let Num_i denote the function Num(i,x) of argument x. Let P_{Num} denote the set of all functions Num_i where i$\in$N, and let R_{Num} denote the subset of all recursive functions from P_{Num}. A numbering Num is called decidable iff there is dec $\in$ R such that, for any i,j$\in$N, dec(i,j) = 1 if and only if $Num_i = Num_j$. For f$\in$R, n$\in$N let f^n denote a code number of the initial segment (f(1),f(2),...,f(n)). Let f,g$\in$P and n$\in$N; then $f =_n g$ iff for any $x \leq n$, both f(x),g(x) are defined and f(x) = g(x) or both f(x),g(x) are undefined; $f \neq_n g$ otherwise. For almost all n$\in$N means for all, but at most finitely many n$\in$N.

The main problem investigated in program synthesis from examples is the following :
Let be given any numbering Num $\in P^2$. One can imagine Num as a programming language and any i$\in$N as being a code of a program of the function Num_i. Let U $\subseteq R_{Num}$ be any class such that any of its functions possesses at least one program in the given numbering. Then, for any function f$\in$U, the task is to find a program i such that Num_i = f solely by processing input/output examples of f, i.e. pairs (x,f(x)) where x$\in$N.

<u>Definition</u>
Let Num $\in P^2$, U $\subseteq$ R.
U is called identifiable with respect to Num iff
there is S$\in$P such that for any f$\in$U,
1) $S(f^n)$ is defined for any n$\in$N,
2) there is i$\in$N such that Num_i = f and $S(f^n)$ = i for almost all n$\in$N.

So, after processing finitely many input/output examples of the function f in the natural order the identification strategy S converges

1) Humboldt-University Dept. of Mathematics DDR-1o86 Berlin PO Box 1297
German Democratic Republic

to a correct Num-program of f. Note that in the definition above it is not required that we should be able to decide whether or not the point of convergence has already been reached. This and other modifications of the given approach are investigated in numerous papers (cf. the surveys /2/ and /15/).

As a motivation for investigating program synthesis from examples we consider the fact that here input/output examples are not only used for testing a program, as it is usual in the stage of program debugging, but immediately in the stage of program construction. Once for testing one needs input/output examples in any case, why one should not use them directly for constructing the program if this is possible and feasible.

As for the possibility on principle for now twenty years we know that important function classes are identifiable by the following result of M. Gold.

Theorem 1 (/11/)

For any Num $\in R^2$, R_{Num} is identifiable with respect to Num.

Consequently, any of the following as well as many other well-known classes are identifiable :

- the class of all primitively recursive functions,
- the class of all functions computable in polynomial time,
- the class of all functions computable in logarithmic space.

Once such important classes are identifiable on principle the question of the complexity of the identification became reasonable and important. There has been investigated a number of complexity measures such as

- the number of changes of the hypotheses, which was studied first in /3/, /4/,
- the number of examples processed by the strategy up to the point of convergence (cf. /5/, /12/, /18/),
- the computation time of the strategy (cf. /1/, /13/, /17/);
- an axiomatic approach to the complexity of identification in the style of M. Blum's complexity theory of recursive functions (cf. /7/) has been developed in /9/, /1o/, /16/.

All these measures and approaches apply to the complexity of the identification process. Alternatively, the complexity of the result of identification has been investigated (cf. /8/, /19/).

In this paper we want to deal with the number of input/output examples processed by the identification strategy up to the point of convergence.

Definition

Let $S \in P$, $f \in R$.

Then let Conv(S,f) denote the least $n \in N$ such that $S(f^m) = S(f^n)$ for any $m \geq n$.

Hence Conv(S,f) is equal to both the point of convergence and the number of examples processed by the strategy S on the function f up to the point of convergence.
In order to investigate this measure there are at least two ways. The first one started by M. Gold /12/ and in a sense finished by H.-R. Beick /5/ deals with the comparison of strategies with respect to their convergence behaviour. M. Gold showed that the classes R_{Num} where $Num \in R^2$, are identifiable by a "best" strategy in the sense that no other strategy can use uniformly fewer examples.

Definition
Let $Num \in P^2$, $U \subseteq R$.
U is called identifiable with respect to Num by a best strategy iff there is $S \in P$ such that
1) U is identifiable with respect to Num by S,
2) there is no $S' \in P$ such that
   - U is identifiable with respect to Num by S',
   - $Conv(S',f) \leq Conv(S,f)$ for any $f \in U$,
   - $Conv(S',f) < Conv(S,f)$ for some $f \in U$.

Theorem 2 (/12/)
For any $Num \in R^2$, R_{Num} is identifiable with respect to Num by a best strategy.

Gold used as a best strategy the so-called identification-by-enumeration strategy which searches for the least number being "consistent" with the given initial segment of the function to be identified :

$$Id_{Num}(f^n) = \text{the least } i \in N \text{ such that } Num_i =_n f.$$

By proving the following result H.-R. Beick completely characterized the best strategies.

Theorem 3 (/6/)
Let $Num \in P^2$, $U \subseteq R$.
U is identifiable with respect to Num by a best strategy iff there is a strategy $S \in P$ identifying U with respect to Num such that for any function $f \in U$ and any $n \in N$
1) $Num_{S(f^n)} =_n f$,
2) $Num_{S(f^n)} \in U$,
3) if $Num_{S(f^n)} = f$, then $S(f^{n+1}) = S(f^n)$.

Consequently, a strategy identifying a class with respect to some numbering is a best one if and only if it works consitent, "class preserving", and it never changes a correct hypothesis. Since for a concrete strategy as a rule these conditions can be checked easily, we are able now to verify whether a given strategy is a best one, let it work enumeratively or not.

On the other hand, for a variety of identifiable classes of functions there cannot be any best strategy on principle, because any strategy identifying them is not class preserving or even not consistent (cf. /14/). At least for these classes, but essentially for all the others, too, it would be desirable, if we could state explicitly how many examples must be considered for constructing a program. This is the second way for investigating the complexity measure Conv, and this is the way we want to deal with in this paper.

In order to realize this conception our intention is the following. Let be given a numbering Num, a class U, and a function b which is intended to bound the admissible number of input/output examples. Then we want to derive necessary and sufficient conditions such that the class U is identifiable with respect to Num within this bound b.

<u>Definition</u>

Let $Num \in P^2$, $U \subseteq R$, $b \in P$.

U is called b-identifiable with respect to Num iff there is $S \in P$ such that

1) U is identifiable with respect to Num,

2) for any $i \in N$ if $Num_i \in U$, then $b(i)$ is defined and $Conv(S, Num_i) \leq b(i)$.

U is called bounded identifiable iff U is b-identifiable for some $b \in P$.

Thus for b-identifying any function Num_i from U the strategy S must not take more than b(i) examples.

This definition is, of course, not the only one to make our intention formally precise, but it seems to be sufficiently general for obtaining results which hold in any concrete case and for hoping to discover some of the points we should check in a concrete case in order to try to improve our general bounds using the more powerful suppositions we than have.

At first we want to present results concerning numberings from R^2. The first one is due to H.-R. Beick.

<u>Theorem 4</u> (/5/)

Let $Num \in R^2$.

R_{Num} is bounded identifiable with respect to Num iff Num is decidable.

In /5/ it is also shown that by choosing the input/output examples not necessarily in the natural order but in an appropriate recursive one, any function Num_i from a class bounded identifiable with respect to Num can be identified using no more than i examples. We note that all re-

sults which follow directly can be generalized to arbitrary recursive orders of the input/output examples.
In order to characterize b-identifiability with respect to $Num \in R^2$ we get a very simple criterion if b is nondecreasing.

Definition

Let $Num \in P^2$, $b \in R$.
Num is called b-distinguishable iff
for any $i,j \in N$, if $Num_i \neq Num_j$, then $Num_i \neq_{max(b(i),b(j))} Num_j$.

Theorem 5

Let $Num \in R^2$, $b \in Nondecr$.
R_{Num} is b-identifiable with respect to Num iff
Num is b-distinguishable.

The next result shows that Theorem 5 is not true for b being an arbitrary recursive function.

Theorem 6

There are $Num \in R^2$ and $b \in R$ such that :
1) Num is b-distinguishable.
2) R_{Num} is not b-identifiable with respect to Num.

Intuitively, the reason is that, for „great" i, b(i) can be "small" thus forcing the strategy to converge sufficiently fast on the function Num_i. Therefore, in order to characterize b-identifiablity for an arbitrary recursive function b the strategy must be able "to foresee" such a situation.

Definition

Let $Num \in P^2$, $U \subseteq R$, $b \in R$.
Num is called (U,b)-foreseeable iff
there is $F \in P$ such that for any $f \in U$ and any $n \in N$
1) $F(f^n)$ is defined,
2) $F(f^n) \geq \min I$ if $I \neq \emptyset$, where I is the set of all $i \in N$ such that $Num_i = f$ and $b(i) \leq n$.

Hence F "foresees" an upper bound on an appropriate hypothesis for f with "small" b(i), and thus F enables the strategy to take into consideration this number i in time.

Theorem 7

Let $Num \in R^2$, $b \in R$.
R_{Num} is b-identifiable with respect to Num iff
1) Num is b-distinguishable.
2) Num is (R_{Num},b)-foreseeable.

The situation in the case of arbitrary partial recursive numberings Num is more difficult at least for the following reasons :

- The halting problem in Num is not decidable, in general.
- In most cases the class R_{Num} is not identifiable with respect to Num or it is even not identifiable with respect to any numbering.
- The functions from P_{Num} which are not to be identified, i.e. the functions from $P_{Num} - U$, can essentially disturb the strategy to converge to a correct program within the given bound b or these "complement" functions can even prevent the strategy to converge at all.

As a consequence we will see from Theorem 8,9 and its corollary that no one of the characterizations for recursive numberings remains valid for arbitrary numberings.

<u>Theorem 8</u>

There is $Num \in P^2$ such that :

1) Num is decidable.
2) R_{Num} is identifiable with respect to Num.
3) R_{Num} is not bounded identifiable with respect to Num.

Note that without condition 2 the result can be obtained simply by choosing Num as a Friedberg numbering of P, since then $R_{Num}=R$ but R is not identifiable with respect to any numbering (cf. /11/).

<u>Theorem 9</u>

There are $Num \in P^2$ and $b \in Nondecr$ such that :

1) Num is b-distinguishable.
2) R_{Num} is not b-identifiable with respect to Num.

In fact, we even show that for any $b \in Nondecr$ there is $Num \in P^2$ such that conditions 1 and 2 hold.

<u>Corollary</u>

There are $Num \in P^2$ and $b \in R$ such that :

1) Num is b-distinguishable.
2) Num is (R_{Num}, b)-foreseeable.
3) R_{Num} is not b-identifiable with respect to Num.

Hence, on the one hand, we have some conditions, namely distinguishability and foreseeability, which are in a sense necessary for b-identification as we shall see. On the other hand, now we know that these conditions are not sufficient. Therefore the question arises : What kind of condition should be added in order to get a characterization ? The next result helps us to find an answer.

Theorem 1o

There are Num $\in P^2$ and $b \in R$ such that :

1) Num is b-distinguishable.
2) Num is (R_{Num}, b)-foreseeable.
3) For infinitely many functions $f \in P_{Num}$ there are at least two numbers $i \in N$ such that $Num_i = f$.
4) R_{Num} is not b-identifiable with respect to Num.

The proof of Theorem 1o implies that if "too much" functions from P_{Num} have at least two numbers, then already this fact can be used to make b-identification impossible. Hence we should search for a way to admit only one number for any function in the "space of hypotheses". On the other hand, once the numbering is given with respect to which the identification has to be done, there is no possibility to change the cardinality of the numbers of the functions enumerated by it. But we can change the "space of hypotheses" itself, that is, we can choose another numbering which has the desired properties guaranteeing fast identification, and then we translate the program constructed in this auxiliary numbering into an equivalent one in the given numbering.
In order to realize this idea we need the following definitions.

Definition

Let Aux, Num $\in P^2$, $U \subseteq R$, $d \in R$.
Aux is called d-initial iff
for any $i, x \in N$, if $x \leq d(i)$ then $Aux_i(x)$ is defined.
(Comment : d-initiality allows to check effectively and without computational delay whether program i is an appropriate one up to input d(i).)
Aux is called strongly d-distinguishable iff
for any $i, j \in N$, if $i \neq j$ then $Aux_i \neq_{max(d(i),d(j))} Aux_j$.
(Comment : If Aux is strongly d-distinguishable, then any function from P_{Aux} has exactly one number in Aux.)
Aux is called U-related to Num iff
there is $r \in P$ such that for any $i, j \in N$, if $Aux_i, Num_j \in U$ and $Aux_i = Num_j$, then r(j) is defined and $i \leq r(j)$.
(Comment : If Aux is U-related to Num, then the Aux-numbers of functions from U are at most "recursively much" greater than the Num-numbers of functions from U.)
Aux is called U-reducible to Num iff

1) $U \subseteq P_{Aux}$,
2) there is $r \in P$ such that for any $i \in N$, if $Aux_i \in U$ then r(i) is defined and $Num_{r(i)} = Aux_i$.

Theorem 11

Let $Num \in P^2$, $U \subseteq R$.

U is bounded identifiable with respect to Num iff

there is $Aux \in P^2$ such that

1) Aux is d-initial and strongly d-distinguishable, for some $d \in R$.

2) Aux is U-related to Num.

3) Aux is U-reducible to Num.

In order to characterize b-identifiability we have to sharpen condition 1 and to modify condition 2 of Theorem 11.

Theorem 12

Let $Num \in P^2$, $U \subseteq R$, $b \in P$.

U is b-identifiable with respect to Num iff

there are $Aux \in P^2$ and $b' \in R$ such that

1) Aux is b'-initial, strongly b'-distinguishable, (U,b')-foreseeable.

2) For any $i,j \in N$, if $Aux_i \in U$ and $Aux_i = Num_j$, then $b'(i) \leq b(j)$.

3) Aux is U-reducible to Num.

Condition 1 implies b'-identifiability of U with respect to Aux and conditions 2 and 3 allow to translate this into b-identification of U with respect to Num.

References

/1/ Angluin, D. : Finding patterns common to a set of strings. Journal Comp. and System Sciences 21 (198o) 1, 46-62.

/2/ Angluin, D. and Smith, C. H. : Inductive inference : Theory and methods. Computing Surveys 15 (1983) 3, 238-269.

/3/ Barzdin, Ya. M. : Complexity and frequency solution of some algorithmically unsolvable problems. Doctoral Dissertation, Novosibirsk State Univ., 1971 (in Russian).

/4/ Barzdin, Ya. M. and Freivald, R. V. : Prediction and limiting synthesis of recursively enumerable classes of functions. Theory of Algorithms and Programs I, Latvian State Univ., Riga, 1974, 117-128 (in Russian).

/5/ Beick, H.-R. : Zur Konvergenzgeschwindigkeit von Strategien der induktiven Inferenz. Elektr. Inf.Verarbeitung und Kybernetik 18 (1982) 3, 163-172.

/6/ Beick, H.-R. : Induktive Inferenz mit höchster Konvergenzgeschwindigkeit. Dissertation A, Humboldt-Univ., Berlin, 1984.

/7/ Blum, M. : A machine-independent theory of the comlexity of recursive functions. Journal Assoc. Comput. Mach. 14 (1967), 322-326.

/8/ Blum, L. and Blum, M. : Toward a mathematical theory of inductive inference. Information and Control 28 (1975), 125-155.

/9/ Daley, R. P. and Smith, C. H. : On the complexity of inductive inference. Techn. Rep. 83-4, Univ. of Pittsburgh, 1983.

/1o/ Freivald, R. V. : On the complexity and optimality of computation in the limit. Theory of Algorithms and Programs II, Latvian State Univ., Riga, 1975, 155-173 (in Russian).

/11/ Gold, M. : Limiting recursion. Journal of Symb. Logic 3o (1965), 28-48.

/12/ Gold,M. : Language identification in the limit. Information and Control 1o (1967), 447-474.

/13/ Gold, M. : Complexity of automaton identification from given data. Information and Control 37 (1978), 3o2-32o.

/14/ Jantke, K. P. and Beick, H.-R. : Combining postulates of naturalness in inductive inference. Elektron. Inf.Verarbeitung und Kybernetik 17 (1981) 8/9, 465-484.

/15/ Klette, R. and Wiehagen, R. : Research in the theory of inductive inference by GDR mathematicians - a survey. Information Sciences 22 (198o), 149-169.

/16/ Schäfer-Richter, G. : Über Eingabeabhängigkeit und Komplexität von Inferenzstrategien. Dissertation, RWTH Aachen, 1984.

/17/ Shinohara, T. : Polynomial time inference of extended regular pattern languages. Lecture Notes in Comp. Science 147 (1982), 115-127.

/18/ Valiant, L. G. : A theory of the learnable. Proc. of the ACM Symp. on Theory of Computing, 1984, 436-445.

/19/ Zeugmann, T. : On the synthesis of fastest programs in inductive inference. Elektron. Inf.Verarbeitung und Kybernetik 19 (1983) 12, 625-642.

ON RECURSIVE OPTIMIZERS

By Thomas Zeugmann [1]

Abstract: Problems of the effective synthesis of fastest programs (modulo a recursive factor) for recursive functions given by input-output examples or an arbitrary program are investigated. In spite of the negative result proved by ALTON we point out that even for function classes containing arbitrarily complex functions sometimes the effective synthesis of fastest programs (modulo a recursive factor) can be achieved.

1. Introduction

The present paper deals with the question of effectively synthesizing fastest programs (modulo a recursive factor) for recursive functions. That means, given a class of functions we ask whether there is a master program (so called "recursive optimizer") translating arbitrary programs into fastest ones of the considered functions. If we are given any complexity measure in the sense of BLUM [2] this question arises naturally. It is a well-known phenomenon that in any Gödel numbering every recursive function has infinitely many programs and among them (w.r.t. the complexity measure) there are arbitrarily "bad" ones.
In ALTON [1] and LOWTHER [7] it has been provedthat, in general, such recursive optimizers do not exist. What we like to present here is the following:
First, we give a sharpened version of Theorem 1 pointed out by ALTON [1]. Second, in spite of this negative result we shall state that even for function classes containing arbitrarily complex functions sometimes the effective synthesis of fastest programs (modulo a recursive factor) can be obtained. Moreover, we present results showing that the choice of the recursive factor is of great influence on the capabilities of recursive optimizers. Basic definitions and notations are given in chapter 2. Results are presented in chapter 3 and 4.

2. Basic Definitions and Notations

Unspecified notation follows ROGERS [8]. $N = \{0,1,2,\dots\}$ denotes the set of all natural numbers. The class of all partial recursive and general recursive functions of one resp. two variables is denoted by P, R, and P^2, R^2, respectively. By (φ,Φ) we denote any complexity measure in the sense of BLUM [2]. Instead of $\lambda x\varphi(i,x)$ we write φ_i. Using a fixed recursive encoding $\langle\dots\rangle$ of all finite sequences of natural numbers onto N we write f^n instead of $\langle(f(0),\dots,f(n))\rangle$ for any

1) Sektion Mathematik der Humboldt-Universität zu Berlin
1o86 Berlin, PO Box 1297, German Democratic Republic

$n \in N$, $f \in P$, where $f(x)$ is defined for all $x \leq n$. A sequence $(j_n)_{n \in N}$ of natural numbers is said to be finitely convergent to a number j iff $j_n = j$ for almost all n and if for any k, such that $j_k = j_{k+1}$, it follows that $j_n = j$ for every $n \geq k$. The abbreviation a.e. stands for "almost everywhere" and means "all but finitely many". We write i.o. as an abbreviation for "infinitely often". In the sequel $\#$ denotes incomparability of sets. The set of all general recursive operators (cf. HELM [5]) is denoted by GRO. We regard the functions $h \in R^2$ as operators of the form $\mathfrak{O}_h(f)(x) = h(x,f(x))$. If $\mathfrak{O}$ is an operator which maps functions to functions, we write $\mathfrak{O}(f,x)$ to denote the value of the function $\mathfrak{O}(f)$ at the argument x.
In order to formalize the concept of a fastest program (modulo a recursive factor) we shall use optimal and weakly optimal programs introduced by ALTON [1] as well as compression indices defined by BLUM/BLUM [3]. For the sake of completeness we give these definitions here.

Definition 1: Let (φ,Φ) be a complexity measure, $\mathfrak{O} \in$ GRO, $f \in R$. Then $i \in N$ is said to be an (weakly) $\mathfrak{O}$-optimal program for f (w.r.t. (φ,Φ)) iff

(1) $\varphi_i = f$

(2) $\forall j[\varphi_j = f \rightarrowtail \Phi_i(n) \leq \mathfrak{O}(\Phi_j,n)$ a.e.$]$

((2) $\forall^{\infty} j[\varphi_j = f \rightarrowtail \Phi_i(n) \leq \mathfrak{O}(\Phi_j,n)$ i.o.$]$)

Then we also say that the function f is (weakly) $\mathfrak{O}$-optimal.

Definition 2: Let (φ,Φ) be a complexity measure, $\mathfrak{O} \in$ GRO, $f \in R$. Then $i \in N$ is called an $\mathfrak{O}$-compression index of f iff

(1) $\varphi_i = f$

(2) $\forall j[\varphi_j = f \rightarrowtail \forall n\ \Phi_i(n) \leq \mathfrak{O}(\Phi_j,\max\{i,j,n\})\ ]$

In this case we also say that the function f is $\mathfrak{O}$-compressed.

Next, we formalize the concept of a recursive optimizer in two different ways. In our first definition only the graph of the considered function is successively available and in the second one, an arbitrary program is given as input.

Definition 3: Let (φ,Φ) be a complexity measure, $\mathfrak{O} \in$ GRO and $U \subseteq R$. Then U is said to be finitely identifiable ($U \in$ FIN), ⟨to be finitely $\mathfrak{O}$-optimal identifiable ($U \in \mathfrak{O}\text{-FINOPT}^{(\varphi,\Phi)}$)⟩, [to be finitely weakly $\mathfrak{O}$-optimal identifiable ($U \in \mathfrak{O}\text{-FINWOPT}^{(\varphi,\Phi)}$)], {to be finitely $\mathfrak{O}$-compressed identifiable ($U \in \mathfrak{O}\text{-FINCOMP}^{(\varphi,\Phi)}$)} iff there is a function $S \in P$ such that $S(f^n)$ is defined for all $n \in N$, $f \in U$ and the sequence $(S(f^n))_{n \in N}$ finitely converges to a φ-number i of f; ⟨finitely converges to an $\mathfrak{O}$-optimal program for f⟩, [finitely converges to a weakly $\mathfrak{O}$-optimal program for f], {finitely converges to an $\mathfrak{O}$-compression index of f}.

Remark: Finite identification originally was introduced by TRACHTENBROT BARZDIN [9] and intensively studied in LINDNER [6].

Definition 4: Let (φ,Φ) be a complexity measure, $\mathfrak{O} \in GRO$ and $U \subseteq R$. Then it is said that U is finitely $\mathfrak{O}$-optimal standardizable ($U \in \mathfrak{O}\text{-FSOPT}^{(\varphi,\Phi)}$), [finitely weakly $\mathfrak{O}$-optimal standardizable ($U \in \mathfrak{O}\text{-FSWOPT}^{(\varphi,\Phi)}$)], {finitely $\mathfrak{O}$-compressed standardizable ($U \in \mathfrak{O}\text{-FSCOMP}^{(\varphi,\Phi)}$)}, iff there is a function $\psi \in P$ such that

(1) $\varphi_i \in U$ implies that $\psi(i)$ is defined

(2) $\varphi_i = \varphi_j$ implies $\psi(i) = \psi(j)$, for all $\varphi_i, \varphi_j \in U$

(3) $\psi(i)$ is an $\mathfrak{O}$-optimal program for φ_i

[(3) $\psi(i)$ is a weakly $\mathfrak{O}$-optimal program for φ_i]

{(3) $\psi(i)$ is an $\mathfrak{O}$-compression index of φ_i}

In the sequel we investigate the capabilities of the introduced recursive optimizers.

3. Basic Results

Theorem 1: Let (φ,Φ) be a complexity measure, $U = \{f/f \in R,\ \varphi_{f(0)} = f,\ f(n) = 0 \text{ a.e.}\}$, $\mathfrak{O} \in GRO$. Then there is no function $\psi \in P$ such that $\varphi_i \in U$ implies that $\psi(i)$ is defined and $\psi(i)$ is a weakly $\mathfrak{O}$-optimal program for φ_i.

This Theorem is in some sense stronger than the corresponding result in ALTON [1]. First, there is a recursive function $h \in R^2$ such that each function from U is h-compressed (cf. ZEUGMANN [10]) and not only h-optimal as it was required in [1]. Second, the program equivalence for functions from U is trivially decidable. Third, we only require the optimizer ψ to work on functions from U and not on all h-optimal functions as in [1]. Finally, the translated program is only required to be weakly $\mathfrak{O}$-optimal for any operator $\mathfrak{O} \in GRO$ and not only to be weakly h-optimal as in [1]. As we shall see below the enlargement from functions $h \in R^2$ to arbitrary operators $\mathfrak{O} \in GRO$ enlarges the family of function classes having even $\mathfrak{O}$-compression indeces considerably. More results concerning this question can be found in [10, 11]. Now one might expect that there is no hope at all to identify or standardize finitely $\mathfrak{O}$-optimal programs but surprisingly we find:

Theorem 2: There is a complexity measure (φ,Φ) such that $\mathfrak{O}\text{-FINCOMP}^{(\varphi,\Phi)}$ contains function classes of infinite cardinality for every operator $\mathfrak{O} \in GRO$.

Although the measure in Theorem 2 is a very natural one, Theorem 2 does not hold for arbitrary measures.

Let I be the identical operator (i.e. $I(f) = f$, for all $f \in P$).

Theorem 3: There is a complexity measure (φ,Φ) such that

$$\text{I-FINOPT}^{(\varphi,\Phi)} = \emptyset$$

Now the problem arises whether results obtained for one complexity measure can be generalized to any measure in a qualitative sense. This question is answered by our next theorem.

Theorem 4: Let (φ,Φ) and (φ^*,Φ^*) be complexity measures and $\mathfrak{O} \in$ GRO. Then there is an operator $\mathfrak{O}^* \in$ GRO such that

(1) $\mathfrak{O}\text{-FINOPT}^{(\varphi,\Phi)} \subseteq \mathfrak{O}^*\text{-FINOPT}^{(\varphi^*,\Phi^*)}$

(2) $\mathfrak{O}\text{-FINWOPT}^{(\varphi,\Phi)} \subseteq \mathfrak{O}^*\text{-FINWOPT}^{(\varphi^*,\Phi^*)}$

(3) $\mathfrak{O}\text{-FSOPT}^{(\varphi,\Phi)} \subseteq \mathfrak{O}^*\text{-FSOPT}^{(\varphi^*,\Phi^*)}$

(4) $\mathfrak{O}\text{-FSWOPT}^{(\varphi,\Phi)} \subseteq \mathfrak{O}^*\text{-FSWOPT}^{(\varphi^*,\Phi^*)}$

Using the latter theorem we are allowed to introduce the following notations:

$$\text{FINOPTH} = \bigcup_{h\in R^2} h\text{-FINOPT}^{(\varphi,\Phi)}$$

$$\text{FINOPTGRO} = \bigcup_{\mathfrak{O}\in \text{GRO}} \mathfrak{O}\text{-FINOPT}^{(\varphi,\Phi)}$$

$$\text{FINWOPTGRO} = \bigcup_{\mathfrak{O}\in \text{GRO}} \mathfrak{O}\text{-FINWOPT}^{(\varphi,\Phi)}$$

and analogously we define the families FSOPTH, FSOPTGRO, FSWOPTGRO as well as FINCOMPGRO and FSCOMPGRO.

Next it can be shown that there is no best operator $\mathfrak{O}$ in the sense that $\mathfrak{O}\text{-FINOPT}^{(\varphi,\Phi)} =$ FINOPTGRO (as well as for the other families introduced above), since we have:

Theorem 5: Let (φ,Φ) be a complexity measure. Then, for every operator $\mathfrak{O} \in$ GRO there is an operator $\mathfrak{O}^* \in$ GRO such that $\mathfrak{O}\text{-FINOPT}^{(\varphi,\Phi)} \subset \mathfrak{O}^*\text{-FINOPT}^{(\varphi,\Phi)}$.

4. Main Results

We shall start by clarifying the relations between finite optimal identification and finite optimal standardization.

Theorem 6: Let (φ,Φ) be a complexity measure and $\mathfrak{O} \in$ GRO. Then it holds:

(1) $\mathfrak{O}\text{-FINCOMP}^{(\varphi,\Phi)} = \text{FIN} \cap \mathfrak{O}\text{-FSCOMP}^{(\varphi,\Phi)}$

(2) $\mathfrak{O}\text{-FINOPT}^{(\varphi,\Phi)} = \text{FIN} \cap \mathfrak{O}\text{-FSOPT}^{(\varphi,\Phi)}$

(3) $\mathfrak{O}\text{-FINWOPT}^{(\varphi,\Phi)} = \text{FIN} \cap \mathfrak{O}\text{-FSWOPT}^{(\varphi,\Phi)}$

Theorem 6 actually shows that finite $\mathfrak{O}$-optimal identification can be decomposed. Instead of directly looking for an $\mathfrak{O}$-optimal program in the identification process, we finitely may synthesize any program for the function to be identified. After that, we can translate it effectively into an $\mathfrak{O}$-optimal one. This theorem was found by a suggestion given by FREIVALDS [4]. Next we point out that the intersection in Theorem 6 is not trivial.

Theorem 7: (1) FIN – FSWOPTGRO $\neq \emptyset$
(2) FSCOMPH – FIN $\neq \emptyset$

As a corollary we get:

Corollary 8: (1) FINCOMPH $\subset$ FSCOMPH
(2) FINOPTH $\subset$ FSOPTH
(3) FINCOMPGRO $\subset$ FSCOMPGRO
(4) FINWOPTGRO $\subset$ FSWOPTGRO
(5) FINOPTGRO $\subset$ FSOPTGRO

On the other hand we have:

Theorem 9: There is an operator $\mathfrak{O} \in$ GRO and a class $U \subset R$ such that
(1) every function from U is $\mathfrak{O}$-compressed
(2) for every function $h \in R^2$ there is a function $f \in U$ not being weakly h-optimal

This theorem has several consequences.

Corollary 10: (1) FINOPTH $\subset$ FINOPTGRO
(2) FSOPTH $\subset$ FSOPTGRO
(3) FINOPTGRO – FSOPTH $\neq \emptyset$

Furthermore, we were able to show that the family FINOPTH even contains function classes not belonging to the family NUM defined as follows: U $\in$ NUM iff there is a function $g \in R$ such that $U \subseteq \{\varphi_{g(i)} / i \in N\}$.
Since the converse is also true, we obtain:
Theorem 11: FINOPTH $\#$ NUM

Finally, we pointed out that FSCOMPGRO $\subset$ FSWOPTGRO but it is an open problem whether the stronger result FSCOMPGRO $\subset$ FSOPTGRO $\subset$ FSWOPTGRO holds.

References

[1] Alton, D.A., Non-existence of Program Optimizers in Several Abstract settings. J. Comp. System Sci. 12, 1976, 368 - 393
[2] Blum, M., Machine Independent Theory of Complexity of Recursive Functions. J. ACM 14, 1967, 322 - 336
[3] Blum, L. and M. Blum , Toward a Mathematical Theory Of Inductive Inference. Inf. and Control 28, 1975, 122 - 155
[4] Freivalds, R., Private Communication

[5] Helm, J., P., On Effectively Computable Operators. ZML 17, 1971, 231 - 244

[6] Lindner, R., Algorithmische Erkennung. Diss. B, Jena 1972

[7] Lowther, J., L., The Non-existence of Optimizers and Subrecursive Languages. Dept. of Comp. Sci., The University of Iowa, Iowa City, Technical Report 75-07, 1975

[8] Rogers, H., Jr., Theory of Recursive Functions and Effictive Computability. Mc Graw-Hill, New York 1967

[9] Trachtenbrot, B., A. and J.M. Barzdin, Finite Automata-behavior and synthesis. Nauka, Moskau 1970 (in russian) or Fundamental studies in Comp. Sci. 1, North Holland/American Elsevier 1973 (in english)

[10] Zeugmann, T. , A-posteriori Characterizations in Inductive Inference of Recursive Functions. EIK 19, 1983, 559 - 594

[11] Zeugmann, T. , On the Synthesis of Fastest Programs in Inductive Inference. EIK 19, 1983, 625 - 642

Vol. 167: International Symposium on Programming. Proceedings, 1984. Edited by C. Girault and M. Paul. VI, 262 pages. 1984.

Vol. 168: Methods and Tools for Computer Integrated Manufacturing. Edited by R. Dillmann and U. Rembold. XVI, 528 pages. 1984.

Vol. 169: Ch. Ronse, Feedback Shift Registers. II, 1–2, 145 pages. 1984.

Vol. 170: Seventh International Conference on Automated Deduction. Edited by R.E. Shostak. IV, 508 pages. 1984.

Vol. 171: Logic and Machines: Decision Problems and Complexity. Proceedings, 1983. Edited by E. Börger, G. Hasenjaeger and D. Rödding. VI, 456 pages. 1984.

Vol. 172: Automata, Languages and Programming. Proceedings, 1984. Edited by J. Paredaens. VIII, 527 pages. 1984.

Vol. 173: Semantics of Data Types. Proceedings, 1984. Edited by G. Kahn, D.B. MacQueen and G. Plotkin. VI, 391 pages. 1984.

Vol. 174: EUROSAM 84. Proceedings, 1984. Edited by J. Fitch. XI, 396 pages. 1984.

Vol. 175: A. Thayse, P-Functions and Boolean Matrix Factorization. VII, 248 pages. 1984.

Vol. 176: Mathematical Foundations of Computer Science 1984. Proceedings, 1984. Edited by M.P. Chytil and V. Koubek. XI, 581 pages. 1984.

Vol. 177: Programming Languages and Their Definition. Edited by C.B. Jones. XXXII, 254 pages. 1984.

Vol. 178: Readings on Cognitive Ergonomics – Mind and Computers. Proceedings, 1984. Edited by G.C. van der Veer, M.J. Tauber, T.R.G. Green and P. Gorny. VI, 269 pages. 1984.

Vol. 179: V. Pan, How to Multiply Matrices Faster. XI, 212 pages. 1984.

Vol. 180: Ada Software Tools Interfaces. Proceedings, 1983. Edited by P.J.L. Wallis. III, 164 pages. 1984.

Vol. 181: Foundations of Software Technology and Theoretical Computer Science. Proceedings, 1984. Edited by M. Joseph and R. Shyamasundar. VIII, 468 pages. 1984.

Vol. 182: STACS 85. 2nd Annual Symposium on Theoretical Aspects of Computer Science. Proceedings, 1985. Edited by K. Mehlhorn. VII, 374 pages. 1985.

Vol. 183: The Munich Project CIP. Volume I: The Wide Spectrum Language CIP-L. By the CIP Language Group. XI, 275 pages. 1985.

Vol. 184: Local Area Networks: An Advanced Course. Proceedings, 1983. Edited by D. Hutchison, J. Mariani and D. Shepherd. VIII, 497 pages. 1985.

Vol. 185: Mathematical Foundations of Software Development. Proceedings, 1985. Volume 1: Colloquium on Trees in Algebra and Programming (CAAP' 85). Edited by H. Ehrig, C. Floyd, M. Nivat and J. Thatcher. XIV, 418 pages. 1985.

Vol. 186: Formal Methods and Software Development. Proceedings, 1985. Volume 2: Colloquium on Software Engineering (CSE). Edited by H. Ehrig, C. Floyd, M. Nivat and J. Thatcher. XIV, 455 pages. 1985.

Vol. 187: F.S. Chaghaghi, Time Series Package (TSPACK). III, 305 pages. 1985.

Vol. 188: Advances in Petri Nets 1984. Edited by G. Rozenberg with the cooperation of H. Genrich and G. Roucairol. VII, 467 pages. 1985.

Vol. 189: M.S. Sherman, Paragon. XI, 376 pages. 1985.

Vol. 190: M.W. Alford, J.P. Ansart, G. Hommel, L. Lamport, B. Liskov, G.P. Mullery and F.B. Schneider, Distributed Systems. Edited by M. Paul and H.J. Siegert. VI, 573 pages. 1985.

Vol. 191: H. Barringer, A Survey of Verification Techniques for Parallel Programs. VI, 115 pages. 1985.

Vol. 192: Automata on Infinite Words. Proceedings, 1984. Edited by M. Nivat and D. Perrin. V, 216 pages. 1985.

Vol. 193: Logics of Programs. Proceedings, 1985. Edited by R. Parikh. VI, 424 pages. 1985.

Vol. 194: Automata, Languages and Programming. Proceedings, 1985. Edited by W. Brauer. IX, 520 pages. 1985.

Vol. 195: H.J. Stüttgen, A Hierarchical Associative Processing System. XII, 273 pages. 1985.

Vol. 196: Advances in Cryptology. Proceedings of CRYPTO '84. Edited by G.R. Blakley and D. Chaum. IX, 491 pages. 1985.

Vol. 197: Seminar on Concurrency. Proceedings, 1984. Edited by S.D. Brookes, A. W. Roscoe and G. Winskel. X, 523 pages. 1985.

Vol. 198: A. Businger, PORTAL Language Description. VIII, 186 pages. 1985.

Vol. 199: Fundamentals of Computation Theory. Proceedings, 1985. Edited by L. Budach. XII, 533 pages. 1985.

Vol. 200: J.L.A. van de Snepscheut, Trace Theory and VLSI Design. VI, 0–140 pages. 1985.

Vol. 201: Functional Programming Languages and Computer Architecture. Proceedings, 1985. Edited by J.-P. Jouannaud. VI, 413 pages. 1985.

Vol. 202: Rewriting Techniques and Applications. Edited by J.-P. Jouannaud. VI, 441 pages. 1985.

Vol. 203: EUROCAL '85. Proceedings Vol. 1, 1985. Edited by B. Buchberger. V, 233 pages. 1985.

Vol. 204: EUROCAL '85. Proceedings Vol. 2, 1985. Edited by B. F. Caviness. XVI, 650 pages. 1985.

Vol. 205: P. Klint, A Study in String Processing Languages. VIII, 165 pages. 1985.

Vol. 206: Foundations of Software Technology and Theoretical Computer Science. Proceedings, 1985. Edited by S.N. Maheshwari. IX, 522 pages. 1985.

Vol. 207: The Analysis of Concurrent Systems. Proceedings, 1983. Edited by B.T. Denvir, W.T. Harwood, M.I. Jackson and M.J. Wray. VII, 398 pages. 1985.

Vol. 208: Computation Theory. Proceedings, 1984. Edited by A. Skowron. VII, 397 pages. 1985.

Vol. 209: Advances in Cryptology. Proceedings of EUROCRYPT '84. Edited by T. Beth, N. Cot and I. Ingemarsson. VII, 491 pages. 1985.

Vol. 210: STACS 86. Proceedings, 1986. Edited by B. Monien and G. Vidal-Naquet. IX, 368 pages. 1986.

Vol. 211: U. Schöning, Complexity and Structure. V, 99 pages. 1986.

Vol. 212: Interval Mathematics 1985. Proceedings, 1985. Edited by K. Nickel. VI, 227 pages. 1986.

Vol. 213: ESOP 86. Proceedings, 1986. Edited by B. Robinet and R. Wilhelm. VI, 374 pages. 1986.

Vol. 214: CAAP '86. 11th Colloquium on Trees in Algebra and Programming. Proceedings, 1986. Edited by P. Franchi-Zannettacci. VI, 306 pages. 1986.

Vol. 215: Mathematical Methods of Specification and Synthesis of Software Systems '85. Proceedings, 1985. Edited by W. Bibel and K.P. Jantke. 248 pages. 1986.